Jane Austen's Journeys

Jane Austen's Journeys

HAZEL JONES

ROBERT HALE · LONDON

© Hazel Jones 2014
First published in Great Britain 2014

ISBN 978-0-7198-0750-3

Robert Hale Limited
Clerkenwell House
Clerkenwell Green
London EC1R 0HT

www.halebooks.com

The right of Hazel Jones to be identified as
author of this work has been asserted by her
in accordance with the Copyright, Designs and
Patents Act 1988

A catalogue record for this book is available from the British Library

2 4 6 8 10 9 7 5 3 1

Typeset in Palatino
Printed in Great Britain by Berforts Information Press Ltd

Contents

Illustrations

12   *The hall of a mansion* by Edward Blore. (See picture credits for further details)

13   *The Temple of the British Worthies* by Thomas Rowlandson (1805). (See picture credits for further details)

14   *Dinner waiting at a neighbour's house* (November 1816). (See picture credits for further details)

Illustration credits

3   © Neville Ollerenshaw 1981. Photographs of the original pictures by Rodney Wright-Watson, © Victor Gollancz Ltd 1981. From *Mrs Hurst Dancing*, Gordon Mingay, illustrated by Diana Sperling. Image reproduced courtesy of Orion Publishing Group Ltd.

6   © Royal Collection Trust/Her Majesty Queen Elizabeth II 2013

7   Reproduced with the kind permission of Alan Rosevear

8   Copyright holder unknown. Reproduced from *The Regency Road: The Coaching Prints of James Pollard* by N.C. Selway, Faber & Faber, London, 1957.

9   Image courtesy of Albion Prints

12   © The Trustees of the British Museum

13   With kind permission of Stowe House Preservation Trust/ Hall Bequest Trust

14   © Neville Ollerenshaw 1981. Photographs of the original pictures by Rodney Wright-Watson, © Victor Gollancz Ltd 1981. From *Mrs Hurst Dancing*, Gordon Mingay, illustrated by Diana Sperling. Image reproduced courtesy of Orion Publishing Group Ltd.

Acknowledgements

A NYONE WHO WRITES about Jane Austen owes a huge debt to Deirdre Le Faye, whose scholarship is unrivalled in this area. I could not have written *Jane Austen's Journeys* without the help of her many published texts and articles, in particular *Jane Austen: A Family Record*, *A Chronology of Jane Austen* and *Jane Austen's Letters*.

I am most grateful to Maggie Lane for writing the Preface, for her unstinting encouragement and advice, her thorough reading of the typescript and her inspirational friendship.

My thanks also go to the following individuals, libraries and institutions: the British Library; all of the lovely staff at Chawton House Library, particularly Jacqui Grainger, Sarah Parry and Corrine Saint; Hampshire Record Office; Jane Austen's House Museum; at Steventon, the Revd Michael Kenning, Geoffrey Mann and Joyce Bown; the Jane Austen groups at Denman and Ammerdown, who tested my theories to the limit; Helen Porter and other friends and travelling companions on Pride and Prejudice Tours.

I recognize the help and support, also the patience and forbearance of my husband David Brandreth and father-in-law Dr T.K. Brandreth, given the scarcity of puddings over the past two years.

Finally, thanks are due to Gill Jackson, Nikki Edwards and Catherine Williams at Robert Hale.

Preface

FILM AND TELEVISION adaptations of Jane Austen's novels show her characters stepping out of elegant carriages or riding horseback without a care in the world. The reality of travel in the early nineteenth century could be very different, as Hazel Jones reveals in this book. Too often it was slow, dirty and dangerous. A friend of Austen's was killed when her horse bolted, and a cousin died when the light carriage she was driving overturned. Other hazards included lost luggage, highwaymen and – when a public conveyance was chosen for reasons of economy – smelly fellow-passengers inside and bitterly cold conditions on top. Maps and road signs were in their infancy, while roads themselves were invariably rutted and bumpy. And then there were the inns, which could hardly be avoided when travelling long distances: without modern appliances at the landlord's disposal, it is not surprising if the sheets weren't laundered very often, or the freshness, variety and cookery of the food left something to be desired.

And yet! There was a rage for travel, which Austen's characters and Austen herself often shared. To venture beyond home territory was a pleasure and an education that those with the means to indulge could hardly get enough of, whether their object was to look at the scenery, visit friends, view great houses, dance at an assembly or stay in one of the new leisure resorts. In this way, good manners were diffused through the

11

middling classes – just the people Austen loves to write about – and opportunities for social climbing and for meeting marriage partners were greatly increased. The novel of manners could hardly exist except within the context of widespread travel.

It is surprising therefore that this topic has not hitherto been explored in the depth it deserves. Hazel Jones has unearthed some fascinating contemporary accounts of travellers in England, some native, some foreign, from the irascible Colonel Byng who managed to find fault with everything and every-where, to the much more easily pleased German lady Johanna Schopenhauer, and the intrepid young Mr James Plumptre whose sightseeing tastes led him to view the new industrial processes. But the value of this book is not only its wealth of evidence, enthralling though this is, but its insights into the way Austen sends her characters on journeys of mental and moral discovery.

In her own forty-one years on this earth, Jane Austen herself managed to see a considerable portion of southern England, urban and rural. Some of this she accomplished by being, as she described herself, a 'desperate walker'; but for journeying further afield, she was reliant on the escort of a male relation. Her letters show that this lack of independence often irked. In her novels, women are similarly constrained, but rarely voice complaint. The contrast between male and female levels of mobility was certainly very great. But a sense of place and a sense of home were attainable by men and women alike, and this is what her most thoughtful characters' journeys – and her own – ultimately yield: a right balance between restlessness and repose, home and away.

Maggie Lane

1

A Laudable Thirst For Travelling

JANE AUSTEN LIVED through a great age for travel. Her own journeys took her through fourteen English counties and fostered an enduring regard for the country's varied landscape and unique architecture, thriving industry and productive agriculture – that combination of beauty and utility praised in *Sense and Sensibility* by Edward Ferrars. Her letters and novels are testaments to what she called 'the laudable thirst ... for Travelling',[1] a rational enthusiasm with which she endowed her heroines before sending them off down the nearest turnpike road, for, as the narrator famously states in *Northanger Abbey*, 'if adventures will not befall a young lady in her own village, she must seek them abroad ...'.[2] With the Continent largely closed down to travellers in the 1790s and early 1800s by the war with France, 'abroad' meant Bath and London, the fashionable seaside resorts and the remote regions of the north and west.

In the novels, the association of character and place – where men and women feel comfortable, where they choose to be – is always significant. Change of location is a test of integrity, calling for adaptation to prevailing social demands while keeping faith with self-esteem and principles. Neither Catherine Morland in Bath, Elizabeth Bennet at Rosings, Anne Elliot in Lyme nor Elinor and Marianne Dashwood in London 'perform to strangers'.[3] The same is true of the dependable male characters. Wherever they happen to be, they are essentially what they always were. In *Emma*, where the heroine barely sets foot outside her immediate neighbourhood, it is duplicitous Frank Churchill who adopts a role to suit his surroundings. On the outing to Box Hill, when Emma joins in the performance against her better nature, social disharmony and individual pain, not least Emma's own, are the consequences. Farther away from home territory, the other heroines' adventures involve far more than merely locating suitable husbands; through their journeys they learn something of the world and discover where, and with whom, they do and do not belong. Travel, pleasurable or otherwise, is always an education in Jane Austen's fiction, both practical and emotional.

From the 1790s into the first two decades of the 1800s, when Jane Austen's characters are out on the roads of England, contemporary travellers were discovering a patriotic enthusiasm for their homeland. With time, leisure and money that would previously have been expended on the Grand Tour of Europe burning holes in their pockets, they set out from their estates, parsonages and town houses to throng the turnpike roads and mail coach routes on their various ways to showpiece houses, watering places, sites of industry and beauty spots. En route and on arrival, they settled themselves into inns or lodgings and planned outings to accessible places within a day's ride or carriage drive. Foreign visitors to these shores marvelled that the whole nation, from Scotland to the far South West of England, appeared to be in constant motion. One observer, a French emigré from America, noted in his travel journal for 1811 that the English were so fond of racketing around the countryside in carriages that they abandoned their homes and took to the roads as often as possible, to 'make the pleasure last as long as they can'.[4] Jane Austen's cousin Eliza de Feuillide recognized the same propensity in herself and identified the travelling urge as a national trait: 'I have my share of the *wandering spirit* our Countrymen are in general possessed with',[5] she wrote with complacent pride.

Hankering after the superficial amusements of Brighton, Dawlish or Weymouth was far from praiseworthy, but in Jane Austen's opinion 'the idlest haunts in the kingdom'[6] were unquestionably superior to watering places in Europe: 'The idea of a fashionable Bathing place in Mecklenburg!' wrote Jane to her brother Frank on naval service in the Baltic in 1813. 'How can people pretend to be fashionable or to bathe out of England!'[7] Tourists inevitably drifted back across the Channel following the cessation of hostilities with France in 1815, but Jane's heart and mind remained steadfastly in favour of her home country. Frank Churchill's complaint that he is 'sick of England',[8] coming immediately after the author's unqualified approval for all things English, sounds a jarring note and foreshadows the following day's discord on Box Hill. Appalling behaviour is hardly to be wondered at from a man who professes a preference for 'abroad' over his native soil. Writing at the beginning of 1817 to Alethea Bigg of Manydown House, Jane hoped that letters received from friends on a tour of foreign health resorts had been optimistic, adding, 'They would not be satisfactory to <u>me</u>, I confess, unless they breathed a strong spirit of regret for not being in England.'[9] In late spring of the same year, she learned that Alethea herself had 'frisked off like half England', as a petulant Mr Churchill had threatened to do, 'into Switzerland.'[10]

Mr Knightley's collection of engravings featuring Venice and Switzerland and the inclusion of Lord Macartney's volume on the Orient in Fanny Price's East Room imply that a curiosity in other lands was more laudably indulged by reading books and studying prints and maps. Letters from Jane Austen's sailor brothers from Bermuda, the Mediterranean, China and the East Indies, like William Price's to Fanny, encouraged a desire to know more about foreign locations visited in the line of duty. Jane read up on Sweden when Frank was stationed there in 1813 and found some comfort in fancying it 'more like England than many Countries; — & according to the Map, many of the names have a strong resemblance to the English.'[11] Many of her letters carry references to travel literature: *An Account of the*

Manners and Customs of Italy; *A Journey from London to Genoa*; Sir
John Carr's *Descriptive Travels in the Southern and Eastern Parts of
Spain and the Balearic Isles*; *Travels in Iceland*; Lord Macartney's
embassies to Russia and China. Anne Grant's *Memoirs of an
American Lady*, which Jane read in 1809, might have influenced
the undated poem she wrote about her niece Anna, comparing
her 'unconfined' spirit to America's 'vast savannah', 'Ontario's
lake' and 'Niagara's Fall'.[12] The previous year, Anna had shocked
everyone by cutting off her hair; at the end of 1809, she acted
against her father and stepmother's wishes by accepting a proposal of marriage, only to change her mind a few months later,
thereby living up to her aunt's description of nature untamed.

Catherine Morland's reading of Mrs Radcliffe's Gothic
novels, on the other hand, colours her understanding of human
nature in England as well as on the Continent. Faced with the
realization that Northanger Abbey in Gloucestershire in no way
resembles Count Montoni's Udolpho and nor is General Tilney
a wife-murderer, she finally reaches the reasonable conclusion
that 'among the English ... in their hearts and habits, there
was a general though unequal mixture of good and bad'. Her
revised opinions are applied with confidence to 'the midland
counties of England', with less certainty to the 'northern and
western extremities', but she cannot quite persuade herself to
believe that horrors are not a daily occurrence in 'the Alps and
Pyrenees ... Italy, Switzerland, and the South of France'.[13]

If far-away places with strange-sounding names held new
thrills and dangers for Jane Austen's contemporaries, navigating
a way along *this* kingdom's highways and byways had long been
a matter of chance, or, more commonly, mischance, but new
atlases and road books based on actual surveys rather than on
ancient charts promised greater accuracy in mapping. County
maps of the seventeenth century had depicted towns and cities
as separate, disconnected places, located in a landscape of hills,
rivers and forests; by the end of the century, John Ogilby's
continuous-strip routes, the first to be published in England, had
appeared. From the 1780s into the next century his illustrated

maps were reduced in size and the information refined for the traveller's convenience.

One section of Ogilby's road map from London to Southampton, for example, depicts the border between Surrey and Hampshire, a paper mill, the churches at Bentley, Binsted, Alton and Chawton, a 'free schole', a few hills, two rivers and a stand of trees. A later version, reproduced in *Paterson's Roads* has no graphics apart from the bridge marking the county border, with the words 'Cross the river Blackwater, and enter Hampshire'. White-gloved index fingers point to right and left, indicating crossroads and country seats – one of which is 'Chawton House, Edw. Knight, Esq.' – listed in the margins. Helpful mileages from London and to the place of destination appear in columns on either side of the route.[14]

By the end of the eighteenth century, turnpike and mail roads linking community to community were the most prominent features on maps and their printed size was generally small enough to slip into the pocket of a greatcoat, with larger editions produced for gentlemen's libraries. Armchair travellers also considered essential a geographical knowledge of their own country. One writer of the time praised the ingenuity and usefulness of these publications:

> I bought … a map of England, folded for the pocket, with the roads and distances all marked upon it. I purchased also a book of the roads, in which not only the distance of every place in the kingdom from London, and from each other, is set down, but also the best inn at each place is pointed out, the name mentioned of every gentleman's seat near the road, and the objects which are most worthy a traveller's notice. Every thing that can possibly facilitate travelling seems to have been produced by the commercial spirit of this people.[15]

Jane Austen's father and his neighbours in the Steventon area invested in travel guides, road books and topographical journals. In the lanes around Godmersham Jane's brother Edward would have seen men with surveyors' wheels, theodolites and compasses, measuring field boundaries, roads and waterways for the first Ordnance Survey maps. Sheets were issued under county titles and the first four published in 1801 were of Kent. The Survey was a military initiative, so initial attention naturally focused on those parts of England most likely to be attacked by Napoleon. Forward planning was critical for rapid troop deployment to potential trouble spots and of crucial importance to national safety. Map-making comprised one aspect of Francis and Charles Austen's education at the Royal Naval Academy in Portsmouth. The Admiralty expected to see clear, accurate representations of foreign and home coastlines in every midshipman's and captain's log. Not only tourists travelling for pleasure worried about getting lost.

The rigours of travelling on horseback or in horse-drawn vehicles and the good health and temper required to withstand the attendant inconveniences were familiar to Jane Austen and the majority of her readers. The novelist did not need to spell out in tedious detail the length of a journey, nor the number of days spent on indifferent roads, but her characters naturally do discuss such matters – '"And what is fifty miles of good road?"' asks Mr Darcy, with his well-sprung carriages and highly-bred horses; '"Little more than half a day's journey."'[16] Mrs Jennings returning from Devon to London with the Dashwood sisters, the Gardiners and Elizabeth Bennet making their way to Derbyshire, Catherine Morland accompanying the Allens to Bath, Willoughby hastening from London to Somerset, all take the required amount of time to reach their destinations. The number of miles that could be accomplished in an hour was roughly seven, but it could take two days to cover a hundred over hilly terrain. Travelling from Dawlish to Bath, for example, would involve an overnight stop and daytime meals at coaching inns, plus at least six changes of horses. The novelist's rigorous attention to routes and journey times ensured that her readers were never diverted from the road she intended them to follow.

An annual income of £1,000 was the generally agreed requirement for living comfortably and maintaining an equipage with the animals to power it, together with the necessary stabling, coach house and servants. George Austen kept a carriage for a while on £600 before he was obliged to part with it; his eldest son James struggled to run two relatively modest vehicles on less; his daughters were grateful for any available mode of transport that might satisfy their urge to travel to and from home, even a donkey cart, but otherwise made do with thick boots. Like the majority of the population, Jane and Cassandra walked more frequently than they rode in carriages. Richer relations and acquaintances possessed the economic advantage of travelling with ease – the Leigh Perrots, Edward Knight, the Bigg-Withers, the Bramstons, the Heathcotes. Carriage and horse ownership in the novels reveal different levels of disposable income – Henry Crawford's barouche and string of hunters, Mr Bingley's chaise-and-four, Willoughby's curricle, John Thorpe's gig – and hints at moral character – Lady Catherine de Bourgh's multiple equipages match her numerous fireplaces and superfluity of windows; Sir Walter Elliot maintains two pairs of expensive carriage horses as non-negotiable markers of baronet status; the chaise, barouche-landau and four horses are essential for nouveau riche Mr Suckling's exploring parties and twice-weekly drives to London from Maple Grove. A laudable thirst for travelling this certainly was not.

Serious travellers liked to be recognized as such; they were keen to justify their reasons for venturing away from home territory, especially when a 'rage of rambling' was preached against in the pulpit. For some, enjoyment might come from criticising other tourists for their lack of taste, their want of judgement, their habit of following each other like sheep, their inferiority as 'foreigners', but the more enlightened expected to learn something of value on their journeys. They climbed hills and descended into mines, viewed the gardens and grounds of great houses and made lists of the owners' furniture and works of art. They equipped themselves with William Gilpin's picturesque tours, packed their watercolour boxes and sketch pads, their pencils and notebooks and set off to discover and record an England that could be framed and displayed on the drawing room wall.

This was the age of the travel journal and women as well as men, the unknown as well as the famous, walkers, riders and carriage passengers, submitted a proliferation of letters and diaries to publishers, as guides for future travellers. While female travel writers in general tended to be somewhat diffident about their ambition to publish their thoughts and experiences, they nevertheless considered their views valid and of interest to others. The urge among these writers to direct and educate was strong and a number of travel books aimed specifically at the young encouraged an interest in travel, while others had the effect of smothering it.

The Tour of Dr Syntax In Search of the Picturesque, first published in 1809, is a humorous poem by William Combe, illustrated by Thomas Rowlandson, featuring a tourist intent on publication taking the well-beaten track to the English Lakes. The publisher to whom he offers his completed journal laughs at his attempt:

> A Tour, indeed! I've had enough
> Of Tours, and such-like flimsy stuff.
> What a fool's errand you have made
> (I speak the language of the trade),
> To travel all the country o'er,
> And write what has been writ before![17]

In *Sense and Sensibility*, Marianne Dashwood regrets 'that admiration of landscape scenery is become a mere jargon'[18] since William Gilpin first defined picturesque beauty. It is preferable, she concludes, to stay silent rather than use the worn and hackneyed language employed by the majority of mindless travellers. Jane Austen knew of Combe's spoof on picturesque tourism, and took heed of the valid criticism made there and elsewhere.

She included in her novels and letters only what she considered to be the necessary details of journeys, but now and again she provides tantalising glimpses of coaching inns and carriages, grand houses and estate grounds, picturesque locations and urban centres, nankin boots, suntanned skin and petticoats six inches deep in dirt. The weather, the state of the roads, the accuracy of maps and guidebooks, the comforts or otherwise of inns, the accessibility of country houses and ruined castles, the friendliness or hostility of the local inhabitants are matters that interested her and her contemporaries as much as they occupy the modern traveller. They were as familiar as we are with the concepts of biographical and literary tourism. Where they visited the sites of Mary Stuart's incarceration and flocked to the places described in William Wordsworth's poems or Sir Walter Scott's historical romances, we trace Jane Austen's footsteps in Hampshire and Bath and track down the locations featured in film versions of her novels. Whether she would consider this a laudable thirst for travelling, I leave it to be settled by whomsoever it might concern ...

2

A Tolerable Proficient In Geography

THERE WAS NO excuse for getting lost in Jane Austen's England, or so the publishers of maps, itineraries and tour guides were keen to assure the travelling public. From the 1780s on, as the road network spread and domestic tourism became increasingly popular, the whole genre of travel literature for both serious and armchair travellers expanded and flourished. Before setting out for popular tourist destinations, those with enquiring minds scoured the circulating libraries, consulted their own collections of geographical texts and purchased the most up-to-date information on locations and routes, but it does not occur to silly Camilla Stanley in Jane Austen's *Catharine, or The Bower*, to carry out any kind of useful preparation for her journey to the Lakes, beyond planning what clothes she should pack: '"I know nothing of the Route, for I never trouble myself about such things—. I only know that we are to go from Derbyshire to Matlock and Scarborough, but to which of them first, I neither know nor care."'

Catharine Percival concludes that Miss Stanley is 'shamefully ignorant as to the Geography of England',[1] but when the Misses Bertram make the same assessment of Fanny Price's lack of geographical knowledge, they do not take into account that she has received scant instruction. The names and locations of

22

European countries, English, Welsh and Scottish counties could be learned from 'dissected maps'.[2] Many children, including the Prince Regent, were taught their first lessons in geography by way of these instructional jigsaw puzzles. Once started on the road to discovery, Fanny continues to educate herself about the world around her, whereas Julia and Maria give up learning at the age of seventeen, when their governess is dismissed. Catherine Morland admits to some interest in the subject, but her ignorance of the route from Northanger to Fullerton exposes her to real danger when the General packs her off in a post chaise to make the seventy-mile journey entirely alone. She must then have wished that she had gained a proficiency in geography that went beyond a cursory dip into the occasional travel commentary.

Camilla Stanley chooses to remain ignorant of routes and regions and, by the time she returns from the north, is likely to have little idea of where she has been or what she has seen. Travel will neither enlarge her mind nor widen her conversation. Elizabeth Bennet determines to be a very different kind of tourist:

"And when we *do* return, it shall not be like other travellers, without being able to give one accurate idea of any thing. We *will* know where we have gone — we *will* recollect what we have seen. Lakes, mountains, and rivers, shall not be jumbled together in our imaginations; nor, when we attempt to describe any particular scene, will we begin quarrelling about its relative situation. Let *our* first effusions be less insupportable than those of the generality of travellers."[3]

In his *Traveller's Oracle*, Dr Kitchiner recommended tourists to keep memorandums in pocket notebooks to remind them of village names and sites of interest visited on their journeys. Without keeping a record, he said, only a vague recollection would exist of the places passed through en route.[4] Kitchiner's advice, together with the study of maps and road books, might have prevented *Love and Freindship*'s hapless Edward losing his way between Bedfordshire and Middlesex. With two mail- and two turnpike roads running through his home county to Hertfordshire and across the border south to his aunt's, a journey of no more than fifty miles, Edward still manages to ride three times that distance west into the Vale of Usk. Rather belatedly, he admits that he is lost, but confidently pronounces himself to be 'a tolerable proficient in Geography'. The young Jane Austen laughed at the ridiculous convention of locating the heroes and heroines of sentimental fiction in romantic loca- tions. She would not subscribe to such blatant contrivance: in her mature novels, romance blossoms successfully and more realistically in Surrey and Northamptonshire, Somerset and Gloucestershire, than it ever did in Andalusia, the Pyrenees, or a 'beautifull Vale ... in South Wales'.[5]

A lack of geographical knowledge equals a lack of sense, a failing Jane Austen strove to avoid at all costs in her writing. In a simple poem written in July 1806 to celebrate her brother Frank's marriage to Mary Gibson, Jane described the exact route of the young couple's journey from Ramsgate to Godmersham, taking in topographical details such as the hill over which the coach ran and the narrow track that swept around Edward's estate:

Canterbury they have passed through;
 Next succeeded Stamford-bridge;
Chilham village they came fast through;
 Now they've mounted yonder ridge.

Down the hill they're swift proceeding,
 Now they skirt the Park around;[6]

Immediately to hand at Steventon, perhaps at subsequent Austen homes too, was Jane's father's copy of William Tunnicliffe's *Topographical Survey of the Counties of Hants, Wilts, Dorset, Somerset, Devon & Cornwall*, a road book published in 1791. Each of the six counties has its own section, with a tinted map, a brief description of the major roads and gentlemen's estates, lists of nobility and gentry and coats of arms. In the Hampshire section, 'the Revd George Austin [sic] DD, of Steventon' is listed as a subscriber.[7] The landscapes of the south and west of England, with which Jane Austen was most familiar, permeate her novels. Place names are carefully chosen to reflect aspects of the geographical location: Combe Magna in Somerset conjures up the densely-wooded, steep-sided valleys of that county; Barton is a Devon term denoting the home farm of a large estate – there are no fewer than seventeen places near Exeter featuring 'Barton' as an element;[8] Highbury in *Emma* echoes other town and village names – Foxbury, Longbury, Maybury, Norbury, Thornbury – near Great Bookham in Surrey, where Jane's relations the Cookes lived.

She experimented with fantastical names in her juvenile texts: 'Crankhumdunberry' in *Frederic and Elfrida*, 'Pammydiddle' in *Jack and Alice*, but she realized even then the value of authentic-sounding locations, like 'Marlhurst' in Sussex,[9] and the effectiveness of using real place names wherever possible. She loved the sheer rightness of a niece's fictional 'Newton Priors' – 'Milton w^d have given his eyes to have thought of it' she responded in an initial critique of Anna's latest attempt at novel-writing.[10] Two months later, the name had gained a hyphen but lost none of its charm: 'I never met with anything superior to it. — It is delightful. — One could live upon the name of Newton-Priors for a twelvemonth.'[11] Errors in geographical location met with swift emendation: 'Twice you have put Dorsetshire for Devonshire. I have altered it.'[12]

The insistence on the authenticity of place names extended to mileages and journey times: events in Lyme would not be spoken of in Dawlish, it was too far away; a hundred-mile journey from Devon to Bath would take two days.[13] In her own novels, places feel very real because they are located geographically in relation to actual towns and cities: Highbury, in Surrey, is sixteen miles from London, seven from Box Hill, nine from Richmond; Longbourn is ten miles off the Hertfordshire stretch of the Great North Road between London and Scotland; Catherine Morland's Fullerton, in Wiltshire, is nine miles from Salisbury; from Lyme to Uppercross, where the Musgroves live, is seventeen miles; Mansfield Park is four miles from Northampton, seventy from London, and so on.

The six-volume Hampshire Edition of the novels, published in 1902, included maps of the relevant counties, together with plans of imaginary neighbourhoods. Attempting to pin down exact locations has always been a compelling exercise for some readers, a number of whom have taken their research into the realms of wishful thinking. In 1900, The Earl of Iddesleigh, who owned Pynes House near Exeter, firmly believed that his house was the model for Barton Park, 'and that I am writing these lines in the room in which Sir John Middleton ate his dinner'.[14] Chatsworth is frequently identified as the model for Pemberley, Worthing and Sidmouth as Sanditon, Cottesbrooke Hall and Stoneleigh Abbey as Mansfield Park. Most readers, however, are content to accept the creative veracity of Jane Austen's fictional locations. Mary Russell Mitford stated that nothing delighted her more than sitting down in one of the author's country villages;[15] for Margaret Oliphant, it proved 'impossible to conceive a more perfect piece of village geography, a scene more absolutely real'.[16] Whatever our personal predilections, we never 'get lost in / the works of Jane Austen'.[17]

Many of her chosen locations were either familiar to her from personal visits, or from books. She gathered information from friends, acquaintances and relations for those about which she knew little, Northamptonshire, for example. In the 1790s, when she was writing *Sense and Sensibility*, she had not been to Devon herself, but the South Devon Militia, recruited in the neighbourhood of Exeter, were quartered in Basingstoke in the winters of 1793/4 and 1794/5. It is likely that Jane danced with the officers at the Basingstoke Assemblies and talked to them of their home county. Even before that time, Richard Buller, a pupil of her father's and son of the Bishop of Exeter, had surely spoken to her of Devon. When she came to revise the draft manuscript at Chawton, she had been to Teignmouth and Dawlish, perhaps to Sidmouth and Buller's rectory at Colyton. Since her father's former pupil also held the curacy at Stoke Canon, it is possible that she visited Exeter and took a carriage drive into the area 'four miles northward' of the city. Parts of London were familiar to her through Henry Austen; Gloucestershire, Surrey and Kent she knew from visits to relations, parts of Wiltshire from carriage journeys between Hampshire and Bath. Two holidays in Lyme provided her with descriptions of Dorset and Somerset. Derbyshire, Sussex and Hertfordshire feature, but are not described in any depth. If Anna insisted on sending some of her characters to Ireland, she should not go with them, advised her aunt, since she knew nothing of the places, people or customs there. She had much better accompany another set to Bath, a more familiar setting to the writer and reader alike.

Jane Austen's own experience of Bath, gained from holiday visits in the 1790s and residence from 1801–5, enabled her to drop street names and Bath locations into the narratives of *Northanger Abbey* and *Persuasion*. The Bath of the earlier novel conforms to the maps of the late 1790s, showing Union Passage and the Bear Inn yard, but no Union Street. John Thorpe and Catherine Morland's gig ride to Claverton Down would have taken the quiet road at the edge of Great Pulteney Street, opposite Sydney Gardens and not far from the Austens' house at No. 4 Sydney Place.[18] There are geographical in-jokes, designed for a readership familiar with Bath and its environs. Sham Castle – the name says it all – on an eminence clearly visible from Great Pulteney Street where the Allens have lodgings and only a short carriage drive away, will not do for John Thorpe's purposes. An easily accessible fake ruin would hold no appeal for Catherine nor allow Thorpe and his sister enough time to wheedle their way into the Morlands' affections, so a much longer journey is proposed, out beyond Bristol to Blaise Castle, an ancient edifice, claims Thorpe, with tapestries, trap-doors and galleries. Catherine's ignorance of the locality is understandable, she has never been there before.

She must rely on the insider knowledge, or lack of it – Blaise was constructed as recently as 1766 – of her companion as he steers his gig away from one folly, toward another. On this physical journey in the wrong direction, however, Catherine reaches the conclusion that John Thorpe is thoroughly disagreeable – an independent step in the right direction.

The drive to Blaise is ill-considered in more ways than one. The two carriages set out just after noon, in January, to cover a distance of forty miles there and back. Three hours would be needed to get there, probably more, given that the horses would rest after about twelve miles. Predictably, they have to turn back at Keynsham, after taking an hour to travel seven miles. If John Thorpe had known the geography of the area, or consulted a tourist guide, he would have discovered that seven miles' travel in the opposite direction would have transported them to the ruined, genuinely medieval castle of Farleigh Hungerford, redolent of murders, poisonings and imprisoned wives. Farleigh was a popular tourist destination, featured in various guidebooks to the Bath area, including *Excursions From Bath*, a copy of which the Austens possessed, and Cruttwell's *New Bath Guide*. The latter publication enumerates 'ruins', 'vaults', 'monuments' and a 'chest of old armour' – more than enough to satisfy Catherine's cravings for the Gothic.[19] The route to Farleigh also passed a Gothic folly at Midford and an abbey at Hinton Charterhouse, both mentioned in the Austens' book and providing more instances of Thorpe's inattention to location in favour of exaggerated claims of his horse's capabilities and his own prowess as a coachman. He is a reader of salacious Gothic horror; works that imparted a knowledge of geography or of authentic Gothic castles would hold no appeal. The eventual destination and the gratification of Catherine's passion for ancient edifices are equally irrelevant to him. His main aim is to detach her from the Tilneys, secure her 'fortune' for himself and her brother for Isabella.

Thorpe's sister is as proficient in the geography of Bath as a determined pleasure-seeker and husband-hunter would be.

28

Four years older than Catherine, 'and at least four years better informed',[20] Isabella knows precisely where to strut and preen, where to shop for fashionable accessories, where to make assignations. She is here, there, everywhere, on the look-out for available young men and towing a naïve Catherine in her wake. The Thorpes' control over Catherine's movements in Bath are potentially hazardous, since they threaten her friendship with Eleanor and Henry Tilney and risk damaging her reputation.

Exclusivity is the name of the game played by Sir Walter Elliot in Bath. He and Elizabeth congratulate themselves on the lofty situation of their house in Camden Place, from where they look down on the city spread beneath them. In social terms, they appear unassailable; in geological terms, they are not entirely secure. Jane Austen's readers would have been familiar with the landslip in 1788, which demolished the last five houses in this crescent. The section of ruined edifice overlooking Paragon was left standing for a number of years, because it appeared to picturesque advantage in the urban landscape. Sir Walter's undermined financial situation is reflected in the unstable ground beneath his feet.[21] Lady Russell has a house in slightly lower Rivers Street, close to the Upper Rooms; the Crofts are in Gay Street, leading off the Circus, an address Sir Walter does not disdain to visit; Colonel Wallis and his pregnant wife are in Marlborough Buildings, a smart enough location to impress Sir Walter, near the Royal Crescent. The Musgroves are in the centre of things, at the White Hart Hotel, and Mrs Smith in Westgate Buildings at the lowest end of genteel Bath, which is all she can afford. Viscountess Lady Dalrymple leases a house in Laura Place, in the fashionable Bathwick development on the eastern side of the river. Sir Walter's rank-obsessed vision appears to determine character placement in *Persuasion*, but a different, easy-going Bath belongs to the sociable Musgroves and Crofts, who are happy enough where they are, able to take full advantage of the pleasures on offer: the theatre, the shops, the lively public spaces. Bath belongs to Anne and Wentworth too, as the fitful progress towards their reconciliation is acted out in Molland's pastry shop, at the Assembly Rooms, the White Hart Inn and in Union Street. The quiet environs of Gravel Walk, where the pair renew their engagement as they take the long way home, is more peculiarly theirs than anywhere else in the city: 'where the power of conversation would make the present hour a blessing indeed; and prepare it for all the immortality which the happiest recollections of their own future lives could bestow.'[22]

A sense of place is always critical in Jane Austen's fiction. The silly errors made by some characters serve merely to emphasize their ignorance and have no serious consequences – Mrs Elton's insistence that Surrey is the only county to be called the Garden of England, for instance, Robert Ferrars' superficial knowledge of Devonshire, or Harriet Smith's notion that Frank Churchill's route from Oxford to Surrey might pass through Bath. Those restless individuals who lose their way, are unsettled and unsettling, or fail to comprehend where they belong, often have a more disturbing influence.

The two who threaten to cause the greatest disruption are Mary and Henry Crawford, neither of whom is at peace anywhere for any length of time. Mary is more to be pitied than her brother. She has no fixed home and is in need of stability, although it appears too late to achieve it and is a deficiency she would never admit. Mansfield Park and its environs hold out an opportunity for her to put down roots, but the pull of London proves irresistible. Within the house itself, she drifts between Fanny and Edmund and the more frivolous set which includes Tom, her brother and the Bertram sisters: from the window overlooking the lawn and the night sky to the glee at the piano; from the peace of the fireside to the noisy group of play-actors. Similarly, she envisages future years divided equally between a rural and an urban existence, an incompatible mix of domestic contentment and social display. Time spent in the Northamptonshire countryside teaches her the value of family harmony – on the surface, at least – and she professes reluctance when she has to leave for London, but she soon falls back into the superficial ways of her fashionable friends. '"I shall not be in any doubtful, or distant, or unapproachable region"'[23] she states on her departure and, geographically speaking, she is correct, but her inner compass swings back to the true north of the city and she comes to embody all three of these moral negatives for Edmund.

Henry Crawford's estate in Norfolk should be a settled home for him and his sister, the focus of obligations towards tenants and land, the outward manifestation of taste and character. But Everingham's fascination for Henry is of short duration; initially while improvements are being instituted to his own specifications and latterly as a place to accommodate him for a few weeks in the hunting season. At a time when estate maps were valued and consulted, there are tracts of land and cottages of which Henry knows nothing until, under Fanny's influence, he takes a brief interest in his responsibilities as a landlord. Like Mary, he is incapable of imagining life confined to one home; residence in London must feature in his annual pleasures. Restlessness is embedded in their DNA. Henry's physical loss of direction near Thornton Lacey benefits Fanny, however; she listens with interest to his description of Edmund's living, the house that will be her home until Mansfield Parsonage is reclaimed. Henry's moral loss of direction, where else but in London, results in the disgraced Maria Rushworth's geographical and social isolation and in his sister's loss of a future home with the man she loves. The final chapter of *Mansfield Park* sends Henry back out into society to break more hearts, while Mary lives companionably with her half-sister and searches in vain for a husband with Edmund's qualities.

Jane Austen's self-aware characters know where they are, acclimatize themselves to their surroundings and recognize the meaning of home. Whenever they lose their geographical bearings, there are always mitigating circumstances: Darcy and Elizabeth drifting in the lanes around Longbourn 'without knowing in what direction'[24] following their engagement; Mr Knightley, his head filled with Emma, gone no one knew where,

'Perhaps to Hartfield, perhaps to the Abbey Mill, perhaps into his woods'[25]; Captain Wentworth, his thoughts in emotional turmoil after baring heart and soul in his letter to Anne, unable to say which way or how far he intends to walk from the White Hart.[26]

George Knightley and his brother John are both described as strongly rooted in their home soil, as they consult the Donwell estate map in order to determine the line of a new footpath and plan in which fields to sow the coming year's crops. In 1811, Jane Austen hunted out an old map of Chawton Great House land for her brother Edward, and noted with delight his success with haymaking, his planned improvements to the garden and his enthusiasm for the county of his birth: 'Edward is very well & enjoys himself as thoroughly as any Hampshire born Austen can desire. Chawton is not thrown away upon him. — He talks of making a new Garden ... We like to have him proving & strengthening his attachment to the place by making it better.'[27]

Jane's own attachment to Chawton, intensified by the loss of an established home at Steventon and the subsequent insecurities of Bath and Southampton, is felt most powerfully in the three later novels, where sense of place, of home, finds full emotional expression. The texts conceived at Steventon focus a little more practically on the heroines' responses to the places they call, or come to call, home. Marianne Dashwood might persuade herself that the loss of Norland will break her heart, but Willoughby's arrival at Barton is enough to push her former home firmly into the background. Tears are shed by both sisters on their final day in Sussex, but no more is said of Elinor's feelings on giving up her home. Marianne's dreams of future residence at Combe Magna and Allingham centre on material considerations – the fitting up of sitting rooms, the keeping of servants and carriages. Elinor chooses wallpaper for her home at Delaford Parsonage, plans a shrubbery and wishes for better pasturage for her cows. When Marianne becomes mistress of Delaford, she succeeds to 'the honours of the mulberry-tree, the canal, and the yew arbour',[28] all somehow more tangible than any emotional attachment to home or husband. The geographical closeness of the sisters and their mother is of greater importance and has pride of place in the final paragraph.

Geographical distance from Mrs Bennet is achieved at the end of *Pride and Prejudice*, a very necessary step for Jane and Elizabeth to take. Neither sister appears particularly attached to Longbourn, it is taken for granted as the place where they live. The threatened loss of their home to Mr Collins seems only to affect Mrs Bennet; Elizabeth and Jane content themselves with attempting to make her see reason by explaining the entail. On their marriages, the sisters live within an accessible thirty miles of each other and, although little is said of Bingley's estate, Pemberley is described in some detail. Darcy has created a comfortable, tasteful home for himself and his sister – and ultimately for his wife – as well as pursuing his estate duties with diligence and generosity. Pemberley is where Elizabeth belongs, a place where she can live in elegance and comfort, away from the narrow confines of Meryton society, which believes itself to reflect 'the world' and its opinions.

Northanger Abbey runs like a well-oiled machine under General Tilney's direction. It is opulently furnished and stocked with the very best that his walled gardens can provide, but it is not a comfortable place for his children to live. Catherine Morland is fortunate enough to see the house that she will inhabit as Henry Tilney's wife and to recognize in her heart that it is more a home than the abbey could ever be. Woodston Parsonage is very similar to Fullerton, an important consideration for one who has passed a happy childhood in the family home, with green gates, a large kitchen garden, a pretty sitting room with windows down to the ground and a view over meadowland and orchard.

No maps, road books or travel itineraries will help any of the heroines to reach their ultimate destinations. They must navigate their way through geographically authentic landscapes with only their moral compasses to guide them to where they ultimately belong. Marianne, Elinor, Elizabeth and Catherine are sent on longer physical journeys to find their eventual homes than Fanny Price, Emma Woodhouse and Anne Elliot. The later heroines have strong ties to the places of their birth and have to make greater readjustments of the mind to earn the deep, fulfilled sense of homecoming granted to them in the final chapters.

Fanny Price's removal from her simple home in Portsmouth, where she felt valued, to Mansfield Park in Northamptonshire, isolates her geographically, from her family and within her uncle's grand house itself. She is accommodated on the upper floor near the servants, left pretty much to herself unless required and given few opportunities to extend her physical knowledge beyond the confines of the park. Dispossessed of home at the age of ten, she seeks to recreate it in the East Room with prints and furniture discarded from better apartments, books selected by and discussed with Edmund, letters and sketches from William and trifling presents from her cousins. In her mind, Portsmouth is still the home she yearns for, until, after an absence of eight years, she suffers almost three months in her parents' stifling, noisy, disorderly house: 'When she had been coming to Portsmouth, she had loved to call it her home, had been fond of saying that she was going home; the word had been very dear to her; and so it still was, but it must be applied to Mansfield. That was now the home. Portsmouth was Portsmouth; Mansfield was home.'[29]

Fanny's return to where she truly belongs is a triumph, but she has first to recognize her own worth as a wife for Edmund and as the daughter Sir Thomas values above Julia and Maria. The journey to Portsmouth enables this process, proving to Fanny that she can be proactive in making an uncongenial home more comfortable for her sister Susan by teaching her to love books. Fanny and Edmund together will be exemplary parents. Yet Fanny's complete security in the acquisition of place and position at Mansfield relies on the exile of others – Maria, Mary Crawford, Mrs Norris. On the death of Dr Grant, she and Edmund move from Thornton Lacey: 'to Mansfield, and the parsonage there, which under each of its two former owners, Fanny had never been able to approach but with some painful sensation of restraint and alarm, soon grew as dear to her heart, and as thoroughly perfect in her eyes, as every thing else, within the view and patronage of Mansfield Park, had long been.'[30] Home for Fanny is a geographical and emotional landscape free from fear, emptied of characters who have threatened her peace. The simplicity of the space she creates for herself in the East Room spreads its influence throughout Sir Thomas' domain, bringing about 'tolerable comfort' for the few remaining at Mansfield Park.

Emma travels less than any other Jane Austen heroine; her scope is limited to Hartfield, Highbury and Donwell. She is mistress of all she surveys – first in consequence with her father, with Mr Knightley and in Highbury society. She longs for a glimpse of the sea, but is otherwise content and at peace with her surroundings. Her view from the doorway of Ford's shop as she waits for Harriet to purchase ribbon and muslin underscores this: 'she knew she had no reason to complain, and was amused enough; quite enough still to stand at the door'.[31]

An innate sense of where she belongs allows Emma to divine immediately Frank Churchill's motive of making himself agreeable by professing a keen interest in his 'own country' after an absence of almost twenty years, while the suspicion enters her mind that he might have returned to it at an earlier date, had he chosen.[32] She is also astute enough to gauge that Augusta Hawkins has probably accepted Mr Elton's proposal of marriage for the sake of gaining a good home. Yet Emma's security sometimes makes her careless of the deprivations and insecurities faced by her neighbours. Miss Bates and her mother have lost their parsonage home and must make do with a set of rooms over a shop; Jane Fairfax appears to have no prospects of a settled existence, merely temporary accommodation as a governess. Emma offers charity in the form of pork and suppers at Hartfield and deigns to call on them when she cannot escape the obligation, but she has no real compassion. Even less forgivable is the threat she poses to Harriet's prospects of a respectable home with the Martins.

Emma is happy at Hartfield and equally happy at Donwell, where Mr Knightley's gardens and house reflect his values and symbolize an ideal England, unadorned, a little unfashionable, proud of its links with the past. Emma's sense of place is particularly strong here; this is where she belongs and although she does not yet realize it in any conscious way, the language of her thoughts conveys the truth: 'It was just what it ought to be, and it looked what it was — and Emma felt an increasing respect for it, as the residence of a family of such true gentility, untainted in blood and understanding ... These were pleasant feelings, and she walked about and indulged them'.[33]

Her unqualified admiration of Mr Knightley's house and grounds comes only four chapters after her heightened awareness of his physical appeal, as she notes his superiority to other men at the Crown ball. In this novel, the heroine is not faced with any dispossession of property; Hartfield is hers for her lifetime. But faced with the loss of Mr Knightley, she realizes that home without him would be a lonely place: 'what would remain of cheerful or of rational society within their reach? Mr Knightley to be no longer coming there for his evening comfort! — No longer walking in at all hours, as if willing to change his own home for theirs! — How was it to be endured?'[34] It is in fact Mr Knightley who becomes dispossessed of home. Attached as he is to Donwell Abbey, he voluntarily gives up residence there for Emma's sake. While her father lives, Hartfield will be their home.

In *Persuasion*, the concept of relinquishing home for love is taken to its logical conclusion: the heroine gets the man she desires, but no property. Anne Elliot possesses a keen sense of Kellynch Hall as a home, for its quiet grounds, poignant memories of her mother and a painfully brief period of happiness with Captain Wentworth. For her father and elder sister, the estate is a possession, conferring privilege and status, a domain, not a home. They abandon it with no regrets. As Anne moves from Kellynch to Uppercross, Lyme and Bath, she considers what home constitutes for others. For the sociable Musgroves it is cheerful noise and bustle, open house and everyone welcome. Generations of Musgroves have inhabited the Great House; they are solid, respectable and contented with who and where they are. More transient, but no less happy homes form a contrast: the Harvilles in their cramped lodgings at Lyme, the Crofts at Kellynch and in Bath. Despite scant financial resources and want of health, Captain Harville's ingenuity transforms an unpromising temporary space into a home for his wife and children. Anne recognizes the influence of Harville's profession on his habits, her head and heart respond to 'the picture of repose and domestic happiness it presented.'[35]

Persuasion considers the domestic virtues of well-travelled naval men back on dry land; men with no fixed address, no estate, no pretensions to inheritance. A keen sense of what home means to them permeates the fabric of the novel. Admiral and Mrs Croft are at home wherever they are. At Kellynch, they effect small improvements for their own and the servants' benefit, take an interest in their livestock and acquaint themselves with the immediate area. For them, home is wherever they happen to be together, whether on-board ship, on a country estate, or in a Bath lodging house. As the Admiral explains to Anne: '"We get away from them all, and shut ourselves into our lodgings, and draw in our chairs, and are as snug as if we were at Kellynch, ay, or as we used to be even at North Yarmouth and Deal."'[36]

Tempted by the bewitching prospect of regaining a much loved home by becoming the wife of Mr Elliot, 'calling it her home again, her home for ever',[37] Anne resists, relinquishing Kellynch to remain true to the man she has always loved. On her marriage to Wentworth, she is warmly welcomed into a community of brothers and sisters, Wentworth's blood relations and naval friends. She gains the family she deserves, but no equivalent of Donwell, Mansfield Parsonage, Pemberley, Woodston or Delaford. For Anne Elliot home is not a geographical certainty, but an emotional one, where the heart belongs.

37

3

Fifty Miles Of Good Road

IN MARIANNE DASHWOOD's opinion, talking '"only of the weather and the roads"' made for dull, spiritless conversation,[1] yet such commonplace subjects were of dual concern for short- and long-distance travellers alike in Jane Austen's time. Anne Elliot is by no means bored by her cousin William when they meet again in Bath, even though he regales her with his route to Lyme from Sidmouth and seeks to 'understand something of hers' from Uppercross. On the contrary, she comes to the conclusion that he has 'improved their conversation very much'.[2] Edward Ferrars' first response to Barton on his arrival there from Plymouth is less engaging and undoubtedly tainted by recent association with Lucy Steele – '"these bottoms must be dirty in winter … among the rest of the objects before me, I see a very dirty lane."'[3] – but on a practical level, he is right. In the winter months, Elinor and Marianne must take their walks on the hills: 'The high downs … were an happy alternative when the dirt of the valleys beneath shut up their superior beauties …'.[4]

A few miles over the border with Somerset, the MP for Taunton attempted to prove that it would cost less money to make the county's roads into waterways than it would to set up a turnpike trust to improve them.[5] Richard Warner, a clergyman and antiquarian travelling in Devon in the early 1800s, found even the turnpike roads execrable:

> Instead of making use of the advantages afforded them by their soil, and breaking the stone into small nodules, which, pressed together by the weight of horses and carriages, would form ada-mantine and impenetrable roads, they carelessly sprinkle these public ways with masses of stone larger than a man's head, and leave them to time and chance to be broken and scattered, to the great danger of the horseman and the discomfort of him who is in a carriage.[6]

Heavy rain and deep snow frequently blocked already challenging highways and byways and in dry conditions the uneven ground set like corrugated concrete. The state of the roads and the damaging impact of the weather were subjects that filled the pages of letters and diaries and found their way into county surveys, newspaper articles and novels. Snow and ice caused many disruptions to mobility, leading in extreme cases to food shortages, as Mrs Lybbe Powys of Hardwick in Oxfordshire recorded in her diary for January and February 1776:

> no horse passed for a month, or cart for two. On the fifteenth day the butcher sent over two men with a little beef and veal, which then began to be scarce even there; not one team at Reading market the Saturday after it began a thing never known. The two London waggons came in with sixteen and fourteen horses; but one horseman that day thro' the turnpike; all stages and machines stopped for ten or twelve days on the very best roads ... Two hundred and seventeen men were employ'd on the Oxford turnpike between Nettlebed and Benson to cut a road for carriages, but then a chaise could not go with a pair of horses, and very dangerous, like driving on glass.[7]

Weather conditions at the beginning of the same year in Hampshire were just as treacherous. The Revd George Austen struggled up the steep lane to Steventon church to conduct the necessary services, but his youngest daughter, born the previous December, was baptized privately at home the day after her birth and not carried up the hill to be christened in church until the weather improved the following April. The snow arrived in North Hampshire even earlier in 1801, Mrs Lefroy recording in her journal on 1 December that her husband had been stranded for two days at Ewshot, twenty miles from Ashe.[8] When snow did not make the roads difficult to negotiate, rain did. 'There has been a great deal of rain here for this last fortnight, much more than in Kent,' Jane wrote to Cassandra, following her return from Godmersham in October 1798, '& indeed we found the roads all the way from Staines most disgracefully dirty. — Steventon lane has its full share of it, & I do not know when I shall be able to get to Deane.'[9] Hampshire's minor roads proved tricky even in clement weather, as Johanna Schopenhauer, a German tourist, discovered on her travels north through the county in the early 1800s:

> From Winchester onwards we encountered very bad roads. In order to make our various expeditions, we were forced to leave the main road and now we had to try to find it again by a maze of almost impassable side-roads. We often left the carriage and walked up the steep hills, as it rattled wearily onwards, and had a small reward for our pains in fine open views.[10]

Year after year, county surveys told a tale of woefully inadequate highway maintenance in the face of climatic certainties. Middleton's Survey of Middlesex in 1797, observed that every winter the Oxford road at Uxbridge was reduced to one barely passable track of fluid sludge, less than six feet wide. The remainder of the road was from one foot to eighteen inches deep in mud.[11] Thomas de Quincey had been driven along such a road in a post chaise many times:

> You stretched a wintry length of lane, with ruts deep enough

to fracture the leg of a horse, filled to the brim with standing pools of rain water; and the collateral chambers of these ruts kept from becoming confluent by thin ridges ... the poor off-horse planting his steps with care, and the cautious postillion gently applying his spur, whilst manoeuvring across this system of grooves with some sort of science that looked like a gipsy's palmistry.[12]

The Revd James Woodforde's diary entries for February 1799 describe a particularly bad winter, with loss of human and animal life, snow drifts blocking most of the routes in and out of Norfolk despite the attempts of hired labourers to clear them and 'Very dismal Accounts on the Papers ... Mail Coaches &c. unable to travel. The Roads in very, very many Places impassable.'[13] Later that year, in flooded Somerset, Miss Maria Goodford of Yeovil found the roads 'almost impassable for a Carriage' but, determined to continue her visits to Mrs Leigh Perrot at the jailer's house in Ilchester five miles away, she took to her horse as frequently as conditions permitted.[14] The snow in Emma's Highbury amounts to no more than half an inch, but John Knightley, irritated at having to leave the fireside on Christmas Eve for a dinner engagement at Randalls, represents in terms designed to terrify his father-in-law the consequences of venturing half a mile from Hartfield:

"Something new for your coachman and horses to be making their way through a storm of snow ... I dare say we shall get home very well. Another hour or two's snow can hardly make the road impassable; and we are two carriages; if *one* is blown over in the bleak part of the common field there will be another at hand."[15]

Mary Musgrove's letter from Uppercross to her sister Anne in Bath touches briefly on the difficulty of travelling in a rural area in the winter months: 'What dreadful weather we have had! It may not be felt in Bath, with your nice pavements; but in the country it is of some consequence.'[16] Yet even well-paved urban centres were not immune to weather-related aggravations and disasters. In January 1809, Bath was badly affected by thawing snow and heavy rain. Coaches were swept away by the ferocity of the floods pouring down the steep hills and the whole city was marooned for weeks.[17] Another hard winter over 1813 and into 1814 stranded the Fowles of Kintbury in Cheltenham: 'We left the other party,' recalled Caroline Austen, who departed from the town with her mother on 6 December, 'and *their* stay was lengthened beyond their intention by a heavy fall of snow after Christmas, which made the roads impassable for a long time.'[18]

Jane Austen has the Churchills make their long-distance move to London from Yorkshire in April, in keeping with Mrs Churchill's frailties, but the more robust Mrs Jennings accomplishes a longer journey on more challenging roads from Devon to the capital over three days in January with Elinor and Marianne Dashwood. Returning from Northampton in 'the dirty month of February' to the Price household in Portsmouth, Fanny and William find themselves fatigued and in need of comforting food by the time they reach Newbury, their overnight destination.[19] Jane Austen herself does not appear to have made lengthy journeys in the winter months, but in early March 1814, she and Henry travelled from Chawton to London through several snowstorms. She reported to Cassandra that the road between Cobham and Kingston had proved 'hard ... dirty & heavy'.[20]

Turnpike trusts and their surveyors had been operating since the early 1700s, but road conditions county to county throughout the century and into the next varied enormously. Riding through England in the late 1760s, Arthur Young denounced the state of the roads in every county. In Yorkshire, they were 'full of ruts', in Bedfordshire, a 'cursed string of hills and holes' and in Wiltshire, 'little better than ponds of liquid dirt'.[21] Mrs Allen knows to her cost the state of the Wiltshire roads between Fullerton and Salisbury: '"A clean gown is not five minutes wear"'[22] in an open carriage over nine miles of squelchy ground. Emma Watson discovers the same in Surrey, as the chair driven by her sister 'splashed along the dirty lane'[23] on its way to the turnpike road into the town. Emma's brother Robert is scandalized when he makes a visit to the family home at Stanton: '"Your road through the village is infamous ... worse than ever it was. By heaven! I would endite it if I lived near you. Who is surveyor now?"'[24] Diana Sperling's watercolour of 29 August 1816, entitled *A specimen of the Buckinghamshire roads*, shows a stranded carriage, its two bemused horses looking askance at a 'string of hills and holes'. The Sperling family had been making their way from Essex to Buckinghamshire, probably along the same road that Arthur Young criticized in 1768.[25]

No central fund existed to pay for road maintenance. Individual parishes were supposed to be responsible for local stretches of highway, but the organization of unpaid labour proved difficult and, understandably, unpopular. Some areas had no access to stone with which to effect long-lasting repairs and transporting it in cost money. An increasing number of landowners had no option but to take matters into their own hands. Jane Austen had witnessed changes to the road system in and around Adlestrop village, undertaken by Leigh relations at the rectory in 1796. At Sotherton, believed by some to be based on the Leighs' Stoneleigh Abbey, Mr Rushworth improves the approach to his estate, allowing Maria Bertram to remark with pride – she can boast little of the man himself – : '"Now we shall have no more rough road ... The rest of the way is such as it ought to be. Mr. Rushworth has made it since he succeeded to the estate."'[26]

The uneven and pitted Northamptonshire roads over which Mr Crawford's barouche bumps and jolts on the summer excursion to Sotherton do not spoil the party's enjoyment. Julia Bertram is entirely comfortable on the box beside Henry, Fanny Price looks about her at the fields, the roadside habitations and people and 'the bearings of the roads' without suffering headaches.[27] The previous winter, if Mrs Norris' account is to be believed in its entirety, the same journey along 'ten miles of indifferent road'[28] in Sir Thomas' coach had required a coachman, postilion and four straining horses, '"where what with frost and snow upon beds of stones, it was worse than any thing you can imagine."'[29]

On main stage coach routes and major links between the more populous places and market towns, the obvious solution was to privatize the road system. In the early years of the eighteenth century, turnpike trusts were set up piecemeal, each one authorized by Act of Parliament. The trustees were required to maintain, repair and improve the roads and empowered to purchase land and materials, remove obstructions, scour ditches, fell trees, make causeways, cut drains, erect bridges, widen roads and make temporary roads as diversions. The statutory breadth of a turnpike road was sixty feet (approximately eighteen metres), including a wide grass verge; lesser highways were forty feet wide and minor carriageways and bridleways twenty feet, barely wide enough for carriages to pass without being scraped by hedges and walls. This was no charitable exercise; the trustees expected to make a profit from road improvement. Turnpike roads were toll roads, with gates, or turnpikes, set up at agreed distances, each one manned by a tollkeeper. The keeper had to work all hours, every day of the year, from a small purpose-built dwelling with toll charges displayed on the wall and windows overlooking the approach roads. Dr Kitchiner recommended travellers: 'Be provided with Pence, Sixpences and Shillings, ready to pay the Tolls — Turnpike-men are not obliged to give any change; and having the Money ready saves Time.'[30]

The author Robert Southey, adopting the persona of a Spanish nobleman called Don Manuel Alvarez Espriella touring England in the early 1800s, described the system in detail:

At certain distances gates are erected, and toll-houses beside them, where a regular tax is paid for every kind of conveyance in proportion to the number of horses and wheels ... These gates are rented by auction: they are few or frequent, as the nature of the soil occasions more or less expense in repairs ... Another useful peculiarity here is, that where the roads cross or branch off, a directing post is set up ... The distances are measured by the mile, which is the fourth of a league, and stones to mark them are set by the way side, though they are often too much defaced by time, or by mischievous travellers, to be of any use.[31]

Jane Austen's mother had this method of signposting in mind when she suggested that her cousin Thomas Leigh set up 'directing Posts' at each intersection of the confusing passageways at Stoneleigh Abbey.[32] From 1767, milestones, finger-posts and boundary markers were compulsory on all turnpike roads, to inform travellers of directions and distances, to help coaches keep to schedule and for levying a charge for the changing of post horses at coaching inns. In *Northanger Abbey*, James Morland appeals to John Thorpe to consider the accurate distances on the milestones between Tetbury and Bath in determining the duration of the journey.[33] Guide- and road books mentioned them as aids on unfamiliar routes. *A Picturesque Guide to Bath* provides a route to Keynsham along the Lower Bristol Road, through Twerton: 'About the four mile stone, the Wells road from Bath branches off to the left'. At the five-mile stone, the estate of Kelston was visible.[34] Each turnpike trust had its own design of milestone, which reflected distinctive local materials and styles. The distances specified on the stones were also used in the calculation of postal charges before a uniform postal rate was introduced in 1840. At the very least, the information on finger-posts might forestall the mortification of gentlemen who 'can never bear to ask' losing their way,[35] and although the eighteenth-century traveller Colonel John Byng complained that those in the north were 'both expensive and ill-looking', he found that they were more reliable than the directions given by local inhabitants, such as the blacksmith he enquired of near Doncaster: 'He order'd me to turn to the left, to turn to the right and to turn so often that he forgot himself. However, I obey'd his first turn, and there found a better guide, a direction post'.[36]

The money collected at toll bars met expenses and repaid loans and the remainder was shared out. Turnpike trusts raised money from investors at four or five percent interest for the initial repair of the roads, then leased out the collection of tolls to contractors, who charged travellers as much as possible and blocked off alternative routes to prevent avoidance. Pedestrians, cattle, horses and all vehicles – mail coaches, troop carriers and those transporting royalty excepted – were subject to a toll at each gate. Local people who needed to use the roads for trade purposes objected to the imposition of charges and to the inescapable annual contribution towards road-mending. Matthew Flinders, an apothecary in Lincolnshire, kept a record of the tolls he had to pay when called on to visit patients. In August 1776, he passed through '16 Toll Barrs' on his horse, for which he forfeited two shillings; the following month, he paid for thirteen turnpikes. Every two years he paid nearly six shillings for 'High Way Assessment', together with intermittent payments towards the labour involved in 'Statute Work' – the repair of local roads.[37] Flinders' diaries show similar amounts paid out on road maintenance and inspection until 1798.

A percentage of Colonel Brandon's £2,000 a year would have contributed to the financing of maintenance on the turnpike road a quarter of a mile from Delaford. In common with other landowners, he would probably not have considered the entertainment value of having a turnpike so close to his estate, but for Mrs Jennings, it is one of Delaford's attractions: '"'tis never dull,"' she enthuses to Elinor, '"for if you only go and sit up in an old yew arbour behind the house, you may see all the carriages that pass along."'[38]

In 1822, William Cobbett travelled the road between Farnham and Alton and noted a group of labourers carrying out repairs near Wrecclesham, 'at the expense of half-ruined farmers and tradesmen and landlords, to break stones into very small pieces to make nice smooth roads lest the jolting, in going along them, should create bile in the stomachs of the over-fed tax-eaters.'[39] Not everyone appreciated having to contribute towards the cost of improving the road system, but most saw the benefits of level highways and the consequent reduction in discomfort, inconvenience and journey times. 'The lane between Deane and Steventon has long been as smooth as the best turnpike road,' wrote James Edward Austen-Leigh in his *Memoir* of 1870,

> but when the family removed from the one residence to the other in 1771, it was a mere cart track, so cut up by deep ruts as to be impassable for a light carriage ... In those days it was not unusual to set men to work with shovel and pickaxe to fill up ruts and holes in roads seldom used by carriages, on such special occasions as a funeral or a wedding.[40]

Road-menders used whatever came to hand to fill up the ruts and potholes; stone from ancient ruins was a favourite material. Colonel Byng noted black iron ore from local smelting works being used on the 'narrow, wet, and stoney' turnpike road six miles from Gloucester in June 1781[41] and James Plumptre walked along roads near the coast in Wales 'mended with shells, cockle and muscle [sic], of which we saw large heaps lying by the road side.'[42] On a summer excursion taken in 1806, Elizabeth Isabella Spence complained that the streets in the town of Usk, more grass than gravel or anything else, were completely neglected and that the state of the road between Abergavenny and Monmouth by way of Raglan was so dreadful that the journey of eighteen miles had taken five and a half hours to accomplish.[43] The repair of Welsh roads, in her opinion, was the worst in the land. On her visit to Milford Haven in 1791, Mrs Mary Morgan compared them unfavourably to English highways:

> The road from Malvern to Hereford was remarkably good; but from thence to Hay, and from Hay hither (to Brecknock), it has

been intolerably disagreeable. Not that it is in itself bad, but they have such a terrible way of *mending it*. Their custom is to throw down vast quantities of huge stones, as large as they come out of the quarry, the size of a man's head, and many of them four times as big. These are spread over the road in heaps, perhaps a mile distant from each other, covering a great many yards of it. You must either drive over them, or wait till the people, who are there with huge hammers for the purpose, have broken them. This they only do into pieces the size of a pretty large flint. Though we had not these enormous masses to go over, which would have endangered our lives, yet our speed was retarded so much as to make me entirely lose my patience.[44]

Even where roads were well maintained, travelling on them was not a quiet experience. In *The Watsons*, Jane Austen describes Emma and Elizabeth's progress in the family's one-horse chair from the muddy lane onto the cobbled turnpike road into the town, 'the jumbling and noise of which made farther conversation most thoroughly undesirable.'[45] Anne Elliot travelling in Lady Russell's carriage over the old bridge into Bath, a route Jane Austen knew well, is deafened by 'the dash of other carriages, the heavy rumble of carts and drays ... and the ceaseless clink of pattens'.[46]

When the Austens were planning their move to Bath from Steventon Rectory in January 1801, they had to consider what they would take with them. Jane related their deliberations to Cassandra: 'We have thought at times of removing the sideboard, or a pembroke table, or some other peice of furniture — but upon the whole it has ended in thinking that the trouble & risk of the removal would be more than the advantage of having them at a place where everything may be purchased.'[47]

Despite improvements in construction and repair, only the foolhardy would risk moving precious furniture and china by road. Mrs Lybbe Powys was astonished when she heard of a family from London attempting a house-move in winter, but not surprised at the outcome. The wagon overturned on the turnpike road near Oxford and 'a deal of damage done in china, &c.'[48] Margaret Graves, moving breakables by road from Devon to Bath in 1793, was more fortunate: 'I have had surprising luck in the moving of my furniture as there is little or no damage to them. The leg of the black Sopha is broke of[f], but as it was one of the hind legs, 'twill be of no other consequence than the expence of repairing it.'[49]

The famous Staffordshire pottery manufacturer Josiah Wedgwood campaigned vigorously for the construction of the Trent and Mersey Canal, so that his fragile goods had a greater chance of reaching Liverpool in one piece before travelling by sea to his showrooms in London. In early June 1811, Jane Austen unpacked a crate of undamaged Wedgwood ware, delivered from London to Chawton by road, and looked forward to the safe arrival of an entire breakfast set. Mrs Dashwood opts to float the few Norland possessions she is entitled to keep to her next home in Devon, rather than risk 250 miles' worth of jolting in a wagon: 'The furniture was all sent round by water. It chiefly consisted of household linen, plate, china, and books, with an handsome pianoforte of Marianne's.'[50]

From the Sussex coast, the Dashwoods' goods would be transported by sea to Exmouth, then along the River Exe to join the canal that terminated at the quay in Exeter. Beyond there, they would once again be in danger of being smashed to smithereens along four miles of bumpy lanes, but there were worse hazards to be faced on the road than wrecked furniture. A lack of lighting made travelling at night or in fog dangerous, especially in rural areas. Carriage lamps were more or less inadequate and horses ran blindly along the road ahead. Sticking steadfastly to the left, according to the rules of the road, was an essential safety measure in the dark. Even so, the following account sounds a touch overconfident:

As soon as it grew dark the coach-lamps were lighted; the horses having no bells this is as needful for the security of other travellers as for our own. But the roads are wide; and if a traveller keeps his own proper side, according to the laws of the roads, however fearful it may be to see two of these fiery eyes coming on through the darkness at the rate of two leagues in the hour, he is perfectly safe.[51]

Good weather and a full moon were the only blessings that could be looked for; those with carriages and those on foot planned outings to balls and to dinner engagements on moonlit nights and hoped for clear skies. Parson Woodforde made an overnight journey with his niece from Norfolk to London in October 1795 and wrote gratefully in his diary the following day: 'I thank God we had fine Weather and a good Moon all last Night and about 10 o'clock this Morning we got safe and well to London.'[52]

All of Sir John Middleton's neighbours take advantage of the moonlight to be 'full of engagements'[53] and Edmund and Julia Bertram walk back to Mansfield Park from the Parsonage after dinner, guided by the moon. Popular cities like London and Bath, where visitors and inhabitants expected to go about the streets safely after dark, were well lit. Oil lamps were installed along all of the main thoroughfares and improvements to them frequently made. On 23 May 1803, *The Times* reported:

> A satisfactory experiment was first made on Friday evening last, at the Upper end of New Bond Street, to dissipate the great darkness that has long prevailed in the streets of this metropolis. It consisted in the adaptation of twelve newly invented lamps with reflectors, in place of more than double that number of common ones; and notwithstanding the wetness of the evening ... that part of the street [was] illuminated with at least twice the quantity of light usually seen.[54]

Lights in shop windows helped to dispel the gloom, especially when the switch was made from oil to gas in 1805. In the children's book *A Visit To London*, published in the same year, the Sandby parents tease their children by telling them that the city has been lit especially for their arrival.[55] Gas street lighting started in Pall Mall in 1807 and from 1812 gradually replaced oil lamps.

The impenetrable darkness on the lonely heaths and high-ways beyond the lights of the capital was far beyond a joke. Shadowy trees and dark ditches harboured highwaymen and footpads, intent on assault and robbery. Jane Austen's cousin Eliza de Feuillide travelled on a cool, moonlit night from London to Tunbridge Wells in September 1796 and afterwards wrote to Philadelphia Walter, 'I reached this place on Saturday night (about eleven) without having met a single Collector, or Mishap of any kind ...'.[56] Travellers through the dark were well aware of the risks they took and those returning to London at night frequently gathered at inns until safety in numbers boosted their confidence in a safe passage. No highwaymen hold up the Allens' carriage on its way to Bath, but not because such an event was unlikely, even in broad daylight. One felon whose exploits featured in newspapers throughout the 1780s must have caught Jane Austen's attention. His name was D'Arcy Wentworth. She also knew of several highway robberies in the Steventon area before she began writing *Northanger Abbey*. The *Reading Mercury* of 19 August 1793, reported: 'many robberies have of late been committed in and about the neighbourhood of Overton, in the county of Southampton, by a person, supposed to be a stranger.'[57] The first victim was the Austens' friend and neighbour, Mrs Mary Bramston of Oakley Hall, whose carriage was held up at 10 p.m. on 6 June near Ashe and she and a female companion robbed. Mrs Bramston wrote of her ordeal to a friend:

> I have been very much frightened lately, by being Stopd returning from drinking tea with Mrs Lefroy, by a footpad, who put his pistol Close to me & said he would blow out my Brains if I did not give him my Money I lost 8 Guineas which I did not like at all, beside its having made my head Ache ever since & I now Start at my own Shadow but am getting better.[58]

On 5 July, at about the same time of night, 'a servant of the Rev. Mr. Lefroy [of Ashe] was attacked by the same person in Kingsdown Lane, the road leading to Kingsclere and Newbury [from Overton], and who, on making some resistance, was much beaten with a bludgeon'.[59] The third reported attack came on 12 July. Mrs Trevor of Lower Seymour Street, London, with two other ladies,

> travelling in their own carriage, were stopped in the vicinity of Popham-lane, by a man in a smock frock, with a handkerchief or crape over his face, and armed with pistols, who robbed them of nine guineas, their gold watches, and ear-rings from their ears, value together about 100£. The villain came out of Popham wood, and tied his horse to a gate, whilst he committed the robbery.[60]

The terrorized neighbourhood fretted for two and a half months, until, in August, a reward of £40 for apprehension of the malefactor was offered. This was enough to dissuade the culprit from further criminal activity in the area and no more was heard of him, but Cassandra and Jane's outdoor exercise must have been sadly curtailed for some while, as Emma's was, after Harriet and Miss Bickerton's encounter with the gypsies on the road to Richmond, 'which, though apparently public enough for safety, had led them into alarm.'[61] Emma has to promise a distraught Mr Woodhouse not to venture beyond the Hartfield shrubbery, even though the gypsies had removed themselves immediately from the area to escape punishment. The increasing enclosure of common land deprived gypsy families of camping places and drove them onto the highway. In 1805, two gypsies were apprehended on suspicion 'of having robbed Mr. Budd and another person on the highway in the neighbourhood of Alton'[62] and *The Times* reported in autumn 1811 that a young woman in service had been approached by a gypsy woman offering to tell her fortune. She refused and was attacked by two men, knocked down, robbed, then stabbed.[63]

A real fear of highway robbery is reflected in General Tilney's 'numerous out-riders' on the journey from Bath to Northanger Abbey. These horsemen would have been armed too; it was legal to carry weapons for self-defence and the more prominently displayed they were, the more of a deterrent they proved to be. Stage coach proprietors advertised the presence of armed guards as an added incentive to travellers; the Post Office supplied all of the mail coach guards with firearms. On a carriage journey to Portsmouth from London in 1794, John Knyveton described how well primed he and his companion were: 'the coachman and I were all armed to the teeth, with a blunderbuss and a bludgeon and a pocket pistol apiece; perils all the way over the dismal wastes of Surrey and many rogues lurking of course in the ditches near the great and busy port.'[64]

The 'dismal wastes' on his route comprised a number of heaths and commons, but the most notorious stretch of road in Surrey ran over Bagshot Heath, near the border with Berkshire and Hampshire. Highwaymen took advantage of the fact that Bagshot itself was an important staging post on one of the main coach roads out of London, with, at one time, fourteen inns. In 1770, when Eliza de Feuillide was a child of eight, her mother had taken a huge risk on Bagshot Heath. Travelling unaccompanied in a post chaise, a dangerous undertaking it itself, she had discovered mid-way across the heath that her trunk had fallen from the roof. The postilion went back to find it, leaving Philadelphia and her little daughter completely unprotected. They sat in the chaise for a while, then decided to walk two miles to the nearest inn, abandoning their other possessions and leaving the coach doors open. Fortunately, the hot August weather proved a deterrent to thieves and their journey continued to London without mishap as soon as the postilion returned.[65]

In all of the bleak areas around London, where travellers were common and the money in their pockets plentiful, highwaymen lurked. No one was exempt – members of the royal family, the Prime Minister, the Lord Mayor of London, titled personages and the Neapolitan Ambassador all fell victim to highway robbers. Hampstead Heath, Windsor Forest, Wimbledon Common, Hounslow Heath, Epping Forest and Shotover Hill promised easy pickings and a rapid disappearance into the no-go districts of the capital city. In 1788, Eliza made the journey with her mother from Berkshire to London, which entailed traversing Hounslow Heath in a storm. On this occasion, bad weather did them and other travellers a favour:

> We returned to Town on Sunday and of all the dreadful storms of Thunder Lightning & Rain I ever remember, I think that we experienced on that amiable place called Hounslow Heath was the worst, however I believe it saved us from being robbed as we afterwards heard that two Highwaymen were at that very moment in waiting for their Prey & nothing but the violent storm prevented their stopping us.[66]

Colonel Byng held the firm belief that travellers relieved of their belongings had only themselves to blame if they were so foolish as to travel at night:

> I read in the papers of several robberies and abuses of travellers upon Hounslow Heath at ten o'clock, and upon Finchley Common at eleven o'clock at night and here are passengers at nine o'clock at night, stopping only till another chaise is got ready. Now such travellers are the encouragers of highwaymen and ought to be punish'd accordingly.[67]

The final years of the 1790s saw an increase in the number of robberies on the road to London and in 1797, another two of the Austens' acquaintances fell victim to highwaymen. The Very Revd Thomas Powys, Dean of Canterbury, was attacked on Hounslow Heath in 1797, 'by several footpads, who robbed him of three 25£ notes, and a King James's Guinea'.[68] Charles Powlett of Winslade forfeited a gold watch and his purse. The *Reading Mercury* reported in November 1798 that, 'no fewer than sixteen post-chaises were stopped on Hounslow heath in three evenings last week'. Three weeks earlier, the newspaper had applauded the success of nightly cavalry patrols in totally eradicating robbery in the Maidenhead area.[69]

The problem persisted into the next century. Twenty years after John Knyveton had taken a brace of pistols and his life in his hands to cross Surrey, Anna and Ben Lefroy, faced with a journey to Hendon across both Bagshot and Hounslow Heaths on the day of their winter wedding at Steventon, chose an early time for the ceremony and travelled in daylight. Predictably, sentimental novels, popular plays and even newspapers glamorized the 'gentlemen of the road'. Sensational stories made for a good read and the bad boys who starred in them earned celebrity status. Dick Turpin, executed in 1739, was imprinted on the collective consciousness as a national folk hero, a daring 'knight of the road', his exploits performed to popular acclaim on stage throughout Jane Austen's lifetime. A journalist on the *Morning Chronicle* reported on another 'gallant' criminal in January 1797:

> a very gallant highway robbery was lately committed on Wimbledon Common upon the person of a young married lady. After receiving her purse, the robber politely demanded an elegant ring which he discovered on her finger. This she peremptorily refused, saying 'She would sooner part with life'; the hero of the turf rejoined, 'Since you value the ring so much, madam, allow me the honour of saluting the fair hand which wears it, and I shall deem it a full equivalent'. The hand was instantly stretched through the chariot window, and the kiss being received, the highwayman thanked her for her condescension and instantly galloped off perfectly satisfied with the commutation.[70]

The man's polite language would appear to indicate that he was an educated gentleman, as a number of highwaymen undoubtedly were. Some were revealed to be the sons of clergymen and younger members of aristocratic families, tempted into a life of crime as a consequence of gambling debts, drinking problems, a distaste for the more acceptable professions or a need, perhaps, for a greater degree of excitement than everyday existence afforded. The notoriety, romance and thrill were rather offset by the consequences if caught. The malefactor was hanged in public, exhibited on a gibbet at the roadside and the corpse left there in chains until decomposed. Jane Austen might have glimpsed such a grisly sight on her journeys. The *Salisbury Journal* in 1783 spelled out William Peare's punishment for robbing a mail coach: 'executed at Fisherton gallows ... and his body will then be enclosed in a suit of chains ... and affixed to a gibbet erected near the spot where the robbery was committed ... as a dreadful memento to youth, how they swerve from the paths of rectitude, and transgress the laws of their country.'[71]

There is no doubt that, despite the threat of snowfall, flood and highway robbery, improved road construction and maintenance opened up the country to long-distance travellers and provided smoother roads than before for a fast mail service. In Jane Austen's lifetime, over 1,100 separate turnpike trusts were created, resulting in 22,000 miles of improved and new roads.[72] But fewer than twenty per cent of roads were maintained by the trusts and many side-roads remained muddy, unrepaired, uneven and impassable, in good and bad weather alike. The 'very rough lane ... half rock, half sand' in which Mr Parker's carriage overturns in *Sanditon* would be familiar to most of Jane Austen's readers.[73] Mr Darcy's 'fifty miles of good road'[74] remained an impossible dream for most, but a revolution in the speed of transport and communications was fast approaching. In 1800, Thomas Telford was given a free hand to create a network of roads over the Scottish Highlands and in eight years constructed more than a thousand miles of serviceable road over bogs, mountains and fells. His experience in Scotland fed into his road-building programme in England. John McAdam, a Scottish civil engineer, began a rival road-building programme in 1815. 'Macadamisation', as his new method of road construction became known, involved binding stones together with crushed, graded gravel on a foundation of larger rocks, with a camber at each side, allowing rainwater to drain away rapidly. Thomas de Quincey enthused that 'All the roads in England within a few years were remodelled ... from mere beds of torrents and systems of ruts, they were raised universally to the condition and appearance of gravel walks in private parks',[75] a rather expansive claim, but McAdam's roads certainly made journeys less uncomfortable.

Did a stretch of good road between Oxford and Randalls deliver Frank Churchill half a day earlier than expected, or bring Edward Ferrars from Oxford to Barton Cottage in double-quick time, or Willoughby from London to Cleveland in less than twenty-four hours? Strength of purpose probably had more to do with the speed of these determined travellers, but wherever improved roads were found, travelling times were significantly reduced. Jane Austen's journey from Steventon to Bath in May 1799 was particularly expeditious, following heavy winter flooding: 'Our Journey yesterday went off exceedingly well; nothing occurred to alarm or delay us; — We found the roads in excellent order, had very good horses all the way, & reached Devizes with ease by 4 o'clock.'[76]

Jane was also keen to suggest changes to her travelling brothers' usual routes. In May 1813, with Charles' imminent visit to Chawton from London in mind, she thought that he would enjoy the road through Guildford rather than Bagshot. She and Henry, making the journey in the opposite direction, 'made enquiries at Esher as to their posting distances. — From Guildford to Esher 14 miles, from Esher to Hyde Park corner 15 — which makes it exactly the same as from Bagshot to H. P. corner, changing at Bedfont, 49 miles altogether, each way.' They discovered that Charles would gain nothing in terms of mileage, but the road itself 'has much more beauty & not more hills. — If I were Charles, I should chuse it ...'.[77]

Mr Darcy obviously considers the route from Hertfordshire into Kent superior to many, as well he might. Both of the main highways from London to the north passed through Elizabeth

Bennet's home county, encouraging the development of a thriving economy, based on catering for travellers. *Cary's Traveller's Companion* of 1791 shows mail coach roads from London passing through Hatfield to the west of Hertford and through Hoddesdon and Ware to the east. Only a few days after his arrival at Netherfield, Mr Bingley travels to London, prompting Mrs Bennet to fear that he would be 'always flying about from one place to another', as, with two excellent roads to choose from, he is able to do.[78] The roads from Surrey into London were equally well maintained, allowing Frank Churchill to dash there and back in a day from Randalls but, for Mr Woodhouse, sixteen or even half a mile of good road is beyond his idea of an easy distance. He will not exert himself to visit his eldest daughter in Brunswick Square and, until the strawberry party takes him to Donwell Abbey, he has not covered the three miles there for two years. His selfish torpor closes down Emma's horizons; for all her wealth, she has travelled less on England's roads than Jane Fairfax.

In a verbal exchange at Hunsford, where Darcy and Elizabeth misunderstand each other's unspoken meaning, they argue about the ease or difficulty with which fifty miles of good road can be covered. Charlotte's new home at Hunsford is conveniently near her family, merely half a day's journey, pronounces Darcy. Only a large income will support frequent journeys of fifty miles, whether over good roads or bad, but a woman might find herself settled too close to her family, replies Elizabeth, blushing, as her imagination jumps to Jane and Bingley and the three short miles between Netherfield and Longbourn. Readers recall this exchange of views when Bingley purchases an estate not far from Darcy's; an easy distance of thirty miles separates the sisters. Darcy hints that Elizabeth – whom he pictures at Pemberley, over a hundred miles from her family home – is not as attached as Charlotte to Hertfordshire. The lady expresses surprise, the gentleman draws back his chair and adopts a cooler tone. A conversation about the state of the roads is anything but commonplace in this case.

4

An Animal Made For Speed

ORSES WERE AS familiar a sight on the roads of Georgian England as cars are today. They were noticed, but not much commented on unless they were thoroughbreds, more Ferrari than Ford, worthy of posing for George Stubbs or Henry Raeburn. All we learn by way of description from Jane Austen is that Mr Bingley makes his first visit to Longbourn on a black mount, Eleanor Tilney's future husband takes a chestnut to Northanger Abbey (Catherine Morland discovers a farrier's bill for a poultice), Frank Churchill owns a black mare and Edward Ferrars, Colonel Brandon and John Willoughby must ride remarkably similar animals, given that Marianne and Elinor fail to recognize which is which on two separate occasions. Perhaps it's a woman thing, although, with the exception of John Thorpe – and Jane Austen knew more than one man who 'all his life thought more of Horses than of anything'[1] – no male character expands on the appearance of his or anyone else's. The gentlemen at Mrs John Dashwood's dinner party in Harley Street discuss breaking horses, among other topics, but only once in the novels is notice taken by a group of men of a particular horse. Mr Knightley, Mr Weston and Frank Churchill comment on Mr Perry's as he rides by, but their remarks go unrecorded.

The majority of the population travelled on foot if they travelled at all but, for those at Jane Austen's level of society and above, men in particular, a horse was an essential possession, for business and for pleasure. Mr Bennet's horses do double duty, on the farm and harnessed to the carriage; working horses were not taxed so this expedience saves him money and was common practice. Mary Russell Mitford reported in 1801, 'I am convinced that more than half the smart carriages in the neighbourhood of Reading are drawn by the horses which work in the team.'[2] Mr Bennet's saddle horse takes his eldest daughter to Netherfield in the rain and Mr Perry's carries him to his patients in Highbury through all weathers. Mr Elton's horse transports him past the windows of admiring female parishioners and to London on the precious errand of delivering Emma's portrait of Harriet to the frame-maker. Both Mr Knightley and his tenant famer Robert Martin ride to the local market town on estate business; Edmund Bertram travels on horseback to Sotherton, to Northampton and to his ordination in Peterborough; Sir John Middleton sends a servant on a pony to collect his mail. Staid Mr Heywood in *Sanditon* 'went no farther than his feet or his well-tried old horse could carry him'.[3] Henry Crawford, Edmund Bertram, John Willoughby and Reginald de Courcy keep hunters and presumably Messrs Darcy, Bingley and Musgrove junior do too. John Thorpe boasts that he has three, but no one equals equestrian-rich Mr Clifford's 'amazing fine stud' of nineteen.[4]

Horse ownership is a good indicator of income, an excess or a lack of it. One of the markers of Mr Coles' elevation to the first circle in Highbury society is his possession of carriage horses; Emma herself notices them twice. The first sighting of Mr Bingley in a chaise-and-four adds interest to Mrs Bennet's calculations. Sir Walter Elliot must relinquish his two pairs because he cannot afford to keep them, but he ensures that they herald his entry into Bath before parting with them. The first question he asks Anne on the Crofts' arrival in Bath is whether *they* had made the journey from Kellynch with four horses. The irony that they can afford such an expense but would never consider parading their wealth in this way completely passes him by. General Tilney's chaise is drawn out of Bath by four very smart animals and accompanied by a number of outriders. Mr Knightley has no spare money to keep carriage horses, he invests his income in improving his land and prefers anyway to walk or ride. In *The Three Sisters*, one of Mary Stanhope's conditions for marrying the odious Mr Watts is that four horses will pull their new chaise and Lady Catherine de Bourgh, as we would expect, owns several horses to pull her several carriages. Jane Austen claimed that she had 'extended her Lights' by rubbing shoulders with another wealthy horse-owning woman in Kent – 'Lady Honeywood, you know ... going about with 4 Horses, & nicely dressed herself — she is altogether a perfect sort of Woman.'[5]

The subject of horse-riding provided a useful opening gambit in conversation: Frank Churchill's initial enquiries on meeting Emma are '"Was she a horse-woman? — Pleasant rides?"'[6] and one of the 'first rudiments of acquaintance' between Catherine Morland and Miss Tilney involves finding out if riding is a common interest.[7] Socially inept Lord Osborne attempts to engage Emma Watson's attention by recommending that she ride, without considering the obvious lack of financial where-withal in the Watson household:

"Ladies should ride in dirty weather. — Do you ride?"

"No my Lord."

"I wonder every lady does not. — A woman never looks better than on horseback."

"But every woman may not have the inclination, or the means."

"If they knew how much it became them, they would all have the inclination — and I fancy Miss Watson — when once they had the inclination, the means would soon follow."[8]

In similar economic difficulties, Marianne Dashwood thought-lessly accepts Willoughby's gift of a mare and only reluctantly agrees to refuse it when Elinor points out that another horse would have to be purchased for an additional servant and a stable built. A groom could expect to be paid £30 a year, a stable boy almost £17.[9] In addition, farriers' and saddlers' costs would have to be met, veterinary fees found, horse-feed supplied and the required tax paid. Servants who looked after the horses were essential members of the outdoor staff and often known by name. Mrs Norris is even more of an interfering busybody in the servants' quarters at Mansfield Park than she is in the house; in the stables she keeps a close eye on John Groom, Charles and Stephen and doctors old Wilcox the coachman's rheumatism. Mr Woodhouse, who has probably never risked an inspection of the Hartfield stableyard, feigns a very convenient deference to *his* coachman, James.

Cost is Mrs Norris' spurious objection to Fanny's acquisition of a horse to replace the old grey pony, but grooms and stables already exist at Sir Thomas' establishment and Edmund suggests selling his road horse in order to buy a suitable mount for his cousin. Horses 'exactly calculated to carry a woman'[10] were specially trained to a side saddle, for the use of which women required training too. Edmund Bertram has already proved himself an apt tutor to Fanny in matters of moral and literary taste, now he indulges his desire to teach vivacious Miss Crawford something physical, as her riding master. The episode where Fanny watches the animated scene from her isolated position on the hill above the parsonage meadow is a crucial one, marking her growing jealousy of Mary and uneasy awareness of Edmund's neglect. Fanny will not acknowledge these feelings, even to herself; they are transposed instead into pity for the horse, 'if she were forgotten, the poor mare should be remembered', a deluded misreading of Edmund's behaviour and unjustified criticism, on this occasion, of Henry Crawford. She watches her cousin directing Mary's use of the bridle and sees, or imagines she sees, him take her hand:

what could be more natural than that Edmund should be making himself useful, and proving his good-nature by any-one? She could not but think indeed that Mr. Crawford might as well have saved him the trouble; that it would have been particularly proper and becoming in a brother to have done it himself; but Mr. Crawford, with all his boasted good-nature, and all his coachmanship, probably knew nothing of the matter, and had no kindness in comparison of Edmund.[11]

To add insult to injury, Mary is a bold, feisty rider, fearlessly springing from the saddle and eager to canter on her second lesson. The old coachman rubs more salt into the wound by comparing Fanny's fear and trembling when she was first mounted with Mary's '"good heart for riding ... I never see one sit a horse better."'[12] The Miss Bertrams think the same: Mary's delight and accomplishment, her pluck and ardour echo their own. Edmund is so bewitched by Miss Crawford's riding prowess that he manipulates Fanny into agreeing to part with the mare yet again, couching his request in such terms that she cannot refuse, while voicing concern for her well-being: '"*She* rides only for pleasure, *you* for health."'[13] Unfortunately, Mary's pleasure, with Edmund's full encouragement, extends into four morning rides in the shady lanes around the Park, depriving Fanny of exercise, company and respite from Mrs Norris' bullying.

Riding was a universally acknowledged benefit to health. It was an activity that also drew admiring glances from the members of both sexes. Two pairs of female eyes follow Edmund's progress to Sotherton; even a staid clergyman-to-be could look good on horseback in a cut-away coat. Darcy and Bingley riding into Meryton are objects of immediate interest and it was screenplay writer Andrew Davies' intention that the two men galloping across the Hertfordshire landscape should create an energetic beginning to the 1995 BBC series of *Pride and Prejudice*: 'part of the justification for showing Bingley and Darcy at that moment ... is to show them as two physical young men. They are young animals on their big horses'.[14] Similar scenes of straining muscles and leather-clad thighs feature in the 1995 Ang Lee film and the 2007 BBC series of *Sense and Sensibility*. In the novel, Willoughby has sexual attraction enough, but subdued Edward Ferrars and dull Colonel Brandon need the help of riding boots to transform them into physically vital characters. Portraits of the time depict mounted squires inspecting their harvesters, military men reining in their steeds and independent gentlemen in the hunting field or nonchalantly leaning against dangerous-looking beasts.[15]

Women in the saddle, displaying Junoesque figures beneath tight-waisted riding habits and well-turned ankles in nankin boots, quicken the pulse of Lord Osborne in *The Watsons*. The Prince of Wales was equally susceptible. He commissioned George Stubbs in 1793 to portray Laetitia, Lady Lade, a renowned horsewoman, calmly seated on a rearing steed. The side saddle made horse control challenging, but ladies who sat astride and used their thighs as men did risked more than just their reputations. The artist Charles Williams hinted at the consequences in distinctly suggestive terms in a cartoon. The name 'Stretchit' appears on a signpost above a young woman straddling a horse. She enquires of the sailor standing in the road, 'Pray Sir is this the way to Stretchit?' to which he replies, 'Shiver my top-sails my Lass if I know a better way.'[16] Cartoonist Thomas Rowlandson took the same joke beyond mere suggestion when he depicted women with legs splayed, enjoying vigorous copulation on horseback.[17]

It was probably beyond Dr John Gregory, clergyman and writer of conduct manuals, to imagine his daughters disporting themselves in any other way than respectably in the saddle. He advised them to take exercise on horseback in the open air as often as possible: 'This will give vigour to your constitutions, and a bloom to your complexions. If you accustom yourselves to go abroad always in chairs and carriages, you will soon become so enervated as to be unable to go outdoors without them.'[18]

This is certainly the kind of healthy outdoor activity that Sir Thomas has in mind for Fanny Price, but not every woman took to the saddle with a good grace. Through her twenties and thirties, Mary Russell Mitford tried 'very honestly and conscientiously' to like riding, but eventually had to admit that she found it 'a detestable recreation, which I abhor the more I endeavour to endure it'.[19] Of Jane Austen's heroines, Anne Elliot prefers to walk, Elizabeth Bennet 'is no horse-woman'[20] and there is no mention of Emma Woodhouse on horseback.

Medical men of the time recommended horse-riding for both sexes. 'Such as can,' stated William Buchan MD, 'ought to spend two or three hours a-day on horseback.'[21] Active diversion out of doors, he added, improved the spirits, increased the appetite and strengthened the body. Colonel Byng, a staunch supporter of touring on horseback as opposed to travelling by carriage, believed that riding improved one's chances of living to a ripe old age:

> My wish is riding; and that I would indulge in all weathers, were my fortune ever so excessive, by purchasing the very best hackneys; for the pleasure and convenience of a journey, for the opportunity of going in any roads, for the preservation of health, and for the procuration (if to be had by any means) of old age. Most of the old men I know have been great riders.[22]

Byng didn't do too badly – he died one month short of his seventieth birthday, having toured the country on horseback until the age of fifty. At least three of Jane Austen's brothers were men after Byng's own heart, Edward, Frank and Charles. They all rode whenever they could and lived long lives, Charles surviving into his seventies, when cholera killed him, Edward into his eighties and Frank into his nineties. Edward took an active interest in his estates and 'made his horse the chief means of getting about', sometimes travelling the twelve miles from his house at Chawton to inspect his land at Steventon, 'a little roll behind the saddle, bringing necessities enough for a night or two.'[23] As a boy, Edward had ridden a pony on even longer journeys, between his home at Steventon Parsonage and Godmersham Park in Kent, the rich Knights sending their coachman on horseback to collect him for the holidays.[24] At the age of seven, his younger brother Francis bought his first pony on which he hunted for two years before selling it at a profit.[25] Charles too relished riding and thought nothing of travelling thirty-eight miles home to Steventon 'on a Gosport Hack'.[26] In his early forties he enjoyed days in the saddle on coastguard duties in both directions along the Cornish coast from Padstow: 'he will spend great part of his time on Horseback, fortunately he is very fond of that exercise,' recorded his mother.[27]

While some learned the art of horse-riding from family members or from their grooms, others took instruction at equestrian schools. Outside London, riding schools were established in the fashionable resorts of Bath, Cheltenham, Buxton and Brighton. Spa and seaside towns were quick to realize that equestrian arenas were a popular attraction for tourists. The first in Bath was erected in 1772:

> At a little distance from the New Assembly-Rooms, in Montpelier Row, is a large and commodious *Riding-school*, kept by Mr Dash, where Ladies and Gentlemen amuse themselves every morning, and are instructed in the art of horsemanship; the days for Gentlemen are Mondays, Wednesdays, and Fridays; for Ladies, Tuesdays, Thursdays, and Saturdays. The terms for those who learn to ride, and ride the managed horse, are three guineas per month, or 5s. 3d. each lesson: Those whose horses are kept at livery here, are allowed to ride them in the school gratis.[28]

Two of Jane Austen's acquaintances brushed up on their horse-riding skills in Mr Dash's indoor arena. 'This morning we have been to see Miss Chamberlayne look hot on horseback' she wrote to Cassandra in April 1805. 'Seven years & four months ago we went to the same Ridinghouse to see Miss Lefroy's performance!'[29] A low platform around the arena accommodated spectators. The *Bath Guide* for 1800 carries the first advertisement for Ryles in Monmouth Street, which operated as a rival to Mr Dash's establishment: 'An extensive and commodious

Riding House in Monmouth Street near the Elephant and Castle where Ladies and Gentlemen take equestrian exercise when the weather will not permit them to go on the roads or mount the downs.'[30]

At Buxton, Johanna Schopenhauer marvelled at the splendour of the stables and the equestrian school:

Buxton's most remarkable sight is the set of magnificent stables built by the Duke of Devonshire, said to be the finest and most perfect of their kind in Europe, and, as far as we know, they may well deserve that fame. Built in a circle, they are surrounded by a colonnade where, as is the custom in England, the horses are protected from the wind and rain and can be taken care of and groomed throughout the day. In the centre of this is a beautiful and commodious riding school. There are also coach-houses, and the whole is of considerable size, almost suggesting that the four-footed spa guests are of prime importance here. A small stream running alongside makes it easy to keep these magnificent stables clean, so doing away with any unpleasant smells.[31]

The riding house in Brighton adjoined an indoor tennis court and several coach and lodging houses, all situated within the Prince of Wales' Chinese-style stables.[32] Every guide to seabathing places made mention of rides in and around the localities; Captain Wentworth found those in the vicinity of Lyme particularly advantageous as a means of disengaging himself from Louisa Musgrove as well as enjoying the fine views. The best that Sanditon could offer by way of physical amusement in wet weather was Lady Denham's chamber horse, a leather upholstered exercise machine, comprising planks of wood separated by concertina springs, on which ladies and gentlemen could bounce enthusiastically. One female correspondent in 1798 informed a friend that she had been obliged to give up using her chamber horse for a while, 'but I look forward to resuming that exercise, which I commenced when unwell near two years since,

& my Physician most strongly recommended it to me. Indeed, I suppose most female constitutions must derive advantage from any such exercise taken so'.[33]

No one could come to much harm on this rudimentary piece of equipment, unlike those who mounted real horses. The sketchbooks of amateur artist Diana Sperling abound with watercolour drawings of family and friends, male and female, measuring their length after yet another toppling. The titles given to these drawings reveal the commonplace incidence of mishaps on horseback: 'Cherish running off with Isabella', 'Harry tumbling off his colt', 'Charles Sperling picking up his sister who had rolled off her donkey'. Horses throw riders into lakes, donkeys deposit theirs in the mud.[34] Jane Austen's neighbours took tumbles enough, and she recorded some of them in her letters. In December 1798, she described James Digweed's injuries, sustained in the struggle to tame a newly purchased young horse: 'the Animal kicked him down with his forefeet, & kicked a great hole in his head; — he scrambled away as soon as he could, but was stunned for a time, & suffered a good deal of pain afterwards. — Yesterday he got up the Horse again, & for fear of something worse, was forced to throw himself off.'[35]

Predictably, hunting claimed a number of casualties. Sir John Middleton says in praise of Willoughby that there is 'not a bolder rider in England'[36] and William Heathcote, rector of Worting in Hampshire, was a fearless horseman to rival him. He was a mad-keen fox-hunting clergyman – a portrait of him from 1790 shows him looking impossibly gorgeous in his fashionably-cut hunting jacket, not a bit concerned about any threat to his personal safety. A 'genteel little accident' in the hunting field in 1800,[37] which resulted in a broken ankle did not amount to much, but in 1802 his hunting career ended when he died at the young age of thirty. His neighbour, William Chute of the Vyne, with whom James Austen hunted on a regular basis, indulged his passion for the sport into his sixties, although the consequences of one particular fall could have been serious. His horse slipped, he fell under its hooves and was trodden on. The other huntsmen gathered round and expressed their concern as he massaged his inner thigh. 'I thought we were going to lose our member', said one of them. 'Did you?' replied Chute. 'Well, I can tell you I thought *I* was going to lose *mine*.'[38] In *Mansfield Park*, Fanny Price's anxiety concerning Henry Crawford's offer of a hunter to her brother is well founded. While Sir Thomas points out the value of the loan – a good hunter cost between £75 and £150 – Fanny sees the danger in William proving unequal 'to the management of a high-fed hunter in an English fox-chase.'[39]

On Jane Austen's birthday in 1804, her friend and former neighbour Mrs Lefroy of Ashe was thrown from her horse and killed near Overton. She had met James Austen earlier and complained about the sluggishness of her mare, but on the way home, the animal had bolted. Her servant attempted to catch the reins but failed, causing the horse to gallop off even faster. In an attempt to save herself, Mrs Lefroy had thrown herself off and hit the ground with some force. 'She never spoke afterwards, and she died in a few hours', reported Caroline Austen, whose mother Mary had recorded the fatality in her diary and later recounted the whole story.[40] Jane was greatly affected by the loss; in 1808 she wrote a poem to commemorate the sad occasion. Fanny Price might fret over William's fate on a highly-strung hunter and Mrs Weston imagine Frank thrown from his mare when he is late for the picnic at Donwell, but no riding accidents find their way into Jane Austen's published novels. The only fatality appears in *Lesley Castle*, when Eloisa Lutterell's fiancé falls from his horse and dies the same day.

Caroline later recorded a near-accident involving a horse at Steventon Parsonage. In 1814, when she was nine years old, she took her turn over the winter months at exercising the horses in the meadow, accompanied by a groom, for an hour each day. She came to the conclusion that it had not been a safe undertaking, even though the horses were steady creatures. They were fed well in the cold weather and when turned out of the stables took full advantage of their freedom. On this occasion, the canter turned into a gallop at full pelt towards a hedge:

the servant's horse, which was first, charged the fence — the man was as much run away with as I was. As his horse cleared the hedge *he* tumbled off behind, and fell exactly in front of mine, which was following with great energy. The surprise checked him, and I was able to manage him, till the man could come to my help ... The hedge and bank were not very high, and I think that I should probably have got over safe — but I was frightened ... I rode though very often with my father and my brother, and I think riding was my greatest pleasure.[41]

It was certainly her father's. James Austen had always hunted, but his habit led to debt when he was first married. An income of £300 per annum would not cover the maintenance of hunters, harriers, wife and child. Despite Marianne Dashwood's insouciance concerning money, she recognized that a hunting enthusiast required a large income. If James did not hunt, he rode almost every day of the year, on parish duties, to visit his neighbours and friends, his parents at Steventon and later, when he was Rector of Steventon himself, his widowed mother and sisters at Chawton. Jane remarked on his interest in horse appropriation in several of her letters. In 1800, he went to Winchester Fair and bought a 'very pretty' carriage horse; in 1808, a yearly allowance of £100 from his Aunt Leigh Perrot enabled him to consider keeping another two. When the Revd George Austen moved from Steventon to Bath in 1801, James acquired his father's horses, prompting Jane to complain to Cassandra:

the brown Mare, which as well as the black was to devolve on James at our removal, has not had patience to wait for that, & has settled herself even now at Deane. — The death of Hugh Capet, which like that of Mr Skipsey tho' undesired was not wholly unexpected, being purposely effected, has made the immediate possession of the Mare very convenient ... [42]

The endearing names given to James' mounts did not save them from an expedient demise but, for the most part, James

Austen was a kind and careful master. In all his years of riding, he seems only to have had two accidents, breaking an arm at some unspecified date[43] and a leg in 1816, but in his early fifties, failing health led to the curtailment of his daily exercise. His years on horseback did not vouchsafe to him the robust longevity granted to his younger horse-riding brothers. In 1818, he planned a riding tour down the Wye Valley, but realized that his hopes of restored vigour could not be realistically fulfilled. Instead, he submitted to travelling to the New Forest in a post chaise, which was 'hateful' to a man who preferred the freedom of riding. The following year, which was his last, James set off on a journey from Steventon to Scarlets, near Reading, but, as Caroline reported, the outcome was the same as the previous year's: 'My father, always desiring the open air, and horse exercise, persuaded himself that he could ride down. He set off before us with his servant ... But at Cranford Bridge we found he had halted, unable to proceed further on horseback, and obliged to take my place in the carriage.'[44]

Like his father, James Edward Austen-Leigh also relished his time on horseback, riding to hounds whenever he could and tending his mount with the greatest care. Caroline recalled how useful the pony was, on the road and in the field; when he died, James Edward, then aged twelve, was heartbroken. His father understood his grief and wrote a poem to comfort him, pointing out that he had treated the pony well and had nothing to reproach himself with:

But you can view, nor conscience blame,
(And may you ever do the same)
Your conduct to your little steed,
For sure I am no Quadrupede
A kinder master knew
Than Pony ever found in you.[45]

In 1818, when James Edward was twenty and studying for his degree at Oxford, he owned a valuable hunter that he offered to sell so that his father could continue to finance Caroline's education when Mrs Leigh Perrot capriciously withdrew her nephew's yearly allowance of £100. Like Edmund Bertram, James Edward's conscience told him that two horses would suffice – 'I could not sit easy on my horse,' he wrote to his father, 'if by giving him up I could secure Caroline a continuance of instruction.'[46] Whether or not he was called upon to make the sacrifice is not recorded. Many years later, James Edward's own son, Cholmeley, at school in Winchester ended a letter to his father with the hope that 'the ponys are well.'[47]

Visitors to England from other countries saw more to praise in our horses and our treatment of them than in their own. François de la Rochefoucauld, travelling in England in the 1780s, claimed that every English gentleman owned superior horses of the best breed and appearance: 'in France we have no idea of their quality: all tall, well-made and with their tails docked, and as well turned-out as those of a rich private person in France, and all go at a spanking pace.'[48] He noted that, in proportion to the inhabitants, the number of horses in England doubled that in France. Even gentlemen at the lower end of the gentry had two carriage horses and at least one horse to ride; clergymen and the unmarried usually kept saddle horses, which would be worth at least forty guineas each if sold in France. Thorough and regular grooming added the finishing gloss to their superb appearance. A man could travel throughout the country with his own horses and no servant to look after them, he stated, and they would get the best attention in the world: 'The people at the inn will take such an interest in them that it can only be explained as part of the general feeling of the nation for these animals.'[49]

Colonel Byng would have disagreed, violently. At the George Inn at Winchester, and at various hostelries across the country in all his years of touring, he found the stabling 'horrid' and spent his evenings checking that his horse was properly groomed, fed and bedded down on clean, dry straw.[50] Ostlers and stable boys could not be trusted, he complained, and if his horse suffered, the inevitable consequence would be that the next day's ride would be spoiled. Byng blamed 'the universal fashion to go post' for bad stabling and poor service; 'the higher that is taxed the better,' he growled, 'and then good road horses again may be had, and good stabling again may be found.'[51]

Rochefoucauld could be accused of viewing the treatment of horses through rose-tinted spectacles. All Englishmen shared an extraordinary love for their horses, he said, and looked after them with such care that they lived long lives.[52] What he believed was true of all Englishmen applied only to private gentlemen with consciences and those who built magnificent coach houses and stables to enhance their grand properties. The stables at Wentworth Woodhouse in Yorkshire were 'more like a palace than a home for horses'[53] and kept scrupulously clean.

Tom Bertram takes more interest in his stables than he does in the affairs of his family, removing himself after dinner and neglecting his guests in order to consult with his groom on the state of a sick horse.[54] Jane Austen's Mr Clifford is remarkably patient with his four carriage horses, which take eight days in all to cover the seventy miles between Bath and Basingstoke, not counting numerous stops for their owner to recover from 'the Consequence of too violent Exercise'.[55] This painfully slow rate of progress would have goaded John Thorpe to overuse his whip but, had he possessed the best horse-driving skills in England, his horse would never have accomplished ten miles an hour in harness between Tetbury and Bath. Thorpe brags that a distance of twenty-five miles has been covered in two and a half hours. The truth, James Morland argues, is nearer twenty-three miles in three and a half hours, a more believable rate of seven miles an hour.[56]

A post chaise with four horses travelling from Falmouth to London in November 1805, with dispatches detailing the English naval victory at Trafalgar, still only averaged seven miles an hour, despite the critical nature of the intelligence. Lieutenant John Lapenotiere made twenty-one stops over 270 miles to change horses and accomplished the journey along the mail coach route in thirty-seven hours. John Willoughby made faster progress over the 120 miles between London and Cleveland, only stopping briefly for '"A pint of porter with my cold beef at Marlborough."'[57] He had left the capital at eight that morning and accomplished the journey with four horses in twelve hours, at a speed of 10 mph.

Mr Woodhouse is always keen to spare his horses any unnecessary haste, although his professed sympathy for them is invariably linked to a reluctance to leave his armchair or allow Emma to go out and about. '"James will not like to put the horses to for such a little way;"' he claims, when faced with the trials of a half-mile journey to Randalls, '"and where are the poor horses to be while we are paying our visit?"'[58] Emma cleverly swings these objections in her favour when the Crown is suggested as the best location for the ball: '"it will be very convenient for the horses. They will be so near their own stable."'[59] In *The Watsons*, on the morning after the ball in the town of D., Mr Edwards' coachman brings out the horses and carriage to take Emma Watson the three miles home. Tom Musgrave, who wishes to convey her in his curricle, protests that this is an extraordinary measure: '"it is a thing quite out of rule I assure you — never heard of before — the old coachman will look as black as his horses."'[60] Tom has ulterior motives, but the fact that he makes this statement in front of Mrs Edwards proves its veracity. Responsible horse owners realized the value of their horses, treated them with care and rarely crossed their coachmen.

John Thorpe's assertion that '"nothing ruins horses as much as rest; nothing knocks them up so soon"'[61] accorded, unfortunately, with common commercial practice. Travelling in a post chaise from Honiton, Don Espriella's horses were changed for an exhausted pair just returned from Exeter, twenty miles away:

> One of them had been rubbed raw by the harness. I ... could not but consider myself as accessory to an act of cruelty; at every stroke of the whip my conscience upbraided me ... English

travelling, you see, has its evils and its dangers. The life of a post-horse is truly wretched; — there will be cruel individuals in all countries, but cruelty here is a matter of calculation: the post masters find it more profitable to over-work their beasts, and kill them by hard labour in two or three years, than to let them do half the work and live out their natural length of life.[62]

With profits to make on the shortest journey times possible, the owners of post, stage and mail coach horses ran them into the ground. Very few lived out their natural existence. Travellers' expectations ran high, influenced by the introduction of Arab bloodstock into English horse breeds in the mid-seventeenth century and the refinement in carriage construction. Mail coaches pulled by four horses *could* achieve speeds of ten miles an hour, but it was a punishing pace. Dr Kitchiner reported that he had travelled a distance of 120 miles in a mail coach in four-teen hours, beginning at six one March morning and reaching his destination at eight in the evening. On that occasion, the horses had averaged nine miles an hour.[63] The average number of years a mail horse survived in harness was three.

Kitchiner recommended carriage owners to keep their horses in good condition:

Some fine fast Horses will go eight miles in an hour, with as much ease as Heavy Horses will six or five — this depends upon their natural Strength and Swiftness — upon the con-dition they are in — and upon what pace they have been accustomed to ... Give them their own time when going up, and don't hurry them down Hill. The Mail Coachmen's maxims are,
"Down Hill Easy;"
"Up Hill Gently."

From Six to Seven Miles an hour is about the rate that good Carriage Horses, who are allowed plenty of good Corn, will travel comfortably to themselves on a good Road.[64]

He set out a programme for a fifty-mile journey, achievable, he claimed, if the roads and the weather were good. He recommended starting out at 6 a.m., travelling for ten miles, then stopping for fifteen minutes to give the horses a mouthful of hay and a little water. After another six miles, a half-hour stop would be required to remove the harness, rub down the horses and administer 'half a peck of corn'. The next stop was to be made after ten miles – with water and hay given. Six miles down the road, a longer stop for two hours, when hay and corn should be given. Ten miles on the next leg of the journey, with a stop for hay and water, then the final eight miles before an overnight rest.[65]

A mercenary post master was responsible for Johanna Schopenhauer's slow rate of progress by carriage to Matlock Spa, over a distance of seventeen miles. The journey over hilly ground, which should have taken two to three hours, in the event took five. The two horses supplied by the post master had already done a whole day's work in harness and were, understandably, 'very tired and all the postilion's urging could hardly get them to move. Very slowly they proceeded, step by step … We really feared that in the end the poor beasts might stop altogether from sheer exhaustion.'[66] Surprisingly, she found the hackney cab horses in London better cared for. Considering that they trotted on a hard surface for more than twelve hours every day, they were in remarkably good condition. She noted that their drivers regularly allowed them to rest and eat their fill of oats.[67]

Ill-treatment caused Mrs Lefroy's donkey to make at least three solo journeys from Winchester back to his home at Ashe. She had sold him to Charles Powlett and his wife, who 'both starve & overwork him'. Twice at the end of 1802 and once at the beginning of 1803, the animal returned to his previous owner, covering a distance of sixteen miles as the donkey trots. Mrs Lefroy persuaded her husband to let her re-purchase 'poor old Jack' and feed him up to his previous good health.[68] It is to be hoped that this particular donkey was not the one who tripped and broke Mrs Lefroy's leg the following September.[69]

As Jane Austen's health failed, she found a donkey carriage invaluable for local journeys, although travelling this way during the winter was impossible. In January 1817, she wrote to her sister, 'our Donkeys are necessarily having so long a run of luxurious idleness that I suppose we shall find that they have forgotten much of their Education when we use them again.'[70] The following March, she talked of riding one of them to accompany Cassandra on short journeys into Alton and across the fields to visit Ben and Anna Lefroy at Wyards. It would be less troublesome, she said, than using the carriage, although there is no record of her having ridden a horse or donkey before. A saddle was made for her and tried out around the Chawton lanes in the last week of the month. The experience – 'the exercise & everything very pleasant' – encouraged her, but that is the final reference made to the experiment.[71]

Mrs Elton harbours the romantic idea of riding to the strawberry-picking day at Donwell Abbey on a donkey, with her 'caro sposo' walking by her side. On a more practical note, she considers a donkey '"a sort of necessary"' in the country, '"for, let a woman have ever so many resources, it is not possible for her to be always shut up at home; — and very long walks, you know — in summer there is dust, and in winter there is dirt."' Mr Knightley informs her that there is neither dirt nor dust on the road to Donwell, but '"Come on a donkey, however, if you prefer it. You can borrow Mrs. Cole's."'[72] There is something absurd in Mrs Elton's pretensions to donkey ownership and Jane Austen probably never imagined that she herself would take to riding one, with her sister walking by, within two years of the publication of *Emma*.

5

Determined On A Curricle

'THERE ARE MANY more Gentlemen who amuse themselves in getting carriages built than in building houses'[1] noted William Felton, London coachmaker, in his two-volume *Treatise on Carriages*. This publication quickly became a must-have addition to any gentleman's collection when it appeared in 1794 and would certainly have been required reading for John Thorpe, Henry Tilney, John Willoughby and Henry Crawford. Included were illustrations of the different types of carriage, showing how they were constructed, together with tempting embellishments, like sword cases, embossed crests and silver-plated buckles, all priced separately. The final section comprised directions for cleaning and maintaining the pristine condition of the paintwork. Mrs Norris, ever solicitous for the well-being of Sir Thomas Bertram's varnish, would familiarize herself with this information in order to direct the coachman's endeavours with his brushes and mops. Felton's establishment operated from Leather Lane, Holborn, where several hundred allied craftsmen – cartwrights, smiths, harness-makers, wood-carvers, painters and upholsterers – occupied premises. The end of the eighteenth century and the beginning of the nineteenth were boom years for the private carriage trade and London gained recognition for constructing the best horse-drawn vehicles in Europe.

The pinnacle of any fashionable personage's ambition was to be seen driving in an elegant equipage through Hyde Park:

The company which then congregated daily ... was composed of dandies and women in the best society ... Many of the ladies used to drive into the park in a carriage called a *vis-à-vis*, which held only two persons. The hammer cloth, rich in heraldic designs, the powdered footmen in smart liveries, and a coachman who assumed all the gaiety and appearance of a wigged archbishop, were indispensable. The equipages were generally much more gorgeous than at a later period, when democracy invaded the parks ... with shabby-genteel carriages and servants. The carriage company consisted of the most celebrated beauties; and in those earlier days you never saw any of the lower or middle classes of London intruding themselves in regions which, with a sort of tacit understanding, were given up exclusively to persons of rank and fashion.[2]

The Prince Regent frequently drove himself round Hyde Park in a tilbury – one of the more dashing open carriages – with his groom by his side. The Prince gained recognition as an excellent driver and 'skill with the ribbons', or reins, was an accomplishment much admired at the Whip Club and the ultra-exclusive Four-in-Hand Club. Only the best drivers were admitted to the last-mentioned establishment and they wore bright yellow striped and spotted waistcoats to advertise their status. One member was Tommy Onslow, a famous dandy, who always drove a black phaeton drawn by jet black horses. 'What can little Tommy do?' – asked a popular ditty of the time – 'Drive a phaeton and two. Can little Tommy do no more? Yes — drive a phaeton and four.'[3] Henry Austen could only dream of such unattainable glory. He kept a carriage in London and, from all accounts, appears to have been the Georgian equivalent of a boy racer. Travelling in a hired post chaise in the rutted lanes near Steventon in his younger days, he shouted at the postilion to go faster, to which the man replied, 'I *do* get on, sir, where I can!'

'You stupid fellow!' was Henry's rejoinder. 'Any fellow can do that. I want you to get on *where you can't!*'[4] His first wife Eliza confided to a cousin in 1798, 'I am sometimes so gracious or so <u>imprudent</u> as to trust my neck to Henry's Coachmanship ...'.[5]

Eliza relished the high life in London. She frequently took her carriage into Hyde Park before she married Henry and recorded in a letter that 'The Princess of Wales & myself' had enjoyed 'an Airing' there. 'We were however so unsociable as to go in different Carriages' she added.[6] A year later, Eliza came to the galling conclusion that the rising cost of carriage owner-ship signalled an end to such pleasures: 'These new Taxes will drive me out of London, and make me give up my Carriage for I cannot afford an increase of House Rent ... in addition to the present expence of a vehicle, and four Guineas more on my Man Servants Account.'[7]

Duties payable on carriages throughout the country in 1796 were prohibitively expensive for all but the wealthy. Jane Austen's eponymous hero Mr Clifford would have been bank-rupted by the taxes on the carriages he owned in 1788, had he still run all twelve of them eight years later. A levy of £8.16s applied to ownership of one four-wheeled carriage, with £9.18s imposed on the second. If three or more were kept, £11 was payable on each carriage after the first. Lady Catherine, Mr Collins boasts, has several carriages and among Mrs Bennet's first intelligible pronouncements on learning of Elizabeth's engagement to Darcy is, '"What carriages you will have!"'[8]

Two-wheeled vehicles were taxed at £3.17s a year for each one kept.[9] In this category, taxed carts attracted the lowest duty of ten shillings, but they were not to be tolerated by those with any pretensions to fashion. They were two-seater bone-shakers of wood and iron, with no springs, no cover and no lining, used by farmers and tradespeople or those unable to afford anything better. The owner's name and place of abode, plus the humiliat-ing words 'A Taxed Cart', were painted in black and white on the back. Jane Austen was offered a lift in one to a local dinner party and was not impressed: 'In consequence of a civil note that morn^g from Mrs Clement, I went with her & her Husband in their Tax-cart; — civility on both sides; I would rather have walked, & no doubt, they must have wished I had.'[10]

She was happier travelling to Canterbury from Godmersham in her brother Edward's chair, a smooth enough drive for her to read aloud a letter from Cassandra as they travelled.[11] Chairs were more up-market than taxed carts, but still open and pulled by a single horse, the equivalent of a small car used today for local outings to the shops. Edward's chair came out regularly in good weather, to transport guests around his estate and to nearby places of interest. It was probably in a much better and newer condition than the dilapidated vehicle in which Emma Watson endures three miles' worth of splashing along a dirty lane in order to attend a ball.[12]

Even stabling in London proved financially ruinous if one did not have mews. The solution was to rent horses, as the Gardiners, the Hursts and the London Knightleys probably do. Mr Woodhouse supplies 'his own horses and coachman ... to bring some of the party the last half of the way' when his daughter and son-in-law make their Christmas visit to Hartfield.[13]

Only the richest carriage owners could afford to keep up appearances in the smartest areas of London; such conspicuous display required dressing in the height of fashionable chic. Ladies' magazines featured costume plates, many of them carriage outfits, designed for those whose means stretched to impractical white satin pelisses, hats trimmed with ostrich feathers, kid gloves and white half-boots.[14] Servants too required appropriately showy attire; a coachman's livery alone could cost over £20 per year. Dr Kitchiner's *Traveller's Oracle* gives a clear idea of what constituted the flashiest uniform that money could buy: a heavy sky-blue coat, edged with crimson and lined with matching blue silk, with a gold-laced collar and buttonholes; buttons gilt and stamped with the family crest; a blue waistcoat and plush breeches with gilt knee-buckles. Also 'A good full-made Box-Coat, with six real capes' for driving in rain and two hats with more gold lace binding.[15]

In addition to trumpeting one's wealth and status, coachmen and grooms were of vital importance in maintaining the safety and smooth running of one's equipage. The Duke of Devonshire paid his head coachman £60 per annum, at a time when many poor curates were existing on £50. A groom might expect to be paid £25.[16] William Kitchiner listed their duties on extended journeys. At the end of a long day, there was no rest for them:

> desire your Coachman to carefully examine every part of the Carriage, and again at the end of each day's Journey; and examine carefully that the Saddle and the Harness fit your Horses: — if their tackle does not sit easy ... they will be fretted, and not able to do half the work they would if it fitted well. From the want of such precautions, many irreparable and fatal Accidents happen.
>
> ... caution your Servant never to trust the cleaning of the Carriage to the Stablemen of the Inn, who, in their careless hurry, and with their old ragged Mops and dirty Cloths, may scratch and deface the pannels more in a few Minutes, than with proper care they would suffer in many Months ... tell him to look after your Carriage and Horses himself.[17]

Those carriage owners who took the reins in their own hands were well aware of the figures they cut as they whipped their horses through the London streets. It was fashionable to copy the dress and speech, the whistling and swearing of the professional coachmen who drove the public stage coaches. One young Regency 'blade' with more money than sense paid fifty guineas to Hell Fire Dick, the driver of the *Cambridge Telegraph* coach, for lessons in spitting.[18] With access to plenty of role models in Oxford and Putney, John Thorpe has obviously learned the manners required for making a spectacle of himself in any urban environment. 'Fearful of being too handsome unless he wore the dress of a groom', Thorpe appears 'a most knowing-looking coachman' on his arrival in Bath.[19] His talk of horses, dogs, the minutiae of carriage construction and chiefly of himself, is peppered with '"d _____ it"' and '"oh! lord"' and 'frequent exclamations, amounting almost to oaths'.[20] He boasts of his own skills as a coachman and of the superiority of his own equipage. Poor Catherine is stunned into silence; she has no opinions to advance and no idea that her companion's vaunted expertise is superficial.

Both Thorpe and his carriage aspire to be something they are not. The gig, in fact, featured at the bottom end of the list of desirable carriages, 'curricle hung' or otherwise. Felton's description of them makes all clear: 'one-horse chaises, of various patterns, devised according to the fancy of the occupier; but, more generally, mean those that hang by braces from the springs; the mode of hanging is what principally constitutes the name of Gig, which is only a one-horse chaise … Curricles being now the most fashionable sort of two-wheeled carriages, it is usual, in building a Gig, to imitate them, particularly in the mode of hanging.'[21]

John Thorpe's gig cost him fifty guineas. A new one was priced at thirty-one guineas, before the necessary extras such as blocks, boots, coach boxes or wheels were added. £15 would be sufficient to cover the purchase of these items and another £6 for the inessential glitter – sword case, lamps, splashing board and silver moulding – which dazzle him into paying more than he need for a second-hand vehicle. Freeman takes full advantage of his 'friend's' ignorance. The sixty guineas Thorpe claims he was offered for it the following day included his horse. Felton knew the risks of buying second-hand from unscrupulous sellers and warned the unwary against such deals: 'many strangers to Carriages will risk a purchase on their own superficial knowledge, taking the appearance for the sufficiency, which is soon proved to consist of rotten materials, nicely surfaced with putty and shewy painting, or perhaps ornamented with a new inside lining and some slight plated furniture.'[22]

Carriages frequently delineate character in Jane Austen's texts and this is added proof, if any were needed, of John Thorpe's thick-headed blustering. He is rather like his sister

Isabella, passing off her old hats as new with the addition of feathers and coquelicot ribbons. For Miss Denham in *Sanditon*, gig ownership is a degradation and she is 'gnawed by the want of an handsomer equipage' than she and her baronet brother can afford.[23] Mr Collins has a gig, chosen presumably because he and Lady Catherine consider it highly suitable for a clergyman in his position. He would use it only for short journeys within the parish and exhibit grateful raptures on his elevation to one of his patroness' more elegant equipages. Admiral and Mrs Croft purchase a gig for their jaunts around the Kellynch lanes. They could afford something better, but this unostentatious mode of transport suits their habit of dawdling away the days in each other's company and their style of driving provides an insight into their easy-going relationship: '"My dear admiral, that post! — we shall certainly take that post." But by coolly giving the reins a better direction herself, they happily passed the danger; and by once afterwards judiciously putting out her hand, they neither fell into a rut, nor ran foul of a dung-cart …'.[24]

Henry Tilney owns the carriage that John Thorpe can only dream of possessing. The curricle was the Porsche of its time, twice the price of a gig and twice as fast, being pulled by two horses separated by a pole: 'none are so much regarded for fashion as these are by those who are partial to drive their own horses; they are certainly a superior kind of two-wheeled carriage'.[25] At least Thorpe knows what he wants. Faced with a choice between the two, Mrs Lefroy's clergyman son-in-law could not make up his mind. Over a two-year period, she charted his maddening prevarications in her letters:

Rice drove his Gig to Andover to consult Rogers about altering it into a Curricle which he fancys will be more convenient … is determined to change his Gig into a Curricle & buy a pair of Horses for it at Newbury Fair … has sold his Curricle to Mr Chamberlayne he now talks of having a Gig built … has got a new Curricle built at Andover it is to come home next week.[26]

In Catherine Morland's opinion, Henry Tilney has made entirely the right choice. She achieves the sum of female happiness riding in his curricle and comparing his method of driving and his travelling outfit with those of the only other young man by whom she has been taken out in a carriage: 'Henry drove so well, — so quietly — without making any disturbance, without parading to her, or swearing ... And then his hat sat so well, and the innumerable capes of his great coat looked so becomingly important!'[27]

Henry can afford to run a curricle, as can Mr Darcy, but neither man makes a huge show of it. William Elliot displays a family crest on the doors of his. Tom Musgrave in *The Watsons*, a confirmed flirt and committed social climber, is nonplussed by Emma Watson's indifference to a spin in his 'neat curricle'.[28] Mr Rushworth's £12,000 a year supports the running of two carriages, one of them a curricle. John Willoughby and Charles Musgrove stretch their funds to own one and Henry Austen probably did the same to keep a curricle in London, upgrading from a gig sometime between 1811 and 1813. He drove Jane in it from Chawton to his house in Sloane Street in May 1813, generously lent it out whenever necessary – 'What a convenient Carriage Henry's is, to his friends in general! — Who has it next?' and allowed Cassandra and the three Bigg sisters use of it for sightseeing in the capital.[29]

The owners of chariots in Jane Austen's novels are both widows – Mrs Jennings and Mrs Rushworth – and both employ them in an urban setting. Felton considered the chariot, with its removable coach box and seating for three passengers, all facing forward, a vehicle most suited to town use. Mrs Jennings' transports her around London. There is something humorous in the conjunction of formidable old ladies and this type of vehicle, something slightly ridiculous in the term 'chariot' which seems to hint at the character of the occupant. Jane Austen makes the most of this in *Mansfield Park*. On the marriage of her son, Mrs Rushworth leaves Sotherton and 'removed herself, her maid, her footman, and her chariot, with true dowager propriety, to Bath'.[30]

Jane Austen's father owned a chariot for several years when the family lived at Steventon. There is some evidence in the payments from Mr Austen's account at Hoare's Bank to various tradesmen in Winchester that indicate he bought it in June 1784 and perhaps exchanged it for a newer model in 1795.[31] Anna Lefroy appears to have misremembered the date of the purchase, which she thought was late 1797 – it would be odd if her grandfather had given up using it by the end of the following year.[32] Jane recorded the event in a letter dated November 1798: 'Our assemblies have very kindly declined ever since we laid down the carriage, so that dis-convenience and dis-inclination to go have kept pace together.'[33] The carriage remained 'laid down' until the sale of the family's possessions at Steventon in May 1801, the notice of which described the equipage as a 'well made Chariot (with box to take off) and Harness'.[34]

For long-distance travel on a regular basis, Felton recommended the post chaise, a well-sprung, four-wheeled closed carriage that could seat two comfortably, three slightly less so. Mrs Jennings travels to Devon in her chaise, but on the journey back to Berkeley Street with the two Dashwood sisters, Betty the maid is sent home by public coach. The body was the same as the chariot's but, instead of a coachman, postilions on the horses' backs were responsible for steering. Travellers could hire horses at the numerous post houses along the route, but it was more convenient to own rather than hire a chaise. Post masters ran their hired vehicles between specific posting inns, so frequent changes were necessary, involving luggage removals each time – 'an inconvenience too great to be submitted to by any gentleman who can afford the additional expence of keeping their own Post-Chaise', Felton argued.[35] Bags and other items frequently went missing. Mrs Morland hopes that Catherine has left nothing in the door pockets of the hack chaises on her journey back to Fullerton from Northanger Abbey. Colonel Byng's travelling companion lost his luggage between the Bell Inn at Bromley and the Rose and Crown at Tonbridge: 'Our baggage was not to be found, nor arrived; or, perhaps, gone

to the Wells ... after much enquiry I discover'd my little portmanteau; at a corner of the hall ... but Mr I.D.'s was not to be
found.'[36]

General Tilney's smart equipage, which transports Catherine,
Eleanor and her maid on the first stage of the journey between
Bath and Northanger Abbey, is a 'fashionable chaise-and-
four'. Catherine admires, as she is meant to, the 'postilions
handsomely liveried, rising so regularly in their stirrups, and
numerous out-riders properly mounted'.[37] This is the kind of
public show that Sir Walter Elliot also insists on, the ostenta-
tious parade he and Elizabeth are not prepared to give up when
their debts demand retrenchments. 'Leading the way to the
chaise and four' is one of the privileges that defines Elizabeth's
status as the eldest daughter of a baronet, a right unlikely to be
relinquished without a struggle.[38] Given the tax on horse ownership, running four when two would suffice is an unjustifiable
extravagance.

Both men would undoubtedly be tempted by the superior
carriage fittings offered in Felton's catalogue: Wilton carpets,
silk linings and fringes, tassels, cushions and upholstery
buttons, festoons and blinds, all to match the colour scheme
of the servants' livery. A 'cave' could be sunk into the floor of
the carriage, for storing a dozen bottles of Madeira wine. Had
either man seen Napoleon's campaign carriage, exhibited at the
London Museum in Piccadilly after Waterloo, he would have
turned green with envy. The exterior of the carriage was 'in
many respects, very like the modern English travelling chariots',
but inside it was ingeniously fitted up with all the comforts and
conveniences of a luxury camper van:

> In front of the seat are compartments for every utensil of prob-
> able utility; of some there are two sets, one of gold, the other
> of silver. Among the gold articles are a tea-pot, coffee-pot,
> sugar-bason, cream-ewer, coffee-cup and saucer, slop-bason,
> candle-sticks, wash-hand bason, plates for breakfast, &c ... by
> the aid of the lamp, any thing could be heated in the carriage.[39]

Beneath the coachman's seat was a small box, two and a half feet long and four inches square, containing a fold-away steel bedstead; mattresses and other bedding were stored in the carriage compartments. A mahogany case held bottles of rum, Malaga wine, perfume, Windsor soap, a looking glass and shaving paraphernalia. A writing desk contained paper, an ink-stand, pens, maps and small telescopes.

On campaigns, Napoleon slept in his carriage as it rolled on through the night. Prince Puckler-Muskau, travelling in England in 1827, rather enjoyed the experience of sleeping in his, despite the prevailing opinion of medical men that exposure to the night air and disturbed rest were prejudicial to the constitution: 'One always sleeps even better on the second night than on the first in the carriage, whose movement works, on me at least, like a cradle on children. I felt very well and cheerful the next morning ... I lit the reading lamp in the carriage and comfortably read through Lady Morgan's latest novel while we rolled at a gallop across the plain.'[40]

For country jaunts, a two-seater landaulet with a retractable half-roof was ideal. On her marriage to Captain Wentworth, Anne Elliot becomes 'the mistress of a very pretty landaulet',[41] which grants her an independent mobility previously denied by her father and elder sister. Like the Crofts, the Wentworths will go out and about together, but in a more stable, four-wheeled vehicle. Mary Musgrove suffers some very painful emotions when she sees her sister's neat, new carriage; it is, after all, worth far more than her husband's curricle. A Wentworth family crest on the door, if the Captain were ever to be made a baronet, would consign her to the sofa for a month. Anne's health would benefit from frequent outdoor exercise and maybe a more robust constitution is what Lady Catherine intends to promote when she sends her sickly daughter out in a phaeton: 'Phaetons, for some years, have deservedly been regarded as the most pleasant sort of carriage in use, as they contribute, more than any other, to health, amusement, and fashion, with the superior advantage of lightness, over every other sort of four-wheeled carriages, and are much safer, and more easy to ride in, than those of two wheels.[42]

Mrs Gardiner petitions Elizabeth Bennet to acquire a 'low phaeton, with a nice little pair of ponies'[43] for conveying her around the park at Pemberley. When Jane Austen revised the first draft of *Pride and Prejudice*, she might have added this reference in remembrance of the Marchioness of Lansdown's phaeton, which created a stir in Southampton whenever it was driven out from Castle Square. The sight stayed in James Edward Austen-Leigh's memory well into his later years:

> a light phaeton, drawn by six, and sometimes by eight little ponies, each pair decreasing in size, and becoming lighter in colour, through all the grades of dark brown, light brown, bay, and chestnut, as it was placed farther away from the carriage ... It was a delight to me to look down from the window and see this fairy equipage put together ... [44]

Maria Lucas is thrown into paroxysms of delight when she sees Miss de Bourgh's low phaeton and ponies at the gate of Hunsford Parsonage. Elizabeth deplores the thoughtlessness that keeps Charlotte out of doors in a strong wind, but she does not take into account that Anne de Bourgh is similarly afflicted; phaetons were open carriages. Lady Catherine obviously believes in a kill or cure regime, but at least she does not insist on her daughter risking her neck in a high phaeton. This version, perched on large wheels and precariously wayward springs, was involved in more accidents than other carriages. They were favoured by young male menaces of the road, idiots such as Edward and Augustus in *Love and Freindship*. The 'unlucky overturning' of their 'fashionably high Phaeton' tips them both out to expire ignominiously in the dust.[45] Cue much running mad and fainting on the ground by their raving wives. The young Jane Austen loved a black joke and carriage accidents were common enough – so much so that wills were often made before setting off on a journey – to provide the necessary material.

In her early twenties, she jokingly hoped that a mishap on the road would prevent a promised visit to the Cookes at Bookham – 'They talk of going to Bath too in the Spring, & perhaps they may be overturned in their way down, & all laid up for the summer.'[46] Yet only six months previously, in August 1798, a tragic carriage accident had hit the Austen family hard. Jane Williams, *née* Cooper, a cousin with whom Cassandra and Jane had attended school and whose marriage at Steventon in 1792 they had witnessed, had been thrown from a light, two-wheeled carriage called a whiskey and killed.[47]

From Mrs Lefroy at Ashe, Jane would have heard of a number of carriage accidents that had proved fatal or near-fatal to those involved: Lucy and Henry Rice, colliding with a wagon at night near Oakley; a young guardsman crushed under the wheels of a furniture removal cart in Canterbury; John Heathcote, trampled to death by his horses near Dartford when the harness of his curricle broke.[48] Apart from the accident in *Love and Freindship* and the humorous reference in *Persuasion* to the Crofts being tossed out of their gig, *Sanditon* is the only other text where characters come to grief on the road. Through his foolish insistence on taking a carriage up a steep, unsuitable track, Mr Parker sprains his foot when the vehicle overturns, meets the Heywood family and is the means of removing Charlotte from a sequestered rural locality to a seaside resort with more promising prospects. No drama here, unlike that indulged in by many writers of sentimental novels. Jane Austen refused to grant her travelling heroines a convenient way of falling in love by falling out of a carriage: not 'one lucky overturn to introduce them to the hero' features in any of her plots.[49] She laughed up her sleeve as she created far from heroic mischances – a coachman who twists his ankle while cleaning his master's carriage and another who exacerbates his rheumatism by driving ten miles in cold weather on uneven roads.[50]

A report of a fatal accident in Leatherhead in October 1806, that Jane Austen probably read in the *Hampshire Chronicle* or in the national press, might have given her the idea for Mr

Woodhouse's horror of the corner into Vicarage Lane, 'a corner that he could never bear to think of'.[51] A carriage, an open barouche-landau, had overset as it negotiated a sharp corner. The top part of it hit a tree and the three women inside were half thrown out. Miss Cholmondeley, with blood issuing from her head, later died of her injuries. An eyewitness testified that 'the carriage was coming at a very great rate; and in turning the corner, swang round upon the two off wheels; that the horses broke their traces and ran away, leaving the carriage broken to pieces'.[52]

Barouches are bad news in Jane Austen's novels. Lady Catherine de Bourgh and the Viscountess Dalrymple both have one; Henry Crawford's barouche adds spice to his flirtation with Julia and Maria Bertram; silly Charlotte Palmer drives about London in one. Fanny Dashwood's ambitions for her brother Edward extend to barouche ownership and Mrs Elton's panegyrics on the Sucklings are larded with references to their spanking new mode of transport, the barouche-landau, not seen in England until after 1800: '"They will have their barouche-landau, of course, which holds four perfectly ... They would hardly come in their chaise, I think, at that season of the year."'[53]

The barouche-landau is mentioned four times in succession, just in case Emma has missed the point. The *Morning Post*, of 5 January 1804, reported: 'Mr. Buxton the celebrated whip, has just launched a new-fangled machine, a kind of *nondescript*. It is described by the inventor to be the due medium between a landau and a barouche, but all who have seen it say it more resembles a fish-cart or a music-caravan.'[54] It held four people, two facing forwards, two back, in addition to the coachman and could be pulled by two or four horses. Like the landau, it had hoods to the front and back so that it could function as an open carriage, a half-open carriage, or a closed carriage. Like the barouche, it was light and elegant.

In January 1809, the Leigh Perrots' indecision over whether or not to purchase a carriage for use in Bath became a matter for family speculation.[55] The Stoneleigh settlement of £24,000, plus an annuity of £2,000 granted to Mr Leigh Perrot on the resignation of his claim to the estate, allowed him to purchase 'Horses & a new Chariot' without having to think twice about the cost. In the winter of 1810/11, the Leigh Perrots moved from their rented house in Paragon and bought their own property in Great Pulteney Street. From the windows of number forty-nine, Mrs Leigh Perrot admired and coveted 'a very Elegant Barouche & 4 beautiful Horses which a Mr Parish used to parade up & down Pulteney Street,' prompting her husband's offer to 'keep such a one for me whenever I pleased as he could now amply afford it'.[56] It appears that a second carriage was still under discussion in May 1811, when Jane wrote to Cassandra of her aunt at Weymouth: 'Mrs Welby takes her out airing in her Barouche, which gives her a headache — a comfortable proof I suppose of the uselessness of the new Carriage when they have got it.'[57]

Mr Leigh Perrot's failing health meant that the plan went no further than the discussion stage. Even so, Jane can be forgiven for feeling a justifiable resentment of the Leigh Perrots' self-indulgence when their sister and nieces were forced into practising strict domestic economy. Jane Austen did not class herself with the Lady Catherines, Selina Sucklings and Mrs Leigh Perrots of this world, who believed that driving around in a barouche was their automatic privilege; nevertheless, she found the novelty of taking an airing in one entertaining: 'the Driving about, the Carriage been [sic] open, was very pleasant. — I liked my solitary elegance very much, & was ready to laugh all the time, at my being where I was. — I could not but feel that I had naturally small right to be parading about London in a Barouche.'[58]

At the age of twelve, Jane wrote *The Memoirs of Mr Clifford* for 9-year-old Charles, listing all of the carriages she could think of. Like little boys of any century, Charles would have been fascinated by anything with wheels and, in this short tale, his sister mentions more types of carriage than she does in her entire published and unpublished output. Very often the generic terms 'carriage' and 'coach' are all we get by way of description. Mr Bennet's coach can carry six: his wife and five daughters visit the Bingleys, Mr Collins and his cousins travel to the Philips' evening party in it. For the Netherfield ball, two carriages are required to carry eight from Longbourn, so presumably one is hired from the Meryton inn. Mr Musgrove senior's coach can also carry six, but because he and his wife are so large, they take up the whole of the forward-facing seat and Mary Musgrove claims that she is squashed between Henrietta and Louisa on the other. Mr Woodhouse's carriage will only carry two comfortably, John Knightley's can hold at least three. Mr and Mrs Wilmot in *Edgar and Emma*, written in 1787, have eighteen children, nine of whom they pack into their carriage on alternate visits, overcrowding on an impossible scale. Jane might have been thinking of this story several years later, when she requested Cassandra to keep her up to date with a neighbour's travel arrangements: 'Let me know how many besides their fourteen Selves & M^r & Mrs Wright, Michael will contrive to place about their Coach'.[59]

In these cases, the designation of carriage is not important; for what purpose their owners use them is. Lady Catherine attempts to exert control through hers – on the Collinses, when she has had enough of their company at the end of an evening, '"we are never allowed to walk home. Her Ladyship's carriage is regularly ordered for us."' – and on Elizabeth Bennet, '"if you will stay another *month* complete, it will be in my power to take one of you as far as London"'. Lady Catherine's attempt to change Elizabeth's mind fails on this occasion, as it does even more comprehensively when she descends on Longbourn in a chaise-and-four to tackle head-on 'the upstart pretensions of a young woman without family, connections, or fortune.'[60]

An early prototype of Lady Catherine appears in *Letter The Third* in the second volume of the *Juvenilia*. Lady Greville rubs Maria Williams' nose in her relative poverty by means of carriage ownership. She is taken to a ball by Lady Greville and allowed 'to sit forwards' – that is, on the best seat – with the purpose of 'confering a great obligation', designed to remind the girl of her social level. In this situation, Maria 'dare not be impertinent' even though she would like to be, given that she is invariably 'abused for my Poverty' whenever she enters her ladyship's coach. There is an echo in this short extract, too, of the episode at Hunsford, where Charlotte is kept out of doors in the wind by Miss de Bourgh. Lady Greville deliberately calls at the Williams' dinner hour and sends in a message by the servant that she will not get out of the carriage, 'but that Miss Maria must come to the Coach-door, as she wanted to speak to her, and that she must make haste and come immediately … Accordingly I went and was obliged to stand there at her Ladyship's pleasure though the Wind was extremely high and very cold.'

Lady Greville has come to 'invite' Maria to dinner, but in such ill-mannered language that even Lady Catherine would blush: '"you may dine with us the day after tomorrow … There will be no occasion for your being very fine for I shant send the Carriage — If it rains you may take an umbrella … You young Ladies who cannot often ride in a Carriage never mind what weather you trudge in, or how the wind shews your legs."'[61]

That the Dashwood women have no carriage is due to the influence of John Dashwood and his wife, Fanny. John thinks himself exceedingly generous in his decision to give his sisters £1,000 each, which, invested at 5% would bring in £150 per annum. Added to the interest on £7,000, left to them by their father, the bereaved women's yearly income would be £650, still below the amount needed to keep a carriage, plus the servants necessary to maintain it. In the event, his wife argues him out of giving them anything. Fanny Dashwood knows that the reduced circumstances in which the women will find themselves will limit the girls' chances of meeting suitable marriage partners: '"They will have no carriage, no horses, and hardly any servants; they will keep no company".'[62]

Kind Sir John Middleton offers Mrs Dashwood the use of his carriage to visit other families in the neighbourhood, but she does not wish to be obligated, so her daughters are confined to the immediate environs of Barton Cottage and the company at Barton Park. Without an independent means of transport, there is no escape route for Elinor and Marianne, they are forced into mixing with Anne and Lucy Steele. Escape is also impossible for those trapped in carriages with uncongenial companions. Emma Woodhouse is particularly unlucky in this respect. On Christmas Eve she travels to Randalls with a complaining brother-in-law and returns with a part-inebriated, wholly unwelcome suitor. Emma's entrapment in a carriage after her rudeness to Miss Bates on Box Hill has more serious consequences. Mr Knightley's reprimand mortifies her into silence; she turns her face away as she is handed into the carriage, the horses are in motion and she is too late to apologize or say goodbye.

Highbury residents with carriages are, for the most part, considerate towards their less wealthy neighbours. Mr Knightley brings his out of storage for the express purpose of taking Miss Bates and Jane Fairfax to the Coles' evening party. True to character, he does not make a parade of his generosity, unlike Mrs Elton, who lets everyone know the full extent of her charity. Mrs Elton's head is so full of herself and her finery that she forgets her promise to collect Miss Bates and her niece on her way to the Crown ball. The omission is duly rectified and Mrs Elton, not in the least shamefaced, proceeds to harangue Mrs Weston: '"What a pleasure it is to send one's carriage for a friend! — I understand you were so kind as to offer, but another time it will be quite unnecessary. You may be very sure I shall always take care of *them*."'[63]

Poor Jane Fairfax is forced into an acquaintance with a woman whose main object is patronage and control. Mrs Elton puts kindness to Jane out of anyone else's power: to Hartfield, to Donwell, to Box Hill, Jane must submit to being taken by Mrs Elton. Emma's compassion for Miss Fairfax when the latter falls ill is genuine and understated. One of the first services she offers, with Mr Perry's blessing, is an airing in the Hartfield carriage. When Jane's engagement to Frank comes to light, Mrs

Weston's carriage provides the means for a confidential discussion between the two women.

Emma too is capable of using her carriage as a method of control. Judging it right for Harriet to visit the Martins, Emma conveys her to Abbey Mill Farm. In this way she can set a limit on how long Harriet will stay – only fifteen minutes – and curtail any dangerous return to friendship: 'they were just growing again like themselves ... when the carriage re-appeared and all was over.'[64] Emma has the good grace to feel uncomfortable about her part in Harriet's ungrateful behaviour to the deserving family, but remains convinced that she is justified in driving a wedge between them.

In this novel, more than in any other, references to carriages develop the plot. Frank Churchill's 'blunder' in revealing the news that Mr Perry was thinking of setting up a carriage reinforces Mr Knightley's suspicion of an alliance between the young man and Jane Fairfax. The non-arrival of the Sucklings' barouche-landau promotes the combination of the two Box Hill parties, which in turn leads to increased ill will and misunderstanding. The news conveyed by the Crown Inn ostler that Frank had hired a chaise to drive back to Richmond a day early prompts Jane Fairfax to accept the post of governess with the Smallridges. Harriet's removal to London in the Hartfield carriage serves a number of purposes – Emma is saved from experiencing more pain on her behalf, Harriet will recover from her crush on Mr Knightley and Robert Martin will find the time and place to make and have accepted a second proposal of marriage.

Marriages and carriages go together; every husband was expected to drive his bride away from the church door in a new equipage. The Bertrams' neighbours notice the lapse in etiquette when Mr Rushworth and Maria leave in a year-old coach, because there hasn't been enough time for a new one to be built. Mr Elton acquires a carriage almost as soon as he acquires Miss Augusta Hawkins; if Mrs Suckling has two carriages, Mrs Elton is certainly going to own one. Willoughby orders a carriage on his approaching alliance with Miss Grey – her £50,000 would allow him to buy the very best – and Mrs Bennet fantasizes about multiple carriages on Jane's engagement to Bingley and Elizabeth's to Mr Darcy. Isabella Thorpe's thoughts focus immediately on a brand new carriage when she accepts James Morland's proposal.

Jane Austen does not go into detail on the appearance of these real or imagined vehicles, but in *The Three Sisters*, she really goes to town. Mary Stanhope's quarrels with Mr Watts centre on her insistence that their carriage be on fashionably high springs and painted blue, spotted with silver, a striking, if rather garish combination. He declares that it will be low-slung and a conventional chocolate brown. Like Isabella Thorpe, Mary Stanhope's view of marriage is entirely materialistic. Unless her carriage is superior to the neighbours', she will refuse to marry. A second carriage is also proposed, a cream phaeton, decorated with wreaths of silver flowers, in which she must be driven out every day. Mary hates Mr Watts, but aims to marry before her younger sisters. She is convinced that if she turns him down, one of her sisters will accept him and Mr Watts is of that opinion too. Their disagreements over the carriage foretell a disastrous match and although a compromise is reached – one carriage, painted brown with a silver border and hung high – neither is happy.[65]

Disagreements, anxieties and manoeuvrings involving carriages are not limited to engaged couples. Mrs Bennet ensures that Jane stays at Netherfield Park overnight by denying her the use of the carriage when rain threatens. In the event, the plan works better than she had hoped; Jane catches a bad cold and has to trespass on the Bingleys' hospitality for several days. It is Mrs Bennet who arranges for the family carriage to arrive long after everyone else's at the end of the Netherfield ball, but her manoeuvrings are innocent when compared with Lucy Steele's. Spotting the Dashwoods' manservant outside the New London Inn in Exeter, Lucy beckons him over to the carriage and announces her change of name to Ferrars. Robert, meanwhile, under Lucy's direction – he is not bright enough to dream up such a plan himself – pulls back into the darkness of the carriage: '"I just see him leaning back in it, but he did not look up; — he never was a gentleman much for talking."'[66] thus tricking Thomas into mistaking him for Edward. News of the marriage, as Lucy intends, will be carried back to Elinor.

Mrs Norris, intent on keeping Fanny Price in her place, 'the lowest and last', begins her bullying of the 10-year-old child on the coach journey between Northampton and Mansfield Park. Her determination to deprive Fanny of any pleasure continues unabated, prompting her to argue with Edmund when he suggests that there will be ample room for his cousin in the barouche bound for Sotherton and to oppose the ordering of the carriage for Fanny's visit to the Grants:

> "My dear Sir Thomas!" cried Mrs Norris, red with anger, "Fanny can walk."
>
> "Walk!" repeated Sir Thomas, in a tone of most unanswerable dignity … "My niece walk to a dinner engagement at this time of the year!"[67]

This is one of Sir Thomas' earliest attacks on his sister-in-law's treatment of Fanny; how relieved he feels when his carriage carries Mrs Norris away from Mansfield Park forever.

6

Regularity And Dispatch

T IGHTLY SCHEDULED STAGE and mail coach journeys meant
that everyone, from the agricultural labourer straightening
his back to watch the public conveyances passing on the road
to the aristocrat waiting for important letters from London, was
more aware than ever before of time. Each mail coach guard
carried an official watch, in order to ensure that schedules
were adhered to, and the large inns on mail routes altered their
clocks to agree. Inn clocks with large dials, referred to as 'Act of
Parliament' clocks, Prime Minister William Pitt having imposed
a tax of five shillings a year on all timepieces in 1797, appear
in many late eighteenth- and early nineteenth-century prints. A
number of Jane Austen's characters consult their watches: Frank
Churchill and Emma Woodhouse, Elizabeth Bennet and Mr
Darcy, Edmund Bertram and Mary Crawford, John and Isabella
Thorpe. General Tilney is a stickler for punctuality – his servants must bring his carriage to the door, have his dinner on the
table and produce cold collations at the exact time specified, or
face the full force of his wrath.

Precise time-keeping could be achieved within a household
and sometimes within a limited neighbourhood, but clocks
throughout the country were not fully synchronized until
the advent of the railways in the mid-nineteenth century. The

consequent imprecision frustrated men of the General's stamp, as Jane well knew. Writing to Cassandra from Kent, she reported on a discrepancy between Godmersham time and Canterbury time and its effect on the irascible husband of a friend: 'Oweing to a difference of Clocks, the Coachman did not bring the Carriage so soon as he ought by half an hour; — anything like a breach of punctuality was a great offence — & Mr Moore was very angry'.[1]

Public transport followed strict timetables and travellers were warned to arrive early at coaching inns: 'It is necessary to be at the place in due Time; for as the saying is, "Time and Tide," and it may be added, "Stage Coaches, stay for no Man." As Clocks vary, you will do wisely to *be there full Five minutes before what you believe to be the true Time*.'[2]

Several European travellers to England commented on the vast numbers of carriages thronging the roads between posting inns and causing congestion in cities and towns. 'You cannot imagine the quantity of travellers who are always on the road in England', commented François de la Rochefoucauld, of a journey between Dover and London in 1784. 'You cannot go from one post to another without meeting two or three post-chaises, to say nothing of the regular diligencies.'[3] 'Chaise after chaise, coach after coach, cart after cart', one German visitor complained of Cheapside and Fleet Street in the 1770s. 'All the world rushes headlong without looking.'[4]

Horace Walpole wrote to a friend in 1791 of the endless tide of 'coaches, chariots, curricles, phaetons, &c.'[5] and many of Thomas Rowlandson's cartoons depict carriage congestion. By the mid-1820s, the unobservant pedestrian in the capital risked life and limb just walking on the pavement: 'if you are not careful to look to right & left, you are in constant danger of being spitted by the shaft of a cabriolet which comes too near the footpath, or crushed to death by some diligence which has broke down & overturned.'[6]

Cheapside, where the Gardiners in *Pride and Prejudice* live, was a particularly hectic area of the City and on a main coaching route. Three busy inns, the Bell, the Cross Keys and the Spread Eagle, were located in Gracechurch Street. *Cary's Itinerary* of 1819 lists the coaches from Cheapside to Edinburgh, Brighton and various towns in Kent, Cambridgeshire, Essex, Surrey and Hampshire. Coaches to Bath and the south west, the Midlands, the north, Wales and Scotland departed from the nearby Swan With Two Necks in Lad Lane.[7] The whole area reverberated all day every day and into the night as well, with the incessant clatter of horses' hooves and iron-rimmed wheels on cobbles. Jane Austen's eldest brother, his wife and two children stayed in a hotel to the north of Cheapside in June 1808, on their way to Godmersham. James caught the Dover coach at 5 a.m. from the Cross Keys, while Mary, James Edward, Caroline and Jane, who joined them that morning, having stayed the night with Henry, travelled in the Austens' new chaise. The overnight accommodation, reported Jane to Cassandra, 'had been found most uncomfortable ... very dirty, very noisy, and very ill-provided.'[8]

A mile and a half to the west of Cheapside, from a window overlooking the teeming junction at Charing Cross one November morning in 1827, Francis Place made a list of the horse-drawn vehicles he could see, totalling 102 horses, thirty-seven carriages – including five stage coaches and seven hackney coaches – and several small carts.[9] With each horse depositing twenty-two pounds of dung a day (over three and a half tons a year) streets in cities were unavoidably smelly and needed constant clearing. Johanna Schopenhauer noted the congestion created by hundreds of vehicles passing in the middle of every road and expressed sympathy for the sweepers fighting a losing battle at every crossroad. She kindly spared them a few coppers – 'something one would have given gladly, even without being asked.'[10]

Twenty-three public coaches a week operated between London and Bath in 1740. By the end of the century, there were over 150.[11] The Bear Inn in Cheap Street, where John Thorpe probably stabled his horse on his visit to Bath, ran 'A Post-Coach to London, every afternoon at 4 o'clock, with a guard. A

Post-Coach to London, every Sunday, Tuesday, and Thursday, at half past three o'clock. A Day and Half Coach to London, every Monday, Wednesday, and Friday, at nine in the morning.' Despite their name, post coaches carried passengers but not mail. They travelled between staging posts – various inns on the route – and changed horses there.

The White Hart Inn just around the corner in Stall Street sent 'A new and expeditious Post-Coach to London every morning (except Sunday) at six o'clock. Also two-day Coaches to London, every Monday, Wednesday, and Friday morning, at eight o'clock.' The White Lion ran post coaches to London every morning and afternoon; the *Mercury* post coach ran from the Christopher Inn and Tavern, in the Market Place twice daily, at 7 a.m. and 4 p.m.; the *Royal Blue* left from the Greyhound every afternoon at 4 p.m.; the Castle Inn and Tavern in Northgate Street scheduled one at the same time, accompanied by a guard and also offered 'A Four-Horse Coach' to the capital every Sunday, Tuesday and Thursday evening at ten o'clock. The Lamb Inn and Tavern, Stall Street, operated the *Prince of Wales*, which left Bath for London at 6 a.m. every day. Another coach with a guard left at 4 p.m.[12] Added to these were the many coaches that left Bath for Bristol, Exeter, Plymouth, Falmouth, Gloucester, Worcester, Birmingham, Oxford, Weymouth, Salisbury, Southampton and Portsmouth. The whole city and its inhabitants must have been in perpetual motion and it is not surprising that Isabella Thorpe is thwarted in her attempt to cross Cheap Street in pursuit of two young men; it was the main east to west thoroughfare of Bath.

The name painted on the side of each stage coach, together with the name of the owner, hinted at speed, excitement and safety: the *Alert*, the *Meteor*, the *Telegraph*, the *Flying Machine*, the *True Blue*, the *Life Preserver*, the *Vivid*. Sometimes the name of the vehicle belied its promise of superior comfort and solidity, as did the *Prince Regent*, in which the governess Agnes Porter travelled through Glamorgan: 'I am sorry to remark that His Royal Highness had not a sound bottom, for the lower part of the coach was like a sieve'.[13] Guards were an added bonus, in terms of safety and entertainment. On tedious journeys, some could be persuaded to fire off their blunderbusses and outside coaching inns they played lively tunes on their bugles. Early one summer morning in July 1827, Francis Place heard three accomplished horn players competing with each other:

At 7 came a coach from the Strand. 'Mathew Melton. Windsor' on the side ... the guard a well dressed man in an olive frock, was playing an air on a keyed bugle horn. The coach drew up at the Ship, nearly opposite to my window, and the guard played, in excellent tone and time the 'Death of the Stag' — and then one of our fashionable airs. Just as he finished, a coach drew up ... and the guard a tall man in a scarlet coat, played on his bugle in excellent stile, 'The Lass of Richmond Hill'. The guard of the Windsor coach as soon as the other commenced playing caught up his bugle and played the same tune at the same time, and tone and manner, both then played a waltz ... another coach drew up and the guard a short man in a drab coat commenced a piece of music which he played exquisitely ...[14]

Coachmen on the stages became bywords for skill and character: Charles Ward, Jack Moody, 'Pop' of the *Light Salisbury*, Jackman of the *Old Salisbury*, Mountain Shaw on Monk's Basingstoke coach to London and back. Jane Austen knew the names of at least three local coachmen – Messrs Falknor, Wise and Yalden. An American travelling in England in the early 1820s was particularly struck by the coachmen he encountered:

I could not but notice the air of bustle and importance of the coachman. He enjoys great consequence and consideration along the road; has frequent conferences with the village housewives, who look upon him as a man of great trust. The moment he arrives where the horses are to be changed, he throws down the reins with something of an air, and abandons the cattle to the care of the ostler; his duty being merely to drive from one

103

stage to another. When off the box, his hands are thrust into the pockets of his great coat, and he rolls about the inn yard with an air of the most absolute lordliness.[15]

Travelling by stage coach was considered unseemly for genteel females. In the late summer of 1796, when Jane Austen was twenty, she wished to travel from Kent to London by this method, rather than wait around until someone could accompany her in a post chaise, but she was overruled: 'As to the mode of our travelling to Town, I want to go in a Stage Coach, but Frank will not let me.'[16] Her brothers and their friends, however, made frequent journeys by stage coach, as she recorded in her letters. John Warren was dropped off at Deane Gate on his way back to London after a winter ball near Steventon and Charles Austen suffered a long wait in the same place a few years later. Both of that day's coaches were full, so he had to trudge home and try again the following day. Frank himself had travelled often enough in stage coaches between Portsmouth and the Wheatsheaf Inn at North Waltham, on his way home from sea.

It appears that Eliza de Feuillide had no scruples about women travelling by stage coach. In the same month and year that Jane had put forward her scheme for leaving Kent, Eliza suggested that Philadelphia Walter could travel home to Seale by public coach from Brighton or London, in order to fit in with Eliza's rather hazy plans:

> Let me now My dear Cousin remind You of my wish to obtain your Company to Brighton ... If I should return to London from Brighton, You may easily come home from London (to which I would carry you) by the Stage — but if I should go elsewhere on quitting Brighton I am almost sure You may reach Tunbridge or Sevenoaks by the Stage, and should it be otherwise it is extremely easy to proceed by the same conveyance to Town and from thence home[17]

Stage coach travel was deeply unfashionable. Externally imposed schedules, overcrowding and the smell from less than clean companions dissuaded those who had a choice from depriving themselves of personal comfort. Colonel Byng preferred travelling on horseback and his objections to stage coaches sound convincing: 'box'd up in a stinking coach, dependent on the hours and guidance of others, submitting to miserable associates and obliged to hear their nonsense, is great wretchedness!'[18]

Most coaches carried six to eight passengers inside and four were legally allowed on the roof, although this number was routinely exceeded. Outside passengers were charged half-fare, but they sometimes paid a high price in terms of their health and safety. In March 1812, a Wiltshire newspaper reported that three passengers had frozen to death on the roof of a stage coach travelling the relatively short distance between Bath and Chippenham.[19] Dr Kitchiner gave sound advice in his *Travellers' Oracle* to those exposed to the elements: 'put on Two Shirts and Two Pairs of Stockings, turn up the collar of your Great Coat and tie a handkerchief round it, and have plenty of dry Straw to set your Feet on.'[20]

Jane Austen's nephews Edward and George were fortunate to have suffered no ill effects from the journey between Steventon and Southampton in the autumn of 1808, when they chose to sit outside on the box, with no extra covering other than what Mr Wise the coachman spared them of his greatcoat. They were 'so much chilled' by the time they arrived at Castle Square that their Aunt Jane was worried they must have caught cold, but in the event the boys proved to be as hardy as John Knightley's sons and the fresh air did them good.[21] Jane's niece Caroline took an unexpected ride on a coach box at the age of fourteen, when her ill father abandoned his horse and took her place in the private carriage: 'I was put outside the coach which soon came by, with my brother on it, and a very delightful way of travelling I thought it was. The coach was very full and I could only be taken by good-nature on the box, between the coachman and a gentleman — they were very careful of me — and in this manner I made my first approach to Scarlets.'[22]

Robert Southey's Don Espriella described his experiences as a roof passenger in hair-raising terms:

> As the day was very fine, D. proposed that we should mount the roof; to which I assented, not without some little secret perturbation; and to confess the truth, for a few minutes, I repented my temerity. We sate upon the bare roof, immediately in front, our feet resting upon a narrow shelf which was fastened behind the coachman's seat, and being further or closer as the body of the coach was jolted, sometimes it swung from under us and at others squeezed the foot back. There was only a low iron rail on each side to secure us, or rather to hold by, for otherwise it was no security.[23]

Passengers could be accommodated in the luggage basket hanging at the back, a precarious position even on a smooth road, but particularly dangerous on steep downhill stretches, where the bags bounced and tumbled. Jane Austen's Gustavus and Philander in *Love & Freindship* are discovered in the basket of the stage coach into which Laura climbs one night. It is so dark that she does not see her fellow travellers until the morning reveals them to be, fantastically but conveniently, her cousins and in-laws, being driven back and forth on the same road from Edinburgh to Sterling by Laura's late husband's aunt and her bankrupt spouse.[24] Jane was reminded of this early composition when she took Mr Yalden's coach from Alton to London in the summer of 1814:

> I had a very good Journey, not crouded, two of the three taken up at Bentley being Children, the others of a reasonable size; & they were all very quiet & civil. — We were late in London, from being a great Load & from changing Coaches at Farnham, it was nearly 4 I beleive when we reached Sloane S^t; Henry himself met me, & as soon as my Trunk & Basket

could be routed [sic] out from all the other Trunks & Baskets in the World, we were on our way to Hans Place in the Luxury of a nice large cool dirty Hackney Coach. There were 4 in the Kitchen part of Yalden — & I was told 15 at top … & in short everybody either <u>did</u> come up by Yalden yesterday, or wanted to come up. It put me in mind of my own Coach between Edinburgh & Sterling.[25]

Mr Yalden drove his coach from Alton to London one day and made the return journey the following day. In the novels, servants are sent to and from their employers' residences in public carriages: Mrs Jennings carries Marianne and Elinor Dashwood to Berkeley Street in her chaise, so Betty has to return by the stage; the Dashwoods' servants precede them to Barton Cottage in a coach; Mrs Norris' housekeeper is sent to fetch Fanny Price from London by the cheapest transport, an indignity for the child and an early indication of her inferior position in the Bertram household. When it is suggested several years later that Fanny return with William to her family in Portsmouth, her penny-pinching aunt decides that a stage coach will be quite good enough for them, but Sir Thomas has learned to value his niece and pays handsomely for a post chaise. Tempted by such luxury, Mrs Norris determines to accompany them, until she recalls that she would have to pay her own fare back to Mansfield. In *Emma*, Robert Martin, a respectable farmer, travels to London and back in a stage coach and Mr Elton takes himself off to Bath in one. Highbury is off the main coaching route, so both men meet timetabled coaches elsewhere. Penurious Mrs Smith in *Persuasion* takes a stage coach to Bath in the winter and catches a bad cold as a result.

When Jane lived at Chawton, the mail coach road between London and Winchester ran past her front door and the turnpike to Southampton and Gosport branched off immediately opposite. The Edwards' house, on a busy thoroughfare in the Surrey town of D. in *The Watsons*, requires its windows to be guarded by posts and a chain, and a narrow strip of fenced ground provided some protection for the Austens' home against damage from collision. This barrier did not stop coach travellers peering in through the windows, however, as Mrs Knight related to her god-daughter Fanny: 'I heard of the Chawton Party looking very comfortable at Breakfast, from a gentleman who was travelling by their door in a Post-chaise about ten days ago.'[26]

There was no inn and conveyances did not stop in the village unless emergency repairs were needed at the blacksmith's next door. Miss Shirreff, who read *Pride and Prejudice* on R.B. Sheridan's recommendation and became a great admirer of Jane Austen's work, used to hope that her carriage would break down as she passed through Chawton, so that she could knock on the Austen ladies' door and introduce herself.[27] The regular stream of passing carriages created an animating sight for Mrs Austen, who stationed herself by the dining room window every morning to watch the world go by. Caroline Austen, contributing to her brother's *Memoir* in her sixties, remembered her grandmother's interest and the thrill she herself had felt as the coaches thundered past: 'I beleive the close vicinity of the road was really no more an evil to her than it was to her grandchildren. Collyer's daily coach with six horses was a sight to see! and most delightful was it to a child to have the awful stillness of night so frequently broken by the noise of passing carriages, which seemed sometimes, even to shake the bed'.[28]

Jane herself took a keen interest in Collyer's coach, which came through Chawton daily, bound for Southampton. She sometimes referred to it as Falknor's, Falknor being the coachman, and made up nonsensical stories with her niece Anna, where the everyday coach featured as the Car of Falkenstein.[29] Collyer's coach performed at least one very pleasurable service for the author, in delivering her second novel, her 'own darling Child', on 27 January 1813. The nearby town of Alton is where coaches and post chaises stopped to change horses, at the George, the Crown or the Swan, the latter the only one thought worthy of mention in *Cary's Itinerary*. By 1805, five stage coaches passed through Alton every day and one started from the town every other day. With this volume of traffic in a busy town, accidents were inevitable. A large crate of goods left in the street caused the mail coach from London to Southampton to overturn in October 1805; luckily, there were no casualties. Four years later, however, six of the fourteen outside passengers on the Southampton coach from London were badly hurt in yet another oversetting. Of those, one woman, crushed partly by the coach and partly by heavy luggage, did not recover.[30]

Stage coach accidents were common throughout the country, some less serious than others. One catastrophe that befell a friend brought out Colonel Byng's warped sense of humour:

> I ascended to his Bed Room; and found him recovering from an accident he was happy to relate, and at which I cou'd scarcely refrain from Laughter.
>
> "Going to town, some day since, in a Stage Coach, The Coach was broken down near this Inn-Door, and Mr T. fell under 5 female Passengers with not much damage; (the Horses running off with the fore wheels;) When the Roof breaking in, sent an upper Cargo upon Him, which added to his former Load, bruis'd him, and cut his Head so much as to confine him here for several Days."[31]

Johanna Schopenhauer calmly recorded a minor accident on her journeys in the North Midlands. A postilion fell and the horses bolted, but, she wrote, 'such an incident is of little import, even though in English novels it is often used as an important motif. Our runaway horses were soon stopped and we reached Derby, admittedly a little shaken, but safe and sound.'[32]

Those who were a cut above stage coach travellers, but had no carriage of their own or chose not to use it on a particular journey, could hire post chaises, usually canary-coloured and nicknamed 'yellow bounders'. François de la Rochefoucauld travelling in England in the 1780s attempted to distinguish between the different ways of getting between A and B: by stage coach, by 'diligencies', which held four passengers and had fixed timetables, and by post chaise, 'harnessed to two horses and driven by a postillion, with two or three passengers. They go extremely fast, they charge eleven English shillings a mile, and do at least eight miles an hour. Sometimes they go for twelve or sixteen miles, after which you change both horses and carriage'.[33]

There was no limit to the distance one could travel on any route, he said. A journey from Canterbury to Edinburgh would pose no problem, but eleven shillings a mile sounds an exorbitant price to pay. The usual cost was one shilling and sixpence per mile with two horses, twice as much with four. Post-boys, or postilions (there was no coachman's box on a post chaise) were paid about three pennies a mile. Dr Kitchiner advised the traveller not to allow them to choose the overnight inns: 'most of them have private motives to prefer some Inns to others — inquire of the Post master or Innkeepers of the first reputation, for a List of the best houses of accommodation which are to be met with in the places through which you pass'.[34]

If two or three passengers chose to travel together, they could share the cost and decide their own schedule. The Misses Steele travel post with Dr Davies from Exeter to London, as Nancy gloats triumphantly on their arrival: '"we came post all the way and had a very smart beau to attend us. Dr. Davies was coming to town, and so we thought we'd join him in a post-chaise; and he behaved very genteelly, and paid ten or twelve shillings more than we did."'[35]

Jane's friend Martha Lloyd had benefited from the same kind of generosity each summer, when she travelled post to Harrogate and shared the cost with Mr Best. For some reason, in 1806, he decided not to go, prompting Jane to write a poem, entitled 'Oh! M^r. Best, you're very bad', in which she pointed out 'The way's as plain, the road's as smooth, / The Posting not increased'.[36] On her own account, she worried about the cost of travelling post the thirty-two miles from Chawton to the Cookes at Bookham in the summer of 1814: 'at any rate it must be such an Excess of Expense that I have quite made up my mind to it, &

do not mean to care ... I know it will end in Posting.'[37]

When Frank Churchill hires a chaise for the sixteen-mile trip to London, ostensibly to get his hair cut, but in reality to buy a piano for Jane Fairfax, he is rich enough to ignore the cost. The journey would have taken two hours each way and necessitated at least two changes of horses. In a fit of pique after the unpleasant day on Box Hill, he hires another carriage to take him back to Richmond earlier than he need go. Miss Bates reveals that the chaise had been sent from the Crown to Randalls the previous evening and that, shortly afterwards, Jane Fairfax had written to accept the post of governess with Mrs Smallridge. Frank chooses to travel by chaise for speed and comfort. Captain Wentworth, Anne Elliot and emotionally exhausted Henrietta Musgrove do the same from Lyme. Louisa's parents must be told as soon as possible of her fall from the Cobb. Mr Musgrove's coach is too heavy and slow for the purpose, so the inn's chaise-and-four horses are rented, an expensive but necessary expedient. Speed is of the essence for Lady Catherine de Bourgh too, when she undertakes her turbo-charged rampage from Rosings to Longbourn in a chaise-and-four. The horses are described as 'post' and, since Elizabeth fails to recognize the carriage, that must have been hired also, probably in London, or perhaps from the Bell at Bromley. It is indicative of Lady Catherine's sense of frustrated authority that she favours acceleration over appearances.

At the other end of the social spectrum, Mrs Long arrives at the Meryton Ball in a hack, or hired, chaise, prompting Mrs Bennet to believe that Darcy has not spoken to her because of it. General Tilney unceremoniously packs Catherine Morland off from Northanger Abbey in a hired carriage, with no servant to accompany her and on a Sunday too, a calculated insult to her clergyman father. She is not conveyed home in a trail of glory like the heroine of a sentimental novel, with a retinue of servants in phaetons and barouches: 'A heroine in a hack post-chaise, is such a blow upon sentiment ... Swiftly therefore shall her post-boy drive through the village, amid the gaze of Sunday groups, and speedy shall be her descent from it.'[38] No one has locked her away or threatened her with ill-treatment, this is no Gothic horror story, yet Catherine's ordeal is frightening enough for a young girl with no experience of travelling alone through unfamiliar territory. Only Eleanor's loan of money to pay for the journey saves her from real personal danger. The tourists who arrive in the less-than-flourishing seaside resort of Sanditon turn up in hack chaises, hinting at a lack of funds to spend in the library or the shops. 'Is there a charm in an hack postchaise?' Jane Austen asked, incredulous that her sister had recovered her health on a fifty-mile journey in one.[39]

Lydia Bennet and Wickham are certainly short of cash when they transfer from a chaise to a hackney coach at Clapham. In London, hack carriages, each identified by a number, could be hailed on the street, or found on stands, like taxis today. Mr Bennet is at first hopeful that he will trace the vehicle in which Lydia has been carried away to the city; that he was unsuccessful is not surprising. At the start of the nineteenth century there were just over one thousand hackney coaches licensed to work in London. Johanna Schopenhauer discovered that this number by no means catered for the high demand, especially in wet weather:

Eleven hundred cabs are available all day long, in ranks specially allotted to them, yet it is often impossible to find one just when it is needed. Perhaps the Italians do not fear the rain as much as do the Londoners, for to the latter getting wet is a horrible idea, so that only a few drops have to fall from the sky for everyone who does not carry an umbrella to take refuge in a cab. Within seconds all the carriages have disappeared and one realizes that the number of eleven hundred is far from enough.[40]

She thought the conveyances looked well enough, although 'the straw with which their floor is covered makes them unpleasant'. The fares were tightly regulated and journeys after dark relatively safe for the solitary traveller:

The police keep a strict eye on the cabbies; they are all numbered and woe betide anyone who goes beyond the official low
cheap fares or offends against the rules in any other way.... No
matter the hour of night, one is quite safe in entrusting oneself
to a cab, even though one may be alone or carrying money or
jewels, provided someone in the house one is leaving takes the
number of the cab in such a way as the driver notices.[41]

Jane Austen herself found hackney carriages an acceptable way
of travelling short distances. She and Henry took one from
Sloane Street to his house in Hans Place and from the bank
to visit friends then return home. They were very convenient
modes of transport, even if they were dirty and had straw on
the floor. Jane's final letter to her brother Charles in April 1817
includes a humorous message to his middle and eldest daughters: 'Tell dear Harriet that whenever she wants me in her
service again, she must send a Hackney Chariot all the way for
me, for I am not strong enough to travel any other way, & I hope
Cassy will take care that it is a green one.'[42]

Another option for getting around London, Bath and other
urban centres was the sedan chair. Johanna Schopenhauer
noted that Bath's steep topography made carriage driving difficult, if not impossible, and that a significant saving could be
made by taking sedan chairs:

Several of the finest streets, Bond Street for example, are
completely paved with hewn stone and not at all suitable for carriages. There is no possibility at all of getting to the Assembly
rooms or the two promenades, North and South Parade, by carriage. However, one need not have fear of too great exertion as
sedan chairs are readily available everywhere: they appear at
the slightest wave of the hand and transport their burden at a
jog-trot to the highest summit.[43]

Like the hackney coaches, sedan chairs were licensed and numbered. The charges levied on passengers were set by magistrates

and calculated by the imperial yard. The *New Bath Guide* of 1790 lists the scale of costs and gives a table of distances: no more than sixpence to be charged for any journey up to five hundred yards, or one shilling for every mile. Rather unfairly, chairmen could be kept waiting for ten minutes in any sixpenny fare without recompense, no more than sixpence could be charged if they were left dawdling for half an hour and abuse of the customer in such cases incurred a fine of ten shillings.[44]

Jane Austen, whose last airings from College Street in Winchester in the summer of 1817 were taken in a sedan chair, covers their use in Bath in *Northanger Abbey* and *Persuasion*. Catherine Morland is conveyed back to the Allens' lodgings in Great Pulteney Street in a chair at the conclusion of her first ball at the Upper Rooms and, after dancing with Henry Tilney at the Lower Rooms, 'she danced in her chair all the way home'.[45] She submits, unwillingly, to John Thorpe handling her into a chair after the play. On ball, theatre and concert nights, chairs waited outside to collect fares, but they were more often to be found under the colonnade in the busy Abbey Yard, near the Pump Room, the baths and the White Hart Inn. Anne Elliot seems determined to avoid sedan chairs altogether. Captain Wentworth advises her to stay dry in one rather than walk back to Camden Place from Milsom Street in the rain, but she prefers the open air. The second occasion she refuses a chair, she has just read Wentworth's letter and Mrs Musgrove, interpreting her pallor as illness, tells Charles to call one: 'But the chair would never do. Worse than all! To lose the possibility of speaking two words to Captain Wentworth ... could not be borne. The chair was earnestly protested against'.[46]

The superior way to travel by public conveyance was in a mail coach. These distinctive vehicles with numbers on the rear boot had maroon doors carrying the royal coat of arms, a maroon lower body, black upper body and red wheels. The words 'Royal Mail' were painted on the side, with the terminal towns en route. In 1784, following John Palmer's trial run between Bath and London, these special vehicles replaced horses and carts, which travelled slowly, with no set timetable. The journey by mail coach took seventeen hours rather than two days. A year later, a writer in the *Bath Chronicle* proudly reported on the improved service:

Our Mail Diligence still continues its course with the same steadiness and punctuality; yesterday its coachman and guard made their first appearance in royal livery, and cut a most superior figure ... it is with much pleasure we see so great a change in the conveyance of our mails, not only in its speed and safety, but in its present respectable appearance, from an old cart and a ragged boy ... [47]

The *New Bath Guide* of 1790 listed the four inns from which eight mail coaches set out each day:

White Hart Inn and Tavern, Stall Street (Mr Pickwick) The Mail-Coach to Salisbury, Southampton, and Portsmouth, every morning (except Sunday) at nine o'clock. The Mail-Coach to Oxford every morning, at ten o'clock.

White Lion Inn and Tavern, Market Place (Mrs Granger) A Mail-Coach to Exeter, every morning at ten o'clock.

Three Tuns and Tavern, Stall Street (Mr Dobson) A Mail-Coach to London, every afternoon at half past five o'clock. A Mail-Coach to Exeter, every morning at ten o'clock.

Lamb Inn and Tavern, Stall Street (Mr Dover) A Mail-Coach to London, every afternoon at 5; another at half past 5. A Mail-Coach to Exeter, every morning at ten ... A Mail Coach to Birmingham, every day at 3 in the afternoon.

The above Coaches are all made light for travelling, and most of them take only four inside passengers. — The Mail, and some afternoon Coaches for London, are guarded, and carry only one outside.[48]

The use of these new, light carriages soon spread across the country, but not everyone viewed their progress with unalloyed pleasure. On his tour into South Wales in 1787, Colonel Byng noted with asperity the 'mischief' caused by the new mail coaches. He blamed them for bringing wealthy tourists into previously inaccessible places, thus causing the cost of provisions to rise: 'Why is every part of the kingdom to be overrun by mailcoaches, where formerly the little post was quietly and regularly served by a postboy? They ruin us thrifty, contemplative travellers!'[49]

Mail coaches carried four passengers inside and none outside to begin with. Later, up to three were allowed. They were speedy and relatively safe. Each one employed an armed guard, paid 10s 6d a week by the Post Office. Tips were plentiful, especially if he was willing to carry parcels illicitly for less than the going rate. The guard's authority was absolute. He determined the time of departure, kept the official watch and blew a horn to clear the road of obstructions, such as other carriages and closed toll gates. Sacks of letters were thrown on and off at designated places where the coach did not stop and there was a hefty fine for anyone who delayed the progress of the King's Mail. At inns where the mail coaches stopped to deposit letters, the proprietors benefited from the trade. Horses needed feeding and grooming and passengers required food. The team of four horses was replaced every ten miles, with ostlers and grooms allowed only five minutes to complete the changeover. An innkeeper who hindered the journey onwards could lose his licence.

The landlord at Winterslow Hut near Salisbury could not be held accountable for the delay on the night of 20 October 1816. Heading for London along the Salisbury to Andover mail route, on the edge of the Plain, the Exeter Mail met with a lioness. The animal, which had escaped from a travelling menagerie, attacked the leading horse and the frightened passengers barricaded themselves into the inn. The guard aimed his blunderbuss, but the menagerie owner persuaded him not to shoot such a valuable investment. The lioness was successfully recaptured and subsequently exhibited with the horse she had mauled, and the mail coach continued on its scheduled journey to London. The guard and coachman became national celebrities for a while when the story was printed in all of the main newspapers. Jane Austen cannot have missed this news, when it happened so close to her brother James' home at Steventon. Letters from the same coach were dropped off at Deane Gate as usual later the same night. This is one of the places where the Austens' mail was delivered and collected by servants, or by Jane before the move to Bath in 1801, on her way to and from Ashe Rectory or neighbours at Oakley and Deane.

In Alton, by 1811, Bartholomew Wilkinson was running the post office from his home in Normandy Street, before moving to the High Street between 1816 and 1820. Jane Austen's letters from Chawton to London, Surrey and Kent would have been dispatched from here. In 1823, records show that the mail to London left at forty minutes past midnight and arrived from London at a quarter to three in the morning.[50]

For passengers, the experience of travelling at speeds of up to ten miles an hour often proved nauseating but, unlike many other public conveyances, mail coaches were cleaned regularly inside and out and their axles greased between journeys. Infrequent stops meant a certain amount of personal discomfort, although less inhibited, or more desperate, passengers could use a special chamber pot called a bordalou and dispose of the contents through a sliding hatch in the floor. One traveller who must have been spared this embarrassing spectacle wrote in almost religious terms of his experience:

These mail coaches of Mr Palmer ... first revealed to me the glory of motion: suggesting at the same time an undersense not unpleasurable of possible though indefinite danger; secondly through grand effects for the eye between lamplight and the darkness on solitary roads; thirdly through animal beauty and power so often displayed in the class of horses selected for this mail service; fourthly through the conscious presence of a central intellect that in the midst of vast distances, of storms, of

117

darkness, of night, overruled all obstacles into one steady co-operation in a national result.[51]

The French government was so impressed by the design of the English mail coach that 900 were ordered in 1817, at a cost of £150 each.[52] Henry Austen chose to return to London in the mail one winter night from Deane Gate, but there is no record of his experience.[53] In Jane Austen's novels, only Edmund Bertram travels by overnight mail coach, from London to Portsmouth, but the majority of her characters write letters that fly around the kingdom at all times of the day, stowed safely in the locked box under the guard's feet. The delivery of letters had improved dramatically throughout the period following John Palmer's innovations. Many towns received daily postal deliveries and even those off the main postal routes could expect a regular service. Emma notices 'a stray letter-boy on an obstinate mule'[54] as she stands in the doorway of Ford's shop, presumably the same boy who carries secret letters between Jane Fairfax and Frank Churchill to and from the nearest mail road at Kingston. In some city areas, deliveries were made to individual houses, as Don Espriella records in a letter from London:

> The post-men all wear the royal livery, which is scarlet and gold; they hurry through the streets, and cross from side to side with indefatigable rapidity. The English doors have knockers instead of bells, and there is an advantage in this ... The bell, by whomsoever it be pulled, must always give the same sound; but the knocker may be so handled as to explain who plays upon it ... The post-man comes with two loud and rapid raps, such as no person but himself ever gives.[55]

The telegram of its day, the express, was the only message reliably delivered to the door countrywide, at any time of the day or night. Teams of messengers on horseback carried urgent communications between places by relay. Mary Russell Mitford had been startled at eleven-thirty one night by a desperate rider, who 'having been called out of his bed and lost his way, had fancied the family must be in bed and asleep too, and that he and his horse had nothing for it but to make as much noise as would, I think, have awakened the seven sleepers.'[56] In *Pride and Prejudice*, Colonel Forster's express mail regarding Lydia's elopement leaves Brighton at eight in the morning to reach Longbourn at midnight. In Northamptonshire, Sir Thomas and Lady Bertram receive news by express of Tom's dangerous illness at Newmarket and, in *Emma*, Frank Churchill sends an express to the Westons informing them of his aunt's death in Richmond.[57]

In villages and small towns, mail had to be collected from a designated shop or inn. Dr Grant at Mansfield Parsonage sends a servant on a pony to collect his.[58] The Eltons' manservant fetches the post from Highbury each morning; if the Vicar's wife had her way, the man would collect the Bates' letters too. In order to put an end to Mrs Elton's interference and divert attention away from herself, Jane Fairfax expounds on the efficiency of the postal system:

> "The regularity and dispatch of it! If one thinks of all that it has to do, and all that it does so well, it is really astonishing! ... So seldom that any negligence or blunder appears! So seldom that a letter, among the thousands that are constantly passing about the kingdom, is even carried wrong — and not one in a million, I suppose, actually lost!"

John Knightley gives his explanation for the smooth operation of the service: '"The clerks grow expert from habit. — If you want any further explanation ... they are paid for it. That is the key to a great deal of capacity. The public pays and must be served well."'[59]

Jane Fairfax's determination to fetch her own letters does not escape Emma, who guesses correctly that a clandestine correspondence is in operation. Her erroneous assumption that the other correspondent is Mr Dixon almost persuades her to make 'an enquiry or two, as to the expedition and the expense of the Irish mails'[60] but on this occasion she manages to hold her tongue.

Frank's letter apprising Jane of his aunt's death does go astray, but the postal system is not to blame. He 'raved at the blunders of the post' until he discovered that the letter had been locked away in his writing desk and not posted.[61] In *Pride and Prejudice*, Elizabeth Bennet is convinced that her elder sister's letter *had* reached Caroline Bingley in London, despite protestations to the contrary, but is unsurprised to discover that Jane's letter regarding Lydia's elopement had been delivered to the wrong address in Derbyshire because 'Jane had written the direction remarkably ill'.[62] The novels teem with characters writing letters, waiting for them, sharing their contents and hoarding them for future reference. *Lady Susan*, written in the 1790s, was constructed as a series of letters, but Jane Austen grew tired of the restrictions such a convention imposed and concluded the piece: 'This Correspondence, by a meeting between some of the Parties & a separation between the others, could not, to the great detriment of the Post office Revenue, be continued longer.'[63]

7

Mention My Name At The Bell

ENGLISH INNS – travellers loved and hated them in unequal measure. They were invariably viewed as a necessary evil on long-distance journeys involving overnight accommodation and meals en route while carriage horses were changed, or fed and rested. Inns throughout the country provided waiting rooms for coach passengers, sometimes separate for those travelling up to or down from London. An archway off the road led to a cobbled yard and an open square of stables, the territory of ostlers, post-boys and stable-hands, often overlooked by galleried bedchambers. Rambling passages led to coffee rooms, eating rooms and private parlours. A large clock in the vestibule sounded the quarter, half and complete hours between the timetabled coaches, while passengers surveyed the road in both directions from the bay windows and porticos. Dr William Kitchiner's opinions of inns were shared by many: 'the generality ... are rather to be endured than enjoyed; and we do not envy the domestic Felicity of those persons who prefer them to their own Home.'[1]

The innkeeper or his wife greeted staying guests on arrival, showed them to their bedrooms and parlours and apprised them of the day's bill of fare, but stage coach passengers stopping only to change horses could find themselves treated with less respect, especially at establishments run by money-grabbing hosts. Shunted in and out of the public dining rooms with little ceremony, they were expected to eat whatever was provided, with scant care for their digestive health, hot meals being bolted down and mouths burned in the process, before the coach set off again. Genteel ladies always ate in a private room, but no other concessions were granted, even in the best inns. When the coach was ready, it left. Landlords charged full price for the food ordered, even if it could not possibly be eaten in the short time allowed. Well-run hostelries took time constraints into account and catered for guests accordingly, providing food that could be served and eaten quickly – cold meats, pastries and cheese. Dr Kitchiner advised travellers to inspect the inn larder before making a judicious choice; Mr Hurst would find little on the Doctor's list of risk-free edibles to satisfy *his* appetite: 'the *Safest Foods* are Eggs, plain boiled or roasted Meat, and Fruit: — touch not any of those Queer Compounds … *Ragouts, Made Dishes, Puddings, Pies,* &c. Above all, be on your guard against *Soup* and *Wine*.'[2]

Colonel John Byng never failed to note the details of inn meals and service, and always pasted his bills into his travel journals. At the White Hart and Star in Andover, he was presented with several inedible dishes: 'a little miserable stale trout, some raw, rank mutton chops and some cold hard potatoes. For the sake of hasty gain innkeepers hire horrid servants, buy bad provisions and poisonous liquors.'

Byng was a glass half-empty kind of man and, in this case, the half he *did* have was not at all to his taste. 'I never dined worse, nor was in a crosser humour about it', he grumbled.[3] He was not above unprincipled behaviour himself, however. On easing open the lid of a gooseberry tart and discovering 'last year's fusty fruit', in order to avoid paying for it, he surreptitiously 'closed it tightly down for the next Comer.'[4] The weirdest concoction he consumed at an inn was snail tea, which he insisted on taking for a chest infection. Whether the cure proved efficacious is not recorded, but the unpleasant dose certainly influenced that evening's journal entry, summing up his jaundiced opinion of inns everywhere: 'How difficult to meet our touring wishes; for if we go to a solitary inn, our spirits flag! if we come to a town inn, it is all noise and confusion. In the lone inn there is a damp, in the town inn heat and stinks.'[5]

For the most part, Johanna Schopenhauer had nothing but good to report of the various hostelries in which she stayed on her travels through England in the early 1800s, but the manner in which inn meals were priced annoyed her. She described how joints of meat, whole fish, vegetables, fruit and cheeses were displayed in a glass cabinet in the hall, from which the traveller made a choice, specified whether it should be boiled, fried or roasted, then waited patiently for it to arrive. So far, so good, but if any kind of meat had been ordered, the entire joint would be brought to the table and the guest expected to pay for the whole of it, even though only a few slices might be eaten.[6] The same joint made an appearance several times over, the landlord charging a little less each time, but covering the cost of the meat several times over.

On their journey from Kent to London, Elizabeth Bennet and Maria Lucas might not be unwilling to mention the name of de Bourgh at the Bell in Bromley, where they stop to change horses. No innkeeper would risk the wrath of Rosings by offending the palates of Lady Catherine's acquaintances. On the final leg of the journey from Gracechurch Street to Longbourn, Elizabeth, Jane and Maria are met at the George Inn[7] by Kitty and Lydia, who travel in Mr Bennet's carriage to collect them. The two younger sisters have hired a private room, dressed 'a sallad and cucumber' and organized 'a table set out with such cold meat as an inn larder usually affords',[8] a simple but adequate meal on the road home and nothing exotic to worry Dr Kitchiner.

According to Austen family tradition, Jane's earliest experience of dining at an inn happened in 1785, when she, Cassandra and Jane Cooper were at school in Reading. Edward Austen and Edward Cooper had apparently arrived unexpectedly and been allowed to take their young sisters to a local hostelry for dinner.[9] As an adult, Jane sampled the facilities on offer at inns on journeys with her family to Kent, London, Bath, Devon, Dorset, Somerset, Wiltshire, Staffordshire and Surrey. The Austens preferred to stay with friends and relations wherever possible, but a few instances of nights spent at inns are recorded in Jane's existing letters. In October 1798, she and her parents stopped at the Bull and George in Dartford on their way home from visiting Edward at Godmersham. This is the fullest description of an inn in Jane's correspondence:

> We have got apartments up two pair of stairs, as we could not be otherwise accommodated with a sitting-room and bed-chambers on the same floor, which we wished to be. We have one double-bedded and one single-bedded room ... We sate down to dinner a little after five, and had some beef-steaks and a boiled fowl, but no oyster sauce.[10]

The evening passed comfortably and quietly, with Mr Austen reading a Gothic novel, his wife dozing by the fire and Jane writing to Cassandra.

Nine months later, Jane stayed in Devizes at one of the coaching inns, either the Bear, the Swan, or the Castle, she doesn't say which, on her way to Bath from Steventon with Edward, his wife Elizabeth and their two eldest children. She tells Cassandra that their rooms were comfortable, but focuses primarily on the bill of fare: 'amongst other things we had Asparagus & a Lobster which made me wish for you, & some cheesecakes on which the children made so delightful a supper as to endear the Town of Devizes to them for a long time.'[11]

Several years earlier, the innkeeper of the Bear had hit on an ingenious plan for persuading his guests to part with a little more money. He offered them the chance to have their portraits drawn in crayon by his son Thomas. Fanny Burney and Mrs Thrale were enchanted and impressed by the 10-year-old when they stayed at the inn in 1780. By the time Jane Austen visited

Devizes, Thomas Lawrence, now Royal Academician and King George III's official court painter, was well on his way to being recognized as the most famous portraitist of his day. What a pity it is that she arrived in Devizes nineteen years too late to sit for her likeness to be taken by an accomplished artist.

The only other overnight stay Jane recorded in her letters appears in early March 1814, when she and Henry travelled from Chawton to London. On this occasion they stopped at Cobham. Again, Jane does not specify the inn, but perhaps it was the White Lion, listed in *Paterson's Roads*.[12] Here, they ate 'a very nice roast fowl &c.' for dinner and found everything 'comfortable'. The following morning, a refreshed Jane wrote to Cassandra that she had 'slept to a miracle & am lovely today'.[13]

Travellers rarely viewed themselves in the mirror the next morning with such pleasure. Stopping off at Honiton to rest for a night on his tour through the south west of England, William Gilpin found sleep denied him:

> This town having been twice burnt down within these last thirty years, the inhabitants take a very effectual method to prevent the catastrophe a third time, by appointing all travellers to the office of watchmen. About twelve o'clock a fellow begins his operations with a monstrous hand-bell, and a hoarse voice, informing us, that all is safe. This serenade is repeated every quarter of an hour, with great propriety; for in that portion of time, it may reasonably be supposed the traveller who is ignorant of the institution, and not accustomed to such nocturnal din in a country-town, cannot well get his senses composed, especially as his ear will naturally lie in expectation of each periodical wail. In the mean time, the sly inhabitant, who is used to these noises at night, enjoys a quiet repose.[14]

The noise of carriages leaving inn yards woke many travellers well before dawn. Back rooms overlooking the stables were to be avoided at all costs, but guests in rooms facing main coaching roads could be equally disturbed during the night by intermittent carriage traffic. Mary Morgan, on her way to Milford Haven in 1791, found sleep impossible at a coaching establishment in St Albans, because of 'stage coaches coming in and setting out from the inn every half hour of the night.'[15] To cater for so much passing trade, the inn staff prepared meals throughout the day and into the early hours, with much clattering of pots and pans accompanied by shouted orders and banging doors. An indisposed friend of Jane Austen's staying at an inn in Bath enjoyed little respite: 'Poor F. Cage has suffered a great deal from her accident. The noise of the White Hart was terrible to her.'[16]

Colonel Byng, not surprisingly, found sleeping at inns a trial. At the George in Winchester, a soft feather bed and dirty blankets robbed him of sleep; at the Crown in Ringwood, a late supper of grey mullet, which he considered overpriced, and a bolster insufficiently stuffed with feathers upset his night's rest completely; in Cirencester, light coming under the bedroom door disturbed him; in Lewes, drunkards forced their way into his chamber. The Black Bull in Cambridge came in for his most splenetic eruption: 'The evening soon settled in for a desperate rain, which I had the pleasure of hearing when in a miserable tent bed, in a dark room opening from an old gallery. This wretched inn, with most of this wretched town, ought to be burnt down!'[17] How Byng would have loved TripAdvisor!

Selina Suckling, claims Mrs Elton, has a horror of sleeping at inns and 'always travels with her own sheets; an excellent precaution.'[18] A woman after John Byng's heart! If anything could guarantee him a tolerable night's sleep, it was his own bed linen. Not that he would have changed the bed himself, of course; his servant was responsible for that. 'My own sheets made me sleep so well that I waked not till … eight o'clock', he reported with some satisfaction after a night at the Crown in Faringdon, Oxfordshire.[19] On meeting the famous landscape gardener Humphry Repton at a Biggleswade inn – and hypocritically condemning him as a dogmatic know-it-all – Byng took him to task for insisting on fresh sheets every night, since they were sure to be inadequately aired. 'My bed was good, and my *own* sheets are dry' he noted smugly in his journal, adding with a touch of sanctimonious malice, 'I shall see Repton laid up by the rheumatism, wond'ring at the cause.'[20]

Given the prevalence of tubercular complaints, for which there was no cure, travellers were right to be wary of damp bedding. Jane Austen's practical friend Mrs Lefroy of Ashe recommended to her son the following method for testing inn sheets: 'remember that if when the bed has been warmed, & the pan is just taken out, you put a glass tumbler into it, turned upside down, if there is any damp, it will appear thick, as if it had been held over steam, but if the glass remains perfectly clear, the bed is dry.'[21]

Dr Kitchiner pointed out another danger lurking in strange beds: 'As Travellers never can be sure that those who have slept in the Beds before them, were not afflicted with some contagious Disease, whenever they can, they should carry their own sheets with them, *i.e.* a light *Eider down Quilt*, and two dressed Hart Skins should be put upon the Mattresses to hinder the disagreeable contact ...'.[22]

Security at inns troubled him too. He advised travellers to wear unassuming clothes and on no account to display any valuable possessions such as rings and watches that might tempt robbers to break into bedchambers. If a bedroom door lacked bolts, a table with a chair on top should be pushed against it to hinder access.[23]

Foreign visitors to England were, in general, impressed by the facilities provided at inns. Count Pecchio, travelling post in England in 1827, marvelled at how every inn on his route kept a fire blazing in all of the rooms and tea and coffee in constant supply. He appreciated the newspapers laid out on tables for guests' amusement and the soft, inviting beds. Such luxury came at a price, however, particularly for an Italian nobleman who maybe flaunted his position and wealth too openly: 'English inns would be real enchanted palaces, if the bill of mine host did not appear to dispel the illusion.'[24]

Johanna Schopenhauer praised the rooms, the beds, the service and the overall cleanliness and claimed that English inns surpassed anything she had encountered in other countries. They were managed efficiently, the staff were helpful and polite and when the chambermaid, ostler, shoeblack boy and waiter lined up at the door with their hands outstretched, one tipped with pleasure. Given this level of support, guests had no need of their own servants, but travellers were generally treated with greater respect if a man, a maid or a groom accompanied them. Genteel women never travelled alone; Mrs Jennings has her maid, Elizabeth Bennet and Maria Lucas are attended to London from Hunsford by Mr Gardiner's manservant. Colonel Byng required his man to ride on ahead to secure a room for the night, lay out a change of clothes and remake the bed with his own sheets. The man would also 'attend to my horse ... and give me consequence.' Mr William Elliot's groom, in attendance at the inns between Sidmouth and Bath, would be responsible for grooming his master as well as the horses.

Unlike Colonel Byng, Johanna Schopenhauer had nothing but good to say about overnight accommodation:

> In the bedroom one pays only for the bed, which is seldom more than a shilling a night — and what a bed! There are the finest mattresses, the best sheets and blankets, with beautiful curtains around the bed, while in front of it lies a pretty little rug. A fine white nightcap and a pair of slippers are never missing and the English travellers, who carry very little luggage, use these without the slightest hesitation.[25]

Few characters are shown in residence at inns in Jane Austen's novels. On their way from Hertfordshire to Derbyshire, the Longbourn party would have required overnight accommodation in several places, but we only see Elizabeth Bennet and the Gardiners briefly at two inns. The first is on the road from the northern reaches of Derbyshire to Lambton. Here, the night before the fateful visit to Pemberley is made, Elizabeth discovers from the chambermaid the all-important information that the Darcy family is not in residence. Subsequently, three nights are spent at the inn in Lambton, but nothing is said of bedchambers, breakfasts or blankets. The Gardiners obviously have a private sitting room, since Mr Darcy, his sister and his friend call on them, allowing Elizabeth to gauge Darcy's feelings for her, divine that Georgiana is shy rather than proud and ascertain that no romantic attachment exists between her and Charles Bingley. On this occasion too, Mr and Mrs Gardiner notice Darcy's admiration for their niece. The informality of the location and the smallness of the assembled party encourage a greater intimacy than could have been achieved anywhere less neutral, under the surveillance of embarrassing relatives or jealous rivals. Neither damp sheets nor a disordered digestion is responsible for keeping Elizabeth awake that night.

In *Persuasion*, Charles and Mary Musgrove, Henrietta and Louisa, Anne Elliot and Captain Wentworth take rooms for a night at one of the inns in Lyme. The party from Uppercross arrives late in the afternoon and the first consideration must be to arrange accommodation and order dinner before walking down to the seashore. Lyme boasted two good inns, the Three Cups and the Royal Lion, both described in the 1810 *Guide To All The Watering and Sea-Bathing Places* as 'respectable'.[26] The former Three Cups at the foot of Broad Street, which burned down in 1844 and was rebuilt farther up the main street on the opposite side, is the likeliest contender. The location of the inn yard shown on old maps accords with the description of Mr Elliot's curricle being driven round to the front door. There would also have been a view from the front windows of Mr Elliot's departure up the hill.[27]

The inn at Lyme, like the inn at Lambton, serves a necessary purpose in bringing characters together in an intimate setting, away from the usual distractions of family and everyday demands. On the very first evening, after supper, Wentworth's naval friends stroll in without ceremony, Captain Harville to entertain the company with anecdotes, Captain Benwick to sit apart with Anne and discuss poetry. Friendships progress rapidly, hearts are opened. The following morning, Anne is admired by a stranger, first on the seashore, then at the inn, where they almost bump into each other. This very brief encounter reveals his excellent manners as well as his obvious attraction to her and Anne's interest is piqued. At breakfast, following the stranger's departure in a curricle, 'amidst the bows and civilities' of the inn staff,[28] the waiter reveals that the gentleman is a Mr Elliot, with a large fortune and a future title. How natural for the heir to Kellynch Hall to be staying at one of the better inns in Lyme, on his way from Sidmouth to Bath and how inventive of the novelist to introduce him in such an intriguing manner. He arouses the reader's interest as well as Anne's and is just as influential as the sea breeze in restoring the heroine's bloom.

The most notable hostelry in the whole of Jane Austen's fiction is the White Hart where the Musgrove family stay in Bath. Mary, Henrietta and Mrs Musgrove are here to buy wedding clothes, Charles to enjoy the theatre and inspect the local gun shops. The atmosphere of a busy inn is created sparingly but effectively; notes are brought in, parcels arrive, people come and go. Captains Harville and Wentworth, also in Bath, together with Admiral and Mrs Croft, resume their old habit of seeking out congenial company. Everyone assembles in a completely believable way in these final chapters, the inn as much an open house as Uppercross. The White Hart in Stall Street had long been recognized in guidebooks as one of Bath's principal inns. In the 1790 *New Bath Guide*, a Mr Pickwick is named as proprietor.[29] The location of the White Hart was very close to the Pump Room; from its windows, Anne sees Mr Elliot and Mrs Clay parting company beneath the colonnade opposite, having emerged from the street linking the baths. On the northern side of Bath Street, behind the classical façade, were the White Hart stables, a notorious area for sexual assignations. Is Jane Austen hinting at Mrs Clay's immorality even here?

More importantly, it is at the White Hart that Anne Elliot's heartfelt eloquence is finally expressed and heard by the only person who can change the course of her life. The scene is set in the Musgrove's private sitting room, where Wentworth and Anne have encountered each other on a previous occasion, amidst part-reconciliation and misunderstanding. No details are given as to furniture and decor, the critical issue depends on spatial awareness, where characters are placed in relation to each other. Mary and Henrietta are out shopping, Mrs Musgrove and Mrs Croft sit talking of the recent engagements, Captain Wentworth writes at a separate table, his back turned on them all, Harville stands at a window, where Anne joins him to consider Benwick's portrait and discuss constancy in love. The bustle, the noise of inn life are muted as Anne reveals her undying attachment to Wentworth, as he drops his pen and retrieves it to begin writing one of the most moving love letters in all literature.

Characters in the other novels spend time at inns, either overnight or for a leg-stretch and meal while the horses are changed, but a number of these occasions involve minor characters and happen off-stage, or are barely touched on. In *Emma*, for example, Mr Woodhouse expresses his anxiety that Frank Churchill has slept two nights on the road from Enscombe to Highbury, but naming the inns would serve no narrative purpose. The important point is that Frank has arrived earlier than expected in his haste to see Jane Fairfax. Elinor and Marianne Dashwood travel in Mrs Jennings' carriage from Devonshire to London, necessitating two nights at inns. Faced with the dinner menu, Mrs Jennings, who is presumably financing the journey, is unable to persuade the sisters to choose between salmon and cod, boiled fowl and veal cutlets. In London itself, Sir John Middleton takes lodgings for the season in Conduit Street. On the corner of this street and Hanover Square was Limmer's Hotel, a celebrated rendezvous for the sporting community who visited London. Here Sir John could be certain of 'a good plain English dinner, an excellent bottle of port, and some famous gin-punch'[30] as well as plenty of talk about pheasants, hares and hunting dogs. A house in Conduit Street with easy access to Limmer's is the ideal place for a sporting man deprived of his country pursuits.

The generality of visitors to London chose to stay in lodgings in preference to taking rooms in hotels. Beds at Limmer's were in great demand, despite the hotel's reputation as the dirtiest in London, and consequently expensive. The smartest hotels in the West End charged excessive rates, for food as well as accommodation. At the Clarendon, Grillon's and the Pulteney, dinners cost around £4 a head in 1814. A bottle of champagne or claret cost a guinea. Evans' in Covent Garden, established at the end of the eighteenth century, was a family hotel for the titled, with 'stabling for one hundred noblemen and horses'. Ibbetson's was cheaper and patronized by academics and the clergy. Fladong's attracted naval men and Stephens' in Bond Street catered for dandies.[31]

Johanna Schopenhauer found private lodgings in London far more reasonably priced and comfortable: 'without the slightest trouble one can find perfectly good lodgings, available to let immediately, complete with kitchen and cellar and all conveniences, large or small, furnished elegantly or simply, just as one pleases. There are even available entire houses, with their own stables and any extras one may require.'[32]

Only a very few London inns could provide accommodation at this level of comfort or cost. John Trusler, in his informative guide for visitors to the city, explained the distinction between inns and hotels. Hotels, he wrote, were 'taverns or inns, under a new name, so called from the hotels in Paris, where you may be rather better accommodated than at the inns in and about London, but at much greater expence.'[33]

He recommended lodgings as the best option, especially for families planning to stay in the capital for more than a few days. The unreasonable expectations of hotel servants where tipping was concerned, quite apart from the hefty bill for bed and board, could be ruinous, he warned. Lady Denham discovered the truth of Trusler's words when she determined to book into a London hotel to avoid staying with 'inferior' relatives:

> She had gone to an hotel — living, by her own account, as pru-
> dently as possible, to defy the reputed expensiveness of such a
> home, and at the end of three days calling for her bill, that she
> might judge of her state. — Its amount was such as determined
> her on staying not another hour in the house, and she was pre-
> paring in all the anger and perturbation which a belief of very
> gross imposition *there*, and an ignorance of *where* to go for better
> usage, to leave the hotel at all hazards ... [34]

Sanditon, naturally, has a hotel. Mr Parker is astute enough to
know that such an establishment can command higher rates
for accommodation and impress the tourists more than a mere
inn. His brother Sidney chooses to stay there rather than at the
Parkers' family home. Here, he can enjoy a degree of bachelor
freedom and play billiards with 'a friend or two'.[35] His preference for male company rather than family, his 'decided air of
ease and fashion' and his expensive habits bring to mind Tom
Bertram and Henry Crawford, rather than Mr Knightley or
Edmund Bertram. He would have made an intriguing hero.

Returning to Barton from Cleveland, Mrs Dashwood and
her daughters are two days on the road, so they probably
find accommodation at an inn somewhere near the border of
Somerset and Devon. One inn in *Sense and Sensibility* is identified – the New London Inn, in Exeter, four miles from Barton,
where the Dashwoods' manservant goes '"with a message
from Sally at the Park to her brother, who is one of the post-
boys."'[36] Here is an authentic reason for spotting Lucy Steele,
now Ferrars, in a chaise at the inn door with her husband, not
Edward, but Robert. The New London Inn, on the north side of
Exeter, was a very fashionable coaching inn, completed in 1794.
Just the place for Robert and Lucy to stay on their honeymoon
journey to Dawlish.

Robert Southey's alias, Don Manuel Alvarez Espriella,
patronized the New London Inn on his way from Cornwall

to London. From the outside, he recorded, it resembled a large convent. Inside, the sumptuous furnishings surprised him: 'There was a sofa in our apartment, and the sideboard was set forth with china and plate. Surely, however, these articles of luxury are misplaced, as they are not in the slightest degree necessary to the accommodation of a traveller'.[37] He concluded that the cost of these superfluous items would appear on his bill.

Jane Austen never fabricates the names of inns in real places. Lady Catherine de Bourgh patronizes the Bell at Bromley on her travels; Henry Crawford books into the Crown in Portsmouth's High Street, popular with naval officers and most likely recommended by his uncle the Admiral; General Tilney stops for two hours to bait his horses at Petty France in Gloucestershire, on his way home from Bath to Northanger Abbey. The inn on this main route, formerly called the Old Posting House, now Bodkin House, was well known to travellers on their way north from Bath. In all of the road books, Petty France is named as the second place for changing or resting horses. In *Emma*, Mr Elton takes himself off to Bath to find himself a wife; his name and the White Hart are marked clearly on his luggage. The Allens and Catherine Morland are delivered to an inn, before finding their way to their lodgings in Great Pulteney Street. If they travelled post from Salisbury, the carriage would take them to the White Hart. If in their own carriage, the same inn would store it and look after the horses. The railways replaced horse-drawn coaches from the mid-nineteenth century onwards and the once-bustling White Hart was pulled down in 1869.

The likeliest place for John Thorpe and James Morland to stay in Bath is the Bear, located where Union Street is now. After roughly forcing his horse to a standstill in Cheap Street, Thorpe hands over his gig to a 'servant', probably an ostler, who 'scampered up' from the nearest inn, the Bear, close by Union Passage.[38] The stables were extensive and obstructed the main thoroughfare from the Pump Room and the baths to Queen Square and the fashionable streets in the higher part of the town. It was a dangerous route for the healthy inhabitants and tourists to tread, quite apart from the many invalids trying to get to the baths. A character in Tobias Smollett's *Humphrey Clinker* comments on the unsatisfactory arrangement:

> the poor trembling valetudinarian is carried in a chair, betwixt the heels of a double row of horses, wincing under the curry-combs of grooms and postilions, over and above the hazard of being obstructed, or overturned by the carriages which are continually making their exit or their entrance — I suppose after some chairmen shall have been maimed, and a few lives lost by those accidents, the corporation will think, in earnest, about providing a more safe and commodious passage.[39]

Smollett voiced these opinions in 1771; the Bath Corporation finally cleared away the Bear to make way for safe, spacious Union Street in 1806.

As well as accommodating and feeding the traveller, inns provided other services too. The regiment of militia in Meryton are welcomed with rapture by the young ladies in the locality, but soldiers had to be fed, watered and supplied with beds in private houses and at inns, for only modest recompense. Innkeepers were sometimes compelled to billet troops, but did their utmost to avoid it; the consequent expense and damage often proved ruinous and paying guests were dissuaded from staying by the disruption. This proved the case in Arundel, where the Schopenhauers had hoped to stay:

> That day we were destined to find all the inns in a state of unrest and commotion. In the one at Arundel the soldiers we spoke of earlier were holding a banquet in the hall next to the room allotted to us. The whole building shook with merriment each time a toast was proposed. In the next room the musicians of the regiment made music loud enough to waken the dead. The waiters had their hands full of bottles and corkscrews and while corks popped, bugles and trumpets sounded, and

the rattle of the kettle-drums threatened to shake the foundations of the house. Added to this were the merry shouts of the Volunteers, now in high spirits, and as we saw preparations being made for a ball, we decided it was all too much for us and we slipped away.[40]

Coaching inns hired out post horses and carriages, but even moderately-sized inns off main coaching routes kept two or three horses and perhaps a chaise for hire. The fictional Crown in Highbury, 'an inconsiderable house' but the most frequently mentioned inn in the whole of Jane Austen's fiction, has an ostler in residence and 'a couple of pair of post-horses', kept more for local use than long-distance journeys.[41] Mr Knightley keeps no coach horses, so on the rare occasions he uses his carriage, as he does for dinner at the Coles', the Crown would provide the pulling power. It is likely that the 'mere common coachman',[42] who conveys Emma to and from Randalls in John Knightley's carriage on Christmas Eve, has come from the same inn.

Inns such as the Crown in small towns and villages all over the country had a vital role in community life. The local gentlemen met there, at card clubs and for parish meetings. In *The Watsons*, 'a quiet little whist club' meets three times a week at the White Hart in Stanton.[43] Items of news, national and foreign, often reached inns by way of passing carriage trade, long before reports appeared in newspapers. Innkeepers spread the information by making proclamations from their doorsteps. Some inns hosted book society meetings, as did the Swan in Alton.[44] Edward Knight conducted his manorial audits at the George, which he also owned, when in residence at Chawton Great House.

Located in something of a backwater, the Highbury Crown nevertheless has a suitable room for a ball, with 'two superior sashed windows' that Frank Churchill notices on his second day there. Built as a ballroom many years ago, but now in a state of sad disrepair, Frank still insists that it is fit for purpose: 'It was long enough, broad enough, handsome enough',[45] although on closer inspection the wallpaper is discovered to be dirty and the woodwork yellow and shabby. The card room proves too small for a proper supper to be laid out in it and will be wanted as a card room on the night; the second largest room in the inn where supper might be eaten is along a draughty passage. These difficulties enable Frank, by clever manipulation of his father, to fetch Jane Fairfax and Miss Bates so that they can give their opinions. In the event, the room is temporarily restored to its former glory. The damp anticipated with horror by Mr Woodhouse is dispelled by a good fire and plenty of candles disguise the stained walls. Those invited admire the decorations, take tea, dance, gossip; Mr Elton maliciously saunters about in front of partnerless Harriet Smith and his wife parades her pearls and lace. Mr Knightley stands at the edge of the room with a group of elderly men, drawing Emma's attention to 'His tall, firm, upright figure'.[46] This is the first time Emma becomes consciously aware of Mr Knightley's physical attractiveness and, after admiring his dancing prowess with Harriet, she is very keen to secure him as her next partner.

Jane Austen had experienced balls like the one held at the Crown since her teenage years. It is a great pity that none of her letters exist from 1810; if they did, one might have described the Alton Assembly, advertised in the *Hampshire Chronicle* of 3 December and held at the Swan Inn a week later.[47] She definitely did dance at The Dolphin coaching inn in Southampton, in 1793 and again in the winter of 1808–9. The Dolphin held assembly balls every two weeks from November to April.[48] In Kent, the Ashford assemblies were held in the main coaching inn, the Saracen's Head. Only seven miles south of Godmersham, they were very convenient for Edward Knight's family.[49] Jane records dancing there in her letters, referring to her 'slender enjoyment' of the experience in 1798, perhaps because of the crowded room and hot weather.[50] The status and wealth of the company there called for the special attention of a hairdresser. Unlike Jane Fairfax, who arranges her own hair for the Crown ball, Jane Austen had to pay Mr Hall for his skills when she attended the

Saracen's Head in 1805.[51] Eight years later, she was relieved to be spared the ordeal of donning her best gown and cap when Fanny changed her plans and decided to stay at home.[52]

8

Excursions Of Pleasure

A T ITS WORST, eighteenth-century English country living was an endurance test of mind-numbing boredom in a cultural and social wasteland. Mr Darcy recognized the need for greater exposure to the wider world when he commented on the 'confined and unvarying nature'[1] of rural neighbourhoods in general and Elizabeth Bennet certainly benefits from her travels into Kent, then Derbyshire, away from the narrow society of Meryton. Long journeys, however, were not always possible, affordable, or necessary when shorter trips more often than not relieved the tedium of everyday existence. Dr Johnson's dictionary gives 'excursion' as a synonym of 'jaunt' and either of these terms applied to a life starved of incident supplied a temporary antidote. Small doses of solitude were more tolerable with escape routes in place, or a party of visitors in prospect. Whether at home, staying with relatives, or at a holiday destination, those with carriages at their disposal could be whisked off on relatively brief excursions of pleasure, to view celebrated country estates or local beauty spots.

Sir John Middleton in *Sense and Sensibility* is fond of such schemes, especially out of the hunting season, when the empty hours require filling with company and distractions. Twice every summer he organizes day-trips to Whitwell, 'a very fine

139

place about twelve miles from Barton', with beautiful grounds and a lake, 'a sail on which was to form a great part of the morning's amusement' for his new neighbours the Dashwoods: 'cold provisions were to be taken, open carriages only to be employed, and every thing conducted in the usual style of a complete party of pleasure.'[2]

Taking a gentle drive to places of interest in the immediate locality conveniently solved the problem of how to occupy house guests between breakfast and dinner, as well as enabling them to explore new territory. 'Excursions were made most days to see something,' recalled Caroline Austen of her visit to Stoneleigh Abbey in 1809. 'Warwick Castle, Guy's Cliff, Combe Abbey and Kenilworth were visited.'[3] In *Pride and Prejudice*, Sir William Lucas is driven out into the Kent countryside each morning in his son-in-law's gig and guests at Godmersham too could expect trips out to places of interest in the area. In 1808, Edward took his brother James on rides around his farmland and plantations, to see a local pond dragged, into Canterbury and to Sandling Park, 'a nice scheme for James, as it will shew him a new & fine Country. Edward certainly excels in doing the Honours to his visitors, & providing for their amusement',[4] Jane wrote to Cassandra. Guests at the Austen ladies' house in Southampton were also treated to entertaining outings. In the same letter, Jane mentions a scheme to take James and his son James Edward to Beaulieu later in the year and congratulates Cassandra on her 'spirited voyage' to show their friend Martha and niece Anna the Isle of Wight.[5] When Elizabeth Austen died at Godmersham in October, her two eldest sons left Winchester School to stay in Southampton for a short while. Their Aunt Jane found plenty to employ mind and body: they played indoor and outdoor games and strolled down to the river. Near the end of their visit they enjoyed 'a little water party',[6] taking the Itchen Ferry to Northam, where both boys rowed up the river and forgot their grief for a while in the pleasantness of the excursion.

With Mary Russell Mitford and her father to entertain at Little Harle Tower for the day, Lady Charles Murray-Aynsley:

ordered her landaulet at twelve, and took papa and me to call at Wallington, the very beautiful seat of Sir John Trevelyan, who has given it up to his eldest son. Mr. T. was at home, and Lady C., in order to show me the house, went in and saw him. It is indeed extremely magnificent, and has been fitted up this summer in all the splendour of Egyptian decoration. There are three very large drawing-rooms, a fine dining-room, study, &c. We then drove to Capheaton (Sir John Swinburne's). The family were out, but we admired the park, and drove home by the lake, which covers forty or fifty acres … The ride altogether was through as picturesque a country as I ever saw.[7]

Any excuse served as justification for going out and about. On the occasion of their fourteenth wedding anniversary in August 1776, Mr and Mrs Lybbe Powys set off in a phaeton from their family home near Banbury, on a mini-break to Stourhead. They had long wished to see Mr Hoare's grand house and grounds and this seemed the ideal time for hatching their scheme. Intent on squeezing every ounce of pleasure out of their five-day tour, they rambled through Berkshire into Hampshire, where they took the opportunity of visiting friends at Heckfield, north east of Basingstoke. They passed close to Steventon on the road past Deane Gate to Overton and on to Andover, presumably tracing the route in a road book, since Mrs Lybbe Powys calls the area 'an unknown country'.[8] She notes a number of houses and parks close to the road that a published itinerary would have provided: Captain Jennings' at Laverstock, Mr Portal's papermill, Lord Portsmouth's Hurstbourne Park, the hunting lodge belonging to Mr Delmé, the recently burned-out shell of Lord Holland's property at Winterslow. In Salisbury, they 'laid out money in the famous steel-work' renowned for the production of particularly fine razors, knives and scissors, took a drive out to Longford Castle and revisited Wilton House. Next to be examined was William Beckford's Fonthill, followed by Stourhead. At Stonehenge, a must-see attraction, they offended the local guide by laughing at his straight-faced account of the

Devil dropping the stones on his way from Ireland. On the final day they climbed the 'vast height' of Kingsclere Hill, within sight of their home county, which they reached that evening, 'perfectly pleased with our excursion, and perfectly happy to return here ... tho' we have great pleasure in seeing fine places, we are so vain as to think few surpass our own'.[9]

The Lybbe Powys were typical of the majority of tourists on excursions of pleasure throughout the kingdom, neither connoisseurs nor antiquarians but amateur enthusiasts, capable of forming their own tastes by making critical judgements on grand estates and comparing them with others and with their own. Travelling gave them a taste for learning more about the country in which they lived, but it also fostered an appreciation of home territory.

Guided tours of country houses increased in popularity in Jane Austen's time and collections of engravings illustrating the domains of large landowners promoted their various splendours. Fierce competition raged between the owners of great estates to gain a coveted place in John Preston Neale's *Views of the Seats of Noblemen and Gentlemen in England, Wales, Scotland and Ireland*, published in several volumes throughout the nineteenth century. Rich men who had commissioned costly improvements to their properties wanted to exhibit their wealth and taste to a wide audience, comprising not only their superiors and rivals, but also private gentlemen farther down the social scale and those in the professions.

The mobile leisured classes spotted country seats wherever they went. They appeared on maps and in itineraries, to be admired from the road and viewed more extensively from within, if convenient to the owner. Once in the grounds, the design of the property, the gardens and the stables could be appreciated at close quarters. In the house itself, the cost of the souvenirs and art brought back from the Grand Tour indicated the owner's taste, together with his choice of home-produced furniture and wallpaper. Every property, from royal residences to modest gentlemen's houses, was of interest. Even the owners

142

of modestly-sized estates needed to feel approved and admired. On tour in South Wales in 1787, John Byng found himself obliged to view Mr Burt's modern house:

> with the air and pomposity of newly acquired wealth ... he rode up and desired us to come in and survey his new-built house, and all his improvements ... and then ... forced us about his mansion. It is a single house ... and, throughout, exhibits a charming effort of bad taste and bourgeoisity. Most glad was I to get away from the owner, his vulgarities, slopes, etc., etc.[10]

Nouveau riche Mr Burt was obviously anxious to establish his place on the social ladder. His pretensions bring Mr Suckling to mind; this is how he would behave if he opened Maple Grove to visitors. Jane Austen certainly questions his taste in *Emma*, when Mrs Elton boasts to Mr Weston, '"last year ... we had a delightful exploring party from Maple Grove to Kings Weston."'[11] To begin with, the idea of 'exploring' is rather pretentious when the location was so well known and the road to it so well travelled; then there is the Revd Richard Warner's description of Kings Weston in *Excursions From Bath*, a copy of which the Austens owned. Warner was not impressed: 'This mansion is a specimen of Sir John Vanbrugh's architecture ... disgusting the eye, both within and without, by its weight and clumsiness.'[12]

The final nail in Mr Suckling's coffin is hammered into place when we recall that John Thorpe names Kings Weston as one of the locations to which he is determined to drive Catherine Morland in his gig. Mrs Elton's overuse of meaningless tourist jargon – one 'explore' and two 'explorings' within a short conversation – is picked up by Mr Knightley. '"You had better explore to Donwell,"' he comments drily, but his humour is lost on the lady, who takes the invitation seriously.[13]

John Byng's passion was all for Roman remains, ruined castles and dilapidated abbeys, but his excursions to view them were not often productive of much pleasure, unless he could pocket a mosaic fragment or two, or purloin the rusty blade of an ancient sword. At Caerphilly Castle, he deplored the pomposity of the local guide and the poor state of the path around the ruin; at Castell Coch, he thought that a tea-room with a view down to the sea should be provided 'and then what a sweet place would it be for a party to come to from Cardiff Castle'. At Raby, an inhabited medieval building, other irritants got under his skin:

> I was met by a fat housekeeper and shown into the Great Hall thro' which carriages drive, passing thro' the house. This sounds grand, but must chill the house with winds ... I hasten'd into the other apartments, which are Frenchify'd, deal-floor'd and modernly glazed, without pictures. 'Have you any picture gallery?' 'No.' 'No chapel?' 'No. That was taken into the hall.' 'No library?' 'Yes, one upstairs, kept lock'd.'[14]

Gothic novels and paintings fostered a taste for unimproved medieval houses, but the owners of these homes understandably made the interiors modern and liveable. In terms of comfort, efficiency and taste, nothing could compare with the late Georgian age. Northanger Abbey's carpets, functional fireplaces, elegant furniture and clear-paned windows are a far cry from Udolpho's gloomy tapestries, massy chests, broken lutes and stained glass. Its only redeeming feature in Catherine's eyes is that, from the outside, Northanger looks every inch an ancient abbey 'just like what one reads about'.[15] Mary Russell Mitford could not say the same of Hexham Abbey, which she visited in 1806 with a family of friends at whose house she was staying. The owner, wealthy Colonel Beaumont, had spent £12,000

> repairing and beautifying this house, in which they only spend about a month in the year... It was a fine specimen of the Saxon Gothic architecture; but he has built upon the same foundation, retained all the inconveniences of the ancient style, and lost all its grandeur. It has on the outside an appearance of a manufactory, and the inside conveys the exact idea of an inn ... yet

Pocket map of the English and Welsh counties in *Cary's Traveller's Companion* (1792). This is the kind of map that could be dissected to make an educational jigsaw puzzle

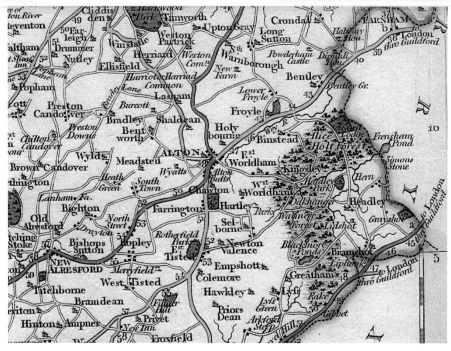

Map of the Alton area (section of the Hampshire map) from *Cary's New Itinerary* of 1821, showing the busy mail and stage coach route that ran past Jane Austen's house in Chawton

Map of the Steventon area (section of the Hampshire map) from *Cary's New Itinerary*, showing the coaching and turnpike roads along which Jane Austen and her family travelled on their way to Bath, London and beyond

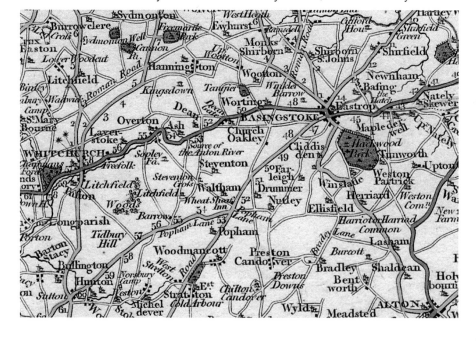

A Specimen of the Buckinghamshire roads (August 1816) from *Mrs Hurst Dancing*. This type of road surface was familiar to carriage travellers in every county

Two smart carriages on an 'excursion of pleasure' to a London lunatic asylum, from *Ackermann's Repository of Arts* (1815)

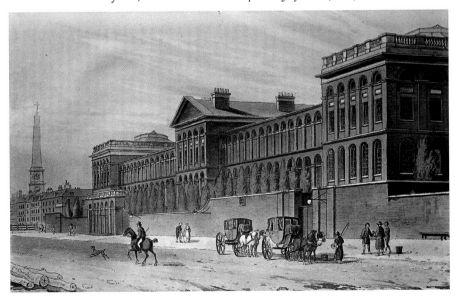

"Henry drove so well"
Chap XX

The curricle ride from Petty France to Northanger Abbey. Henry
Tilney's coachmanship far surpasses John Thorpe's in Catherine
Morland's opinion

'A lady never looks better than on horse-back'. The Prince Regent commissioned George Stubbs to paint the renowned horsewoman Laetitia, Lady Lade, in 1793

A serious oversetting on the Brighton road in 1822. Coaching accidents happened frequently enough to frighten travellers into writing their wills before they left home

A post chaise toiling uphill in 1817. Two-horse power proved insufficient over steep terrain and carriage passengers were often forced to alight and walk. Four horses were an expensive option, but enabled travellers to keep their seats

White carriage dress was fashionable if unsuitable. A costume such as this, featured in *Ackermann's Repository* of 1815, would soon be spoiled by dirt

Two relatively sensible walking outfits, advertised in *Le Beau Monde* (1807), although the flimsy shoes are fit only for urban streets

BATH, from the private Road leading to Prior Park.

At a viewpoint not far from here, Catherine Morland 'rejected the whole city of Bath as unworthy to make part of a landscape'

The housekeeper of a country house conducting a tour in the early 1800s. Tourists at showcase houses expected to view the furniture and works of art and be told how much each item cost

Thomas Rowlandson's drawing of 1805 portrays tourists relaxing at The Temple of the British Worthies at Stowe, one of the must-see places to visit

A 'sloppy lane' in November. This is the kind of lane along which Jane Austen and her sister Cassandra walked between Steventon Rectory and family and friends at Deane and Ashe

this is the occasional residence of a man with an income of a hundred and ten thousand pounds ... [16]

A large income might be the best recipe for happiness, but it did not guarantee good taste, as Mrs Lybbe Powys discovered on her excursion to Wilton and Fonthill on her way to Stourhead. Wilton she found 'too gloomy', 'magnificently uncomfortable' and reminiscent of 'a statuary's shop'. On the principal floor at Fonthill she noted

> immense riches, almost too tawdrily exhibited. There are many good pictures and many very indifferent ... the best at Fonthill are of the small kind, fit only for lady's cabinets ... The chimney-pieces all over the house are elegant to a degree; even those in the attics must have cost an immense sum, all of statuary or Sienna marble; but what hurts the eyes most exceedingly is that every hearth, even in the best apartments, are common black and white, which seems such a saving of expense in the very article where profusion has been so lavish'd that 'tis perfectly amazing.[17]

Parties touring large houses of any age often nourished expectations that were not met. Colonel Byng invariably anticipated some mark of respect or favour towards himself, but was rarely gratified. At Fairford Park, he complained that the gardener had shown him grapes, nectarines and pineapples in the hot houses, but not offered him a taste of any. If there was anything negative to say of the places on his travels, Byng usually said it. In the summer of 1785, he took friends to Lord Guildford's house near Banbury. Unfortunately, the owner had just arrived home from London and the visitors were denied admittance. Byng was incensed: 'Very rude this, and unlike an old courtly lord! Let him either forbid his place entirely, open it always, or else fix a day of admission: but, for shame, don't refuse travellers, who may have come twenty miles out of their way for a sight of the place.'[18]

Sometimes, the viewing party were treated to food and an audience with the landholder; Byng's bad experiences were not common to all. Louis Simond gained entry to Mount Edgecumbe, even though he arrived on a day when the property was shut: 'we were told it was necessary to write to Lord M.E. A note was dispatched, and word returned that we were welcome, and a key given to us, opening all gates, with directions to find our way, and no guides to overlook us, which is a refinement of politeness.'[19]

Byng took his revenge in his journals by recording each inattention to hospitality, every dereliction of duty to house and grounds. At Eastwell Park, he praised the fine views inland and of the sea but, on being turned away from the house, 'as Mr Finch Hatton with "much company were at home; and dinner would soon be ready" (half-past five o'clock! An elegant transfer of London hours!!)' Byng turned splenetic and recorded in his notebook: 'Every part about this place lies in neglect and disorder, with neither a wish to preserve, repair nor keep clean!'[20]

The Finch Hattons were neighbours of the Knights at Godmersham; Jane's brother Edward would have known the family when Byng made his unsatisfactory visit in 1790. The same vilified Mr Finch Hatton was in residence when Edward moved into Godmersham Park in 1797 and the families called upon each other regularly. Jane accompanied her brother and sister-in-law to Eastwell in August 1805, for which occasion Elizabeth hired Mr Hall, a hairdresser from London, to flourish his scissors and brushes. She obviously considered it a smart enough venue to warrant such trouble and expense; Jane wrote to Cassandra of her own hair being 'thoroughly dress'd'.[21] Her letter contains no hint of dirt, neglect or disorder at Eastwell. She had dinner, listened to Miss Hatton playing the piano and remarked on her hostess's lack of conversation, but said nothing of the décor.

There is no evidence, apart from Mrs Austen's mention of a planned excursion to Warwick Castle,[22] that Jane Austen was ever a tourist in a grand house, although she must have felt like one at Godmersham and Stoneleigh Abbey before they became familiar to her. There is a possibility, however, that she was shown around Kenwood House in Hampstead, North London, the home of Lady Elizabeth Murray, later lady of few words at Eastwell. Fanny Burney paid a visit to Kenwood in 1792, as many tourists did, to admire the Adamesque architecture and the excellent collection of paintings. The owner of Kenwood was Lord Chief Justice Mansfield, famous for his verdict of 1772, which ruled that a black slave who had escaped to England could not be returned to slavery in Virginia. Mansfield was Lady Elizabeth's great-uncle and guardian. Also under his roof lived another great-niece, Dido Bell. An enslaved black woman called Maria Bell was probably her mother. It is a widely-aired suggestion that Jane Austen saw a double-portrait of Lady Elizabeth and Dido, the girls occupying equal space in the painting although obviously not equals, which subsequently prompted Jane to explore the relationship between differently circumstanced cousins in *Mansfield Park*.[23] Whatever the case, Jane Austen is likely to have visited Hampstead, where her Aunt Philadelphia, cousin Eliza and Eliza's son Hastings were buried; Henry Austen talked of 'a drive to Hampstead' when Jane was in London searching for portraits of Mrs Bingley and Mrs Darcy.[24] Perhaps, just perhaps, she looked for them among the paintings in Kenwood House too.

On the other side of the house-visiting equation, landowners opening their private dwellings to complete strangers, no matter how genteel, encountered problems. Horace Walpole's Strawberry Hill, built in the 1750s near Twickenham, proved a huge draw for the country house tourist, but by 1783, Walpole's patience with an unending stream of visitors was wearing thin:

> I am tormented all day and every day by people that come to see my house, and have no enjoyment of it in summer. It would be even in vain to say that the plague was here. I remember such a report in London when I was a child, and my uncle Lord Townshend, then secretary of state, was forced to send guards

to keep off the crowd from the house in which the plague was said to be — they would go and see the plague. Had I been master of the house, I should have said ... 'You see the plague! you *are* the plague.'[25]

The following year, he published a set of rules for admission: tickets to view the house on a specific day to be applied for in writing; each ticket to admit four adults only, no children; only one party to be allowed in each day; opening hours between noon and three, from 1 May to 1 October; notice to be given if the party decided to cancel.[26] Tourists were not dissuaded, Strawberry Hill's appointment book for 1784–96 recorded annual averages of 250 to 300 people.[27]

Tourists were interested in any house to which they could gain access, but were willing to make special journeys to see the A-list country properties: Blenheim, Fonthill, Wilton, Stourhead, Chatsworth, Kedleston, Haddon, Stowe, Woburn. Understandably, tempers became frayed when they were turned away at the door. In the 1790s, with footfall increasing yearly – the number of visitors to Wilton as early as 1776 had reached 2,324 by the month of August[28] – several of these places implemented set viewing times: Blenheim opened daily from two till four; Woburn Abbey on Mondays only; Fonthill from twelve to four every day. The information on opening hours was made available at local inns and published in local newspapers.[29] Admission remained largely an informal affair at properties like Jane Austen's Pemberley and Sotherton, with some rooms closed if the family were in residence. The Gardiners drive their carriage to Mr Darcy's front door, apply for admittance and wait in the hall for the housekeeper. Some country house visitors sent their servants to make the request for entry. In *Sense and Sensibility*, the party bound for Whitwell from Barton Park are prevented from setting out on their excursion by Colonel Brandon's departure to London. Whitwell belongs to his brother-in-law, who has left 'strict orders' that no one is to be allowed onto the estate without Brandon in attendance.[30]

Willoughby takes this opportunity to sneak Marianne into Allenham without the owner's permission and show her over the gardens and every room in the house. Elinor points out the impropriety, the impoliteness, of entering Mrs Smith's home uninvited, especially when she was in residence, but Marianne's enthusiasm for what she has seen overrides her sister's censure.

Housekeepers were responsible for conducting guided tours of the rooms open to view and they all expected tips. Horace Walpole wrote to the Countess of Ossory in 1783 that his house-keeper Margaret, 'gets such sums of money ... that I have a mind to marry her, and so repay myself that way for what I have flung away to make my house quite uncomfortable to me.'[31] Many, like fictional Mrs Reynolds at Pemberley and real Mrs Garnett at Kedleston, were civil and well informed, but some proved inarticulate, ignorant and grasping. Complaints that the housekeeper knew nothing of the art on display were rife; the availability of handbooks was much appreciated. Stowe sold two, Wilton had one translated into Italian, Blenheim had a French version. A number of properties provided lists of the items in each room, although they were not always accurate. In the library at Kedleston, Johanna Schopenhauer admired a Rembrandt and a number of others that remained unidentified, since the catalogue was riddled with errors.[32] Where was Mrs Garnett on this occasion?

Sometimes the housekeeper knew more about the paintings and furniture than the owner. At Sotherton, the party from Mansfield Park and Parsonage are guided through the rooms by Mrs Rushworth, 'who had been at great pains to learn all that the housekeeper could teach, and was now almost equally qualified to shew the house.'[33] Her tedious recital of the family's history interests no one but Fanny Price, to whom house-visiting is a new experience. Was Jane Austen ever exposed to the same dull recitation of trivial facts and dates? She certainly provides a convincing example in the word-for-word lesson Mrs Rushworth has taken the trouble to learn: '"This chapel was fitted up as you see it in James the Second's time. Before that period, as I understand, the pews were only wainscot; and there is some reason to think that the linings and cushions of the pulpit and family-seat were only purple cloth; but this is not quite certain."[34]

Completely oblivious to her visitors' lack of interest, Mrs Rushworth determines to show them over the whole house, until her son points out that the grounds must also be viewed. If Rosings ever opened its doors to visitors, Lady Catherine could safely leave the enumerating of its glories, its fireplaces, staircases and glazing bars to Mr Collins. She herself behaves like an ill-mannered country house visitor in the Bennets' house: 'As they passed through the hall, Lady Catherine opened the doors into the dining-parlour and drawing-room, and pronouncing them, after a short survey, to be decent looking rooms, walked on.'[35]

General Tilney would never trust any of his staff to do full justice to his grounds and house. In his kitchen gardens and hot-houses, he steered Catherine 'into every division, and led her under every wall, till she was heartily weary of seeing and wondering'.[36] He is just as relentless a guide in the house, propelling Catherine more for his own gratification than for hers, through very grand, very noble rooms, itemizing the cost of each object with a minuteness that stuns rather than impresses his guest. His wish that she should only see the most opulent accommodation is misinterpreted by Catherine as a guilty reluctance to venture into his dead wife's bedchamber. The Abbey is a show house, not a home, and Catherine, in common with discerning tourists who visited such properties, comes to the realization that her own taste tends towards the more modest and unpretending.

Excursions of pleasure were not limited to visiting great houses; like other pleasures overindulged in, they could become exhausting. Mary Crawford stifles her yawns as she is led from room to room at Sotherton; she has already 'seen scores of great houses',[37] too many to care for any of them. After the fatigues of 'being hurried from one splendid object to another, without the power of viewing anything at my leisure',[38] Mary Morgan found greater satisfaction in a morning spent on the Malvern Hills in Worcestershire. She describes the kind of pleasures to be had at any famous landmark:

> It is very entertaining to see the hill speckled over with parties that are wandering about it. Some in one place with glasses in their hands, as if possessed with the insatiable curiosity of extending their view beyond the clouds ... Two or three in another place, chatting and laughing at each other's labours in ascending the steep. Some sitting on seats at different distances, enjoying the clear sky, and the purity of the ambient air.[39]

The excursion to Box Hill in *Emma* brings little pleasure, despite the fine weather and the general anticipation of happiness. Like Malvern, Box Hill was a well-known location for sightseers. Mr Weston's party shares the space with at least one other group, which arrives in an Irish jaunting car, perfect for 'gentlemen to go a pleasuring with their families'.[40] It had room for a picnic table and seats for up to six people, ideal for fair-weather excursions to nearby beauty spots. Expectations are high and 'every body had a burst of admiration on first arriving',[41] but the feel-good factor does not last. The tensions and misunderstandings between Frank and Jane taint the atmosphere, as does the thinly-veiled mutual dislike of the Eltons and Emma. Harriet is dull and quiet because Mr Knightley is occupied with Miss Bates and Jane Fairfax; Frank Churchill is overbearingly attentive to Emma. Mr Knightley, critical and disappointed, watches from the side-lines. The party splits into exclusive divisions, beyond the harmonizing influence of fine views and picnic treats. The worst tear in the social fabric is caused by Emma's humiliation of Miss Bates, for which she is castigated by Mr Knightley and returns to Hartfield chastened and depressed. The excursion to Box Hill provides questionable enjoyment for anyone. Removal from the organized world, where no one oversteps the boundaries, into a relatively unstructured setting, allows the open expression of irritation and impatience to fracture the surface harmony. The consequences of the Box Hill excursion reverberate throughout the remainder of the novel.

Few outings away from familiar territory are productive of satisfaction in Jane Austen's novels. Those who derive any kind of pleasure from them are usually the untrustworthy characters, Isabella and John Thorpe, Mary and Henry Crawford, Sir Walter and Elizabeth Elliot. For Mrs Norris any excursion is productive of pleasure, especially when it allows her to direct operations with maximum officiousness and minimal financial outlay. For Mrs Elton, the pleasure of an outing lies in 'bustle and preparation ... regular eating and drinking, and pic-nic parade'. Cabbage beds would have tempted her to Donwell; she 'only wanted to be going somewhere.'[42] Male restlessness is held up for disapproval too: Tom Bertram's escape from his responsibilities as the eldest son to the races in Brighton and Newmarket and the seaside at Ramsgate; Mr Knightley's scorn of Frank Churchill's being 'for ever at some watering-place or other'.[43] Henry Crawford is the character who travels most in pursuit of pleasure. His whole existence is a series of excursions in search of novelty and gratification.

The Revd Thomas Gisborne, whose conduct manual Jane Austen read in 1805, might have been describing Henry when he castigated men for ignoring their obligations to dependents in favour of flitting from place to place:

> The duties of the Master of the family, of the Parent, of the Landlord, of the Country Gentleman, are on many occasions grossly neglected in consequence of immoderate indulgence of a propensity to roving. The occupier of the land, deprived of the friendly intercourse, which formerly subsisted between him and the owner ... is degraded into a dependent on the caprice of a steward.[44]

Visits to industrial sites provided a worthier experience of novelty than jaunts to the races or fashionable seaside resorts, but they could hardly be called pleasurable. An interest in the manufacture of profitable goods was considered patriotic and instructive tours of foundries, mills, mines and factories featured in every serious traveller's journal. 'To have been at Newcastle, and men of curiosity too, without seeing a coal-pit, would have been a sin of the most unpardonable nature',[45] wrote one man who did not shirk his duties as a tourist. John Byng went into an iron furnace near Monmouth and requested a tour around Richard Arkwright's cotton mill outside Bakewell, but was denied access. Parties demanding guided tours had become too numerous, he was told, and distracted the workers from their labour.

James Plumptre ventured into a Derbyshire lead mine in 1793, which entailed a precipitous climb up ladders hammered into the cavern walls and a scramble 'through holes in rock just big enough to admit the body'. After this heart-pounding experience, he and his companions worked off the adrenaline by loudly singing 'God Save the King' and 'Rule Britannia', as they made their way back to safety.[46] In 1799, he visited Heaton Colliery and was foolhardy enough to proceed into the pit immediately after a fall of stone had trapped and injured one of the miners. The descent was scary enough for Plumptre to keep his eyes closed until he reached the bottom. He described clearly and calmly how the mine was worked, but later added a note to explain why his guide had pulled down the candle that Plumptre had raised to illuminate the rock strata. Highly flammable gas in mines caused explosions, leading to huge loss of life, 'ninety souls at least', noted Plumptre, in the Chester-le-Street pit disaster of 1708: 'I had enquired of Mr Daglish before I descended if there was the least danger to be apprehended from the fire damps, and he assured me none at all; I was therefore less cautious than I ought to have been'.[47]

He gained first-hand knowledge of the extensive workings of a mine, but came back up to light and air with a sense of relief. Intrepid female travellers also went down mines and into other hazardous working environments. Elizabeth Spence marvelled at the copper works outside Swansea, the spectacle

153

of 'the liquid ore ... pouring from the raging furnaces' was, she thought, 'truly sublime'.[48] Over the course of one day, Johanna Schopenhauer watched women and children working in a Manchester cotton mill, descended into a coal mine and visited a pencil factory. In Leeds, she saw carpets being woven.[49] All of this exposure to industrial processes began to pall after a while and, on being refused admittance to an iron works, she admitted: 'we were not particularly disappointed. It is a fact that while travelling one tends to look at things just because they happen to be there, without real pleasure or inclination. One is inspired merely by some sense of duty, and often wishes afterwards that one had not taken the trouble.'[50]

Mary Morgan had fully resolved to go down a coal-pit in South Wales, but her courage failed her when she discovered that someone had recently suffocated in the very mine she planned to see. She confessed: 'I did not like the idea of being arrested by death so suddenly, particularly in taking a view of the infernal regions; this would have been paying too dear for my curiosity.'[51] This was one excursion she abandoned with relief, but she was happy to visit lunatic asylums and prisons, as were others. Salutary lessons might be learned and the reforming spirit of the governors approved, but they afforded little by way of pleasure except for those who went to deride and laugh. Jane Austen's brother Edward took her to Canterbury Gaol in 1813, on his tour of inspection as a visiting magistrate. Jane wrote to her sister, 'I was gratified — & went through all the feelings which People must go through I think in visiting such a Building.'[52] More pleasurable was the shopping expedition afterwards.

Literary tourism flourished in Jane Austen's day, with countless numbers drawn to the birthplaces and graves of famous writers and the locations of their fictional works. No one passing through Warwickshire would dream of missing an excursion to Stratford upon Avon. 'William Shakespeare was born in this house' announced the board hanging over a butcher's shop in an insignificant backstreet. Pilgrims were told that the old wooden chair in the kitchen was Shakespeare's own – Colonel Byng was credulous enough to buy a piece sliced off one leg – and that the bedstead upstairs was where the playwright's mother had given birth to him. Sections of the mulberry tree that once grew in the garden, at least that's what tourists were told they were acquiring, were also sold.

Tourist numbers to the English Lakes, already high as a result of William Gilpin's picturesque tours, increased on the publication of William Wordsworth's *A Guide Through the District of the Lakes* in 1810, together with his lakeland-inspired poetry. By 1818, John Keats was complaining of contamination by 'bucks and soldiers, and women of fashion-and-hat-band ignorance'.[53] Mild-mannered Gilpin had regretted the number of empty-headed travellers on his tour to the Lakes as early as 1772, noting in his journal that 'these parts are too often the resort of gay company ... who have no ideas, but of extending the sphere of their amusements — or, of varying a life of dissipation.'[54] Rambling in the same region twenty years later with a copy of Gilpin's Lakes tour under his arm, Joseph Budworth reported that nothing had changed. Visitors in search of quick thrills dashed past the recommended viewing points in their picturesque guides 'with an exclamation or two of "Oh! how fine," &c.; or ... the day after we were upon Windermere, "Good God! how delightful! — how charming! — I could live here for ever! Row on, row on, row on"'.[55]

Who knows whether Edward Knight travelled to the English Lakes with Mr and Mrs Knight and a party of twelve merely for pleasure or, like most travellers, for a mixture of entertainment and education? This was, after all, Edward's last holiday with his adoptive parents before his marriage. Edward's eldest son missed seeing the Lakes on his way back to Godmersham from Scotland with his Uncle Henry Austen in the early autumn of 1813, but his Aunt Jane realized that the beauty of the scenery would have been lost on him. He thought more of 'Growse & Partridges than Lakes & Mountains' and was 'no Enthusiast in the beauties of Nature'.[56] Given his love of firearms, Jane's nephew would have relished the twelve brass swivel guns firing cannonballs from a boat on Ullswater, creating the sound of thunder as the echoes reverberated around the surrounding hills.[57]

Any kind of literary link, no matter how spurious, promoted an influx of fashionable visitors. Elizabeth Spence appreciated Haddon Hall in Derbyshire all the more because she believed that Ann Radcliffe had used it as a model for Count Montoni's louring fortress in the Apennines: 'this ancient mansion ... exclusive of its being one of the finest specimens of antiquity this country produces, is the place Mrs. Radcliffe has made the subject of her pen in describing the Castle of Udolpho. This circumstance alone would render it highly interesting to the admirers of her writings'.[58] Catherine Morland would have loved it!

The Scottish Highlands attracted those taken in by the Ossian poems, the literary hoax perpetrated by James Macpherson in the 1760s. Later in the century, avid readers of Sir Walter Scott's *The Lady of the Lake*, published in 1810 and relished by Captain Benwick among countless others, flocked to the Trossachs:

> The whole country rang with the praises of the poet – crowds set off to view the scenery of Loch Katrine, till then completely unknown; and as the book came out just before the season for excursions, every house and inn in that neighbourhood was crammed with a constant succession of visitors. It is a well-ascertained fact that from the date of the publication of *The Lady of the Lake* the post-horse duty in Scotland rose to an extraordinary degree, & indeed it continued to do so regularly for a number of years, the author's succeeding works keeping up the enthusiasm for our scenery which he had thus created.[59]

No wonder Jane Austen complained of unfairness when Scott turned his talents to writing novels, the 'succeeding works' mentioned above.[60] Today, Scott's readership is easily outnumbered by Jane Austen's and the compulsion to locate her life and her fictional creations in the English landscape grows ever stronger. Appreciative readers in the 1850s began to search for their favourite author's burial place in Winchester Cathedral, 'the shrine of Jane Austen', one woman called it.[61] The verger at the time had no idea what all of the fuss was about and had to inquire of a visitor, '"Pray, sir, can you tell me whether there was anything particular about that lady; so many people want to know where she was buried?"'[62] Nowadays there is no chance of missing the famous ledgerstone; the spot is flanked by display boards presenting chronological information on the author's life and homes, a brass wall tablet and a memorial window. 'Janeite jaunts' to the cathedral will, the marketing manager hopes, reverse the trend of falling visitor numbers and top up the cash in the coffers.[63]

In his *Memoir of Jane Austen*, published in 1870, James Edward Austen-Leigh located his aunt firmly in Hampshire. This is where she grew up and lived for most of her life and where he and his sisters had most contact with her. Steventon Rectory had been as much his home as Jane Austen's; the lime tree he had planted with his father was over half a century old when he began the *Memoir*, although the house itself was long gone. Not a stone remained of Jane's first home, but that did not deter Constance and Ellen Hill, who set out in 1901 from their cottage in Hampstead on a very special excursion of pleasure, 'to follow the author to all the places where she dwelt'.[64] The description of their meandering journey through the Hampshire lanes in a one-horse chaise could have been penned a hundred years previously by Johanna Schopenhauer. They consulted finger-posts and studied maps, but were bewildered by the spider's web of byways criss-crossing the county. They discovered when they stopped to ask the way, as Colonel Byng had before them, that local people knew nothing beyond their immediate environs. By more luck than judgement, they reached Deane Gate before dark and 'fell asleep that night with the happy consciousness that we were really in Austen-land'.[65]

Their pleasure was in no way dimmed by the lack of a tangible birthplace. Their response is littered with exclamatory enthusiasm: 'This is the place! ... This is the site of the old parsonage-house where Jane Austen was born! ... There is the very terrace described!'[66] Armed with the Brabourne edition of Jane's letters and the Austen-Leigh memoir, Constance located the relevant references while Ellen recorded each sacred place in her sketchbook – the church, the pump, the old manor house. They almost fainted with rapture when they encountered a descendant of the Littleworth family, long-time servants to the Austens.

Austen-Leigh specifically warned Austen tourists away from the cottage at Chawton – 'I cannot recommend any admirer of Jane Austen to undertake a pilgrimage to this spot'[67] – and with good reason. It was divided into labourers' dwellings immediately after Cassandra's death in 1845 and not restored to a recognizable home until the middle of the last century. The Hill sisters glossed over the state of the house when they visited the village, preferring to picture it as it was in Jane's day and quoting extensively from descriptions in the letters and the *Memoir*. If they were disappointed by the dilapidated appearance of the cottage, it is only detectable by omission. They describe the 'unchanged' rooms in the Great House in more detail, particularly the 'oak room' above the porch, 'especially associated with Jane Austen'.[68] Their final excursion followed Jane to 8 College Street in Winchester, where they maintained a resolutely cheerful air in the face of illness and death: 'We almost fancied we could see Miss Austen seated in the window writing to her nephew'.[69]

The motivations of present-day tourists on excursions of pleasure to Austen locations are little different to the Hills'. The urge to imagine the author's everyday experiences in these significant places is irresistible, although modern visitors are generally more critical of Austen-Leigh's attempt to confine his aunt's life to 'a Victorian idyll of "pleasant nooks and corners"'.[70] Despite Lord Brabourne's attempt to swing locational interest towards Kent in the 1880s, with the publication of the Knight family collection of his great-aunt's letters, the main pilgrimage route still runs through Hampshire. Annual visitor numbers to Jane Austen's House Museum in Chawton since the year 2000 average 30,000; the number of signatures in the Steventon Church visitors' book over the same period averages 1,000. Signs marking the boundaries with West Sussex, Berkshire, Dorset and Wiltshire proclaim that Hampshire is 'Jane Austen's County'.

One of the earliest tourists intent on pinning down an exact novel location was Alfred Lord Tennyson, who walked the nine miles from Bridport to Lyme Regis on 23 August 1867, 'led on ... by the description of the place in Miss Austen's *Persuasion*'.[71] He particularly wished to see the steps from which Louisa Musgrove had fallen. Other readers followed him to Lyme, including the Misses Hill, who speculated on the location of the inn at which the Musgroves stayed – they decided on the Royal Lion – and of Captain Harville's house. On this subject, their landlady at Bay Cottage 'looked upon the whole matter as settled beyond a doubt. She talked of the Harvilles, the Musgroves, Anne Elliot and Captain Wentworth as if they had been in her house but the season before, and pointing to a bedroom on the first floor, exclaimed eagerly, "That is the room where the poor young lady was nursed."'[72]

The blurring of reality and fiction continues in full force today, as coach and minibus tours transport Jane Austen film and DVD addicts to instantly recognizable Longbourn, Netherfield, Hunsford, Rosings and Pemberley; Norland, Cleveland and Barton Park; Hartfield and Mr Elton's rectory; the Great House at Uppercross and Sir Walter's house in Bath. Attractively produced maps and guidebooks direct our steps through the Bath of *Northanger Abbey* and *Persuasion* and the London of *Sense and Sensibility*, along the Devon lanes at Barton and the streets of Fanny's Portsmouth, to the village of Meryton and the seashore at Lyme. Jane Austen's life and works, located, mapped and marketed, constitute in themselves unmissable excursions of pleasure.

9

North To Pemberley

J ANE AUSTEN PROBABLY had no direct personal knowledge of
  Derbyshire, but a familiarity with the county could date from
her years at Steventon and her friendship with Anne Lefroy.
Mrs Lefroy's brother, Sir Samuel Egerton Brydges, was co-editor
of *The Topographer* and copies of the journal were kept in the
Lefroys' library at Ashe Rectory. A writer in the first volume
of 1789 described a tour from Oxford to the Derbyshire Peak
District, made in 1786. His route lay through Banbury, Edgehill,
Warwick, Kenilworth, Coventry, Ashby de la Zouch, Derby,
Matlock and Buxton, the whole journey being accomplished in a
post chaise in four days, necessitating early morning starts and
the hire of four horses over more difficult terrain. The writer
visited the castles at Warwick and Kenilworth and a china manufactory at Derby on his way to Chatsworth and Dovedale.[1]

In 1806, Jane paid a five-week visit to her cousin Edward
Cooper at Hamstall Ridware in Staffordshire, barely twenty-five
miles south of Dovedale, but no evidence exists that she crossed
the border between the counties. Six years previously, Edward
Cooper had taken his mother-in-law on a picnic to Needwood
Forest, from where Dovedale could clearly be seen, so perhaps
Jane caught a glimpse of Derbyshire from the same vantage
point.[2] Her cousin's children all went down with whooping

cough during her stay, which might explain a curtailment of any extended travel plans. Yet to Derbyshire Elizabeth Bennet is sent, with the author issuing the following disclaimer: 'It is not the object of this work to give a description of Derbyshire, nor of any of the remarkable places through which their route thither lay; Oxford, Blenheim, Warwick, Kenelworth, Birmingham, &c. are sufficiently known.'[3]

For the purposes of the novel, attention is directed instead to the small town of Lambton and the imposing Pemberley estate, where Elizabeth will find her future happiness as the wife of Mr Darcy. However narrow the focus, the geographical context is informed by Jane Austen's scrupulous research on the route through the area, taking in 'the celebrated beauties of Matlock, Chatsworth, Dovedale' and 'the Peak'.[4] These signposts to actual places on the road from fictional Longbourn to fictional Pemberley serve to ground the characters in reality and lend credibility to the journey north.

One of Jane Austen's favourite writers was William Gilpin, the intrepid Vicar of Boldre in the New Forest, who travelled throughout England in the latter half of the eighteenth century in search of landscapes worthy of making a picture. His travel guides sparked off a mad scramble to the relatively wild places of the country, specifically to discover the picturesque. For his guide to the English Lakes, published in 1786, Gilpin journeyed to Cumberland and Westmorland (today's Cumbria), via the 'remarkable places' on Elizabeth Bennet's journey north. He returned south by way of Derbyshire, where his unqualified enthusiasm for the landscape encouraged others to make the journey to this relatively neglected county. By 1793, the region had become so popular that James Plumptre, intent on designing a fashionable outfit for his walking tour, noted to himself that he would be keeping more civilized company there than he had in Wales the previous year.[5]

In the decades that followed, Derbyshire appeared in travel journals covering journeys to the Lakes, the Midlands and the north of England. When Jane Austen came to revise her first draft of *Pride and Prejudice* before publication in 1813, she reported to Cassandra that she had 'lopt & cropt' lengthy sections of narrative in the second volume.[6] Perhaps she cut out an extended depiction of the county in the light of increased public knowledge of the area. Visits to the High Peak, where many of the so-called seven wonders of Derbyshire were located, were invariably undertaken and described in detail. A book designed for the education of young ladies helpfully listed them:

These wonders are seven in number, the first is Chatsworth-house, the seat of the Duke of Devonshire. Mam-tor is the second, a hill under which are several lead mines; but the wonder consists in that there are perpetually shivering down from the hill, earth and great stones, in such quantities, and with so loud a noise, as to frequently frighten the neighbouring inhabitants, yet the hill is never visibly diminished. Elden-hole is the third wonder; if a stone is thrown into this hole as large as a man can lift, as soon as it strikes the rock, it will bound from side to side, till out of sight; but the sound may be heard some time after, gradually decreasing till it ends in a murmur. The fourth wonder is Buxton Wells ... the wonder consists in having another fountain, at the distance of six feet, which is cold when the other is hot. Tideswell, or Weeding well, is the fifth wonder, which is a spring that ebbs and flows at uncertain times ... The sixth wonder is Pool's-hole, the entrance of which is almost hid among bushes and brambles, so very low ... yet it is so high in the inside, that in many places the roof is not to be seen ... Peak's-hole is the last wonder, a cavern in a rock, so dark, that people are always near it with lighted candles, ready to conduct those whose curiosity may prompt them to enter the cavern.[7]

Johanna Schopenhauer, touring the region in the early 1800s, did venture into the cave, although the experience frightened her enough to make her wish she hadn't. She wrote about her ordeal for the edification of future travellers to the area.

Stepping off the coach at Castleton, she and her party had been 'seized upon' by a guide and 'hurried to the Peak Cave'. Each member of the party carried a candle to light the way to the back of the cavern, where the guide pointed out impressive stalactites, before leading them farther into the subterranean depths through a narrow, low passage in the rock, over slippery, uneven ground. For the next stage of the underground journey, they climbed into a boat, where they had to lie flat and be pushed. Schopenhauer's description is stiflingly claustrophobic:

> We moved under rocks, scarcely a hand's breadth away from our heads and appearing to be about to break off at any moment. On the other side there was not an inch between us and the bank. Never had the impression of being buried alive seemed clearer to us than in this coffin-like little boat with the black roof of rock looming over us. Our guide had to wade along, stooping; one knock against the rock above would have rendered him unconscious and we should have found ourselves alone in the most horrible situation.[8]

The worst was yet to come:

> The guide pointed to where the deep and awful footpath led down across the slippery stalagmites. 'This is the Devil's Cellar', he said, suddenly seizing one of us by the arm. 'I am the master here,' he continued with a nasty laugh. 'Here I can do as I please; I wish I had Napoleon here!' It is no use denying that we were frightened for it was only too clear that here he was indeed the master and we had long since noticed that he had taken us to be French.

One of the party had the foresight to remind him that a number of their companions were waiting for them outside, who would raise the alarm if some misfortune befell them. The guide then backed off, but on their return to the inn, the shaken tourists were regaled with the spine-chilling story 'that several years earlier a lady and gentleman arrived at the cave in a "whisky", drawn by a single horse and unaccompanied. They fastened the horse outside, went into the cave and were never seen again.'[9]

The Gardiners' proposed tour to the Lakes is curtailed by Mr Gardiner's business commitments, which allow only a three-week absence from London. Derbyshire is their revised destination and, despite the initial disappointment, they and their niece make the best of it, Mrs Gardiner looking forward to revisiting the scene of her childhood, the village of Lambton, within a few miles of Bakewell and only five from the Pemberley estate. In this entirely believable manner, Jane Austen removes Elizabeth from her family, grants her the companionship of people for whom she need not blush and makes possible an encounter with Mr Darcy on his home territory.

Beginning their journey in the Hertford area, Elizabeth and the Gardiners might reach Chatsworth, the most northerly destination on their itinerary, in five days, allowing time for sight-seeing on the way. The journey back to Longbourn, completed in anxious haste and by a more direct route, takes only two. In its early stages, their tour of pleasure would most probably have taken them on the turnpike road through Hatfield, St Albans, Watford and Amersham, which linked fictional Meryton with Oxford. Travelling was an expensive business and carriage ownership was not common, but the London-based Gardiners, like the Knightleys in *Emma* and Jane's banker brother Henry, probably kept their own carriage. Elizabeth's face is tanned by the time she reaches Pemberley, so presumably it had a retractable roof.

At Oxford, Jane Austen was on familiar territory. Two of her brothers had been students at St John's College and she and Cassandra had attended boarding school in the town for a few months in 1783. Perhaps James Austen, still resident in his college, conducted a tour for his little sisters through the 'dismal chapels, dusty libraries, and greasy halls' that give Jane's Sophia Sentiment 'the vapours for two days afterwards'.[10] Five years later, both James and Henry Austen escorted their pretty cousin

Eliza de Feuillide around several of the colleges, where Eliza imagined herself a Fellow in a black gown and square cap, with daily access to St John's delightful gardens. The wonder of Oxford for Eliza centred on seeing herself in it, attended by two handsome young men and no doubt admired by many others.[11]

Elizabeth and the Gardiners might have broken their first day's journey there and visited some of the colleges. Gilpin does not elaborate on the town's domestic or ecclesiastical architecture, in fact, he dismisses the multiplicity of buildings and gardens in a single sentence. Louis Simond, a Frenchman travelling through Oxford thirteen year later, was less polite. The place did not answer his expectations as an illustrious seat of learning; on the contrary, the buildings appeared 'old, dusty, and worm-eaten'[12] and the students indolent.

The following day's journey would take the Longbourn party on to Woodstock and Blenheim, the immense pile designed by Vanbrugh for the Duke of Marlborough. Here Jane Austen could imagine the Gardiners as tourists, taking advantage of the opportunity to view the house and grounds. After her tour of Oxford in 1788, Eliza de Feuillide spent a day at Blenheim, 'a most charming place' she recorded in a letter, but although she praised the hall and library, she found the furniture 'old fashioned & very shabby'.[13] Gilpin admired the grandeur of the gardens, while regretting their artificiality; in the house, he commented on a few notable paintings. Louis Simond's more extensive tour of Blenheim in the spring of 1811 was conducted by six money-grabbing guides outside and one self-opinionated upper servant inside. This 'coxcomb' pointed out the obligatory Gobelin tapestry, 'in very bad taste, as usual', and propelled his guest at speed through a multitude of richly furnished rooms.[14] Simond records that the entire visit cost him an extortionate nineteen shillings, the equivalent of approximately £60 today. He would have been even less happy had he read of Mary Morgan's visit in 1795, where she admitted to indulging a sense of patriotic superiority as she seated herself 'under a majestic oak, and there contemplated, with the secret triumph of an

Englishwoman, a noble bust of Louis the Fourteenth', appropriated by the Duke of Marlborough on his victory over the French at Tournay.[15]

Johanna Schopenhauer intended to walk through the park at Blenheim, but the enterprising landlady at the inn had other ideas. She made arrangements for a phaeton drawn by two rather frisky-looking white horses to collect the party, assuring her guests that it was practically impossible to tour the park on foot. In the event, Schopenhauer agreed: 'The park is so large that one-and-a-half hours were barely enough to complete the trip. The white horses were less wild than they had seemed at first and the considerable height of this, no longer fashionable, uncovered vehicle made it easy to look around in all directions and enjoy to the full the varied views.'[16]

At the gate, a guide joined them, walking beside the carriage and stopping it frequently to deliver William Collins-like proclamations on the view:

> 'over there you can see water with a fine straight bridge across it and to the right of it is a high column on which you can read about the Duke's exploits, the battles he fought and won. On top of the column stands his statue which looks small but is in fact 10 feet high.' He went on in this way for some time until we got rather bored. Everything we were to see later on at close quarters was now being shown to us from a distance, instead of allowing us time to admire the truly varied and charming view from the entrance. Alas it was impossible to stop the stream of his obviously prepared speech.[17]

For this tedious eloquence, the party resigned themselves to paying handsomely. Inside, they quickly became tired of looking at a proliferation of 'columns, vases, stairs, railings and towers'[18] and eventually effected an escape, despite being pressed to view Blenheim's vast collection of Japanese and Chinese porcelain.

The road between Oxford and Warwick was a well-maintained mail route, along which the Gardiners' carriage would make good progress. Wherever possible, however, carriage owners tended to choose turnpike roads, because the distinctive red-wheeled, maroon and black mail coaches, with the royal coat of arms on their doors, took precedence over other types of transport and causing any kind of delay incurred a heavy fine. At Warwick, Gilpin recorded his appreciation of the elegant buildings and the distant view of the castle. The grounds surrounding the habitable part of the edifice satisfied his sense of the picturesque, with their irregular walls and ivy-clad towers. He admired Guy, Earl of Warwick's armour and tilting spear, wandered through the extensive gardens down to the river, sketched the castle glimpsed through noble trees and went away well pleased.[19]

Colonel John Byng, visiting Warwick in 1785, typically found more to damn than praise. The grounds of the castle required draining and planting, the apartments within were 'superbly fitted up, but too much glittering with gold', the chapel was 'not enough in the Gothic taste' and the housekeeper 'old growling superannuated'.[20] Mrs Home had been housekeeper at the castle for twenty-one years when Byng visited and, despite her perceived surliness and decrepitude, continued in the post for another forty-nine, amassing more than £30,000 in tips.

The majority of tourists to Warwick Castle had nothing but praise for the place. Elizabeth Isabella Spence found fault with the pavements in the town in 1809, but rhapsodized over the 'noble hall', 'magnificent apartments' and 'antique solemnity' of the Castle.[21] The Gardiners would surely not have missed the opportunity to visit such a famous location. Mrs Austen, Jane and Cassandra looked forward to a visit there from Stoneleigh Abbey, where they were staying with relatives in August 1806. Unfortunately, there is no written record of their impressions of Warwick, but the remains of Kenilworth they did find entertaining.[22] Despite Jane's love of Gilpin's writing, she satirized his more ridiculous pronouncements on architectural wrecks. Of Henry VIII and Cromwell's destructions he wrote, with no trace of irony:

What share of picturesque genius Cromwell might have, I know not. Certain however it is, that no man since Henry VIII has contributed more to adorn this country with picturesque ruins. The difference between the two masters lay chiefly in the style of ruins in which they composed. Henry adorned his landscapes with the ruins of abbeys. Cromwell with those of castles.[23]

In her *History of England*, written when she was fifteen, Jane Austen claimed that Henry VIII had knocked down so many abbeys for the sole purpose of enhancing the view:

The Crimes & Cruelties of this Prince, were too numerous to be mentioned ... & nothing can be said in his vindication, but that his abolishing Religious Houses & leaving them to the ruinous depredations of time has been of infinite use to the landscape of England in general, which probably was a principal motive for his doing it.[24]

Perhaps the Austen ladies revived this joke as they walked around Kenilworth. Predictably, Gilpin was in raptures over what he described as 'one of the most magnificent piles of ruin in England'.[25] Yet as an edifice it did not suit his picturesque sensibilities: 'Neither the towers, nor any other part, nor the whole together, unless well aided by perspective, and the introduction of trees to hide disgusting parts, can furnish a good *picture...*'.[26] His most stringent criticism, however, was reserved for artificial ruins, or follies, as they came to be known. If mosses and lichens failed to grow on the stones, if ivy refused to clothe the buttresses or shattered battlements, if heaps of ruin were not scattered around convincingly, then 'Built in the year 1772' might as well be carved on the gate.[27]

The next place mentioned on the Gardiners' itinerary is Birmingham, a place the Austen ladies surely passed through on their way north to Hamstall Ridware from Stoneleigh. Louis Simond spent two whole days there, with a local merchant as his guide to the various hardware and glass manufactories. Simond was fascinated by the ingenious inventions: 'patent carriage steps, flying down and folding up of themselves as the door opens or shuts; chairs in walking-sticks, pocket-umbrellas, extraordinary cheese-toasters'.[28] Today, it seems strange that the growing urban sprawl of Birmingham should appear on an early nineteenth-century tourist itinerary, but scenes of industrial activity provided novelty; the steam-driven machines were awesome, the heat and noise stunning to a degree never experienced before.

Johanna Schopenhauer, visiting Birmingham in 1800, noted the small-scale production lines existing in every house, turning out items like pencils, buttons and needles. The whole town was smoky and dirty from the proliferation of factories, every day was noisy from hammering and knocking and every night disturbed by the shouting and singing of the released workforce. She visited Matthew Boulton's Soho establishment, which provided enough work every day for 800 people. English copper coins were minted there, also coins for the East India Company, for America and a number of foreign courts. Apart from the mint, Soho had a large factory for plated goods of all kinds, a glassworks, and a factory for making steam engines.[29]

Mrs Elton dismisses Birmingham as 'not a place to promise much',[30] but Jane Austen and her contemporaries knew otherwise. It was home to new inventions and inventive men and promised a great deal in economic terms. Mr Gardiner might have found something of interest to occupy an hour or so here; unsurprisingly, Gilpin did not. He commented disparagingly on the unpleasing red brick houses and factories, and the hundreds of men employed in making trinkets such as toothpick cases and snuff boxes.

Above Birmingham, Gilpin branched off on the road to Manchester, from where he made his way to the Lake District, whereas Jane Austen, her mother and sister continued on the same coaching route as the Gardiners, towards Lichfield. North of the town, a road branched off to Dovedale; to the south, another led to Burton and Derby. Somewhere on the road north, the Austens would have to alight to travel west to Hamstall. It is frustrating that Jane encompasses all of the subsequent towns the Gardiners would have passed through after Birmingham in a vague '&c.'.

From Burton, Derby was the obvious next stop, followed by Matlock. Here, Simond recorded the wild beauty of craggy outcrops and rushing water, the mineral springs that gave the place a certain cachet as a spa resort and the number of large goitres he had spotted. A lack of iodine in the diet caused unsightly swelling around the throat and in Derbyshire the problem was endemic, so much so that the condition became known as 'Derbyshire Neck'. The shops at Matlock specialized in fashioning 'Derbyshire petrifactions'[31] into souvenirs for tourists, objects Elizabeth Bennet has in mind when she initially feels uncomfortable about visiting Darcy's home county: '"But surely," said she, "I may enter ... with impunity, and rob it of a few petrified spars without his perceiving me."'[32]

On his way south from the Lakes in 1772, Gilpin felt his imagination take fire in the sublime environs of Matlock Vale's rocky ramparts and woods. Johanna Schopenhauer's spirits were revived by them: 'It may be that Matlock's springs are not very effective, but this is not necessary to the finding of new energy and vitality in this heavenly place'.[33] Elizabeth Spence devoted a number of pages of highly-wrought outpourings to Matlock:

> On opening my window this morning what a sublime land-scape burst upon my view! ... Here the air is so soft, that once again I seemed to inhale the gentle breath of summer ... The grand and romantic cliffs spreading into wild forms, and beautifully fringed with trees ... presented a scene calculated to awaken in the dullest mind enthusiastic admiration ... The woods, the rocks, though majestically bold, are wholly divested of terrific gloom; and the eye, instead of fearfully retiring from their gaze, delights to repose on objects so enchanting.[34]

No description of this part of the county finds its way into *Pride and Prejudice*, but it is satisfying to imagine Elizabeth's mind expanding in the unfamiliar beauty of the landscape, before Pemberley opens her eyes and heart to Mr Darcy's qualities. Not all of Derbyshire was unspoiled, however. While appreciating the 'sweet scenery of Matlock vale', Colonel Byng, travelling through the region in 1790, noted rural despoilation in some areas:

> these vales have lost all their beauties; the rural cot has given way to the lofty red mill and the grand houses of overseers; the stream perverted from its course by sluices and aqueducts will no longer ripple and cascade. Every rural sound is sunk in the clamours of cotton works, and the simple peasant (for to be simple, we must be sequester'd) is changed into the impudent mechanic ... the intention of retirement is much lost here; and the citizen or the Tourist may soon seek in vain for quiet and wild scenery ...[35]

Byng saw the dramatic quality of the changing landscape too, comparing the illuminated mills to three-decked man o' war sailing ships, but he realized that industrial development came at a cost. On the road between Derby and Matlock, at night, Johanna Schopenhauer was disconcerted by it:

> Everywhere the fires from the brick works blazed, hovering in the night air like fiery spectres and making the darkness more evident without actually lighting it up. At times the fires made the horses shy as we travelled up and down steep hills, with the roaring of the torrents reminding us of the precipices by the roadside. The noise of many mills, of all the water-wheels in this area of factories, together with the rushing of the waters, the wind, the rain, the blazing lime kilns, all this combined to make the night a truly frightening one.[36]

From Matlock, the Gardiners and Elizabeth would travel to

Dovedale. Gilpin found the whole area 'picturesquely beautiful, in a high degree'[37] with its hanging woods and majestic grey rocks, attractively speckled here and there with richly tinted herbage. James Plumptre applied the term 'sublime' to the scene that met his eyes at Dovedale in the late summer of 1793 – woods, cascades and vast perpendicular rocks 'like the ruins of some stupendous fabric.'[38] With three weeks at their disposal, Elizabeth and the Gardiners might have spent a number of days in Dovedale before continuing to Buxton, the High Peak, Tideswell and on to Chatsworth.

Contemporary views appear to agree on the faded grandeur of the Duke of Devonshire's largest residence. As early as 1772, Gilpin described it as the glory of a past age. He mentions a carved chimney-piece in one of the state rooms, decorated with dead fowl by Grinling Gibbons, and a floor-to-ceiling fresco in the chapel, and that's it.[39] Twenty years later, James Plumptre noted 'nothing striking'. Some of the rooms were large and handsome and the fountains worth seeing once, to gratify curiosity, and that, he claimed, was all that could be said of the place.[40] Louis Simond was a little more complimentary in his praise of the palace-like house and the pretty bridge over the river, but yet another wretched Gobelin tapestry offended his eye, together with numerous 'daubs' on the walls, parading as masterpieces.[41] By the time Aunt Gardiner suggests a visit to Pemberley, Elizabeth complains that she has seen quite enough of great houses, and although this is an excuse to avoid the embarrassment of meeting with Mr Darcy, it probably contains more than a grain of truth.

Chatsworth had, however, a romantically compelling claim to fame, which for many fans of Mary Stuart eclipsed its lack of decorative elegance. The Scottish Queen was held prisoner here in the East Wing between 1569 and 1584 at her cousin Elizabeth I's pleasure. Mary Stuart attracted much sympathy in Jane Austen's time, not least from Jane herself:

Oh! what must this bewitching Princess whose only freind

172

was then the Duke of Norfolk, and whose only ones now Mr Whitaker, Mrs Lefroy, Mrs Knight & myself, who was abandoned by her son, confined by her Cousin, abused, reproached & vilified by all, what must not her most noble mind have suffered when informed that Elizabeth had given orders for her Death![42]

Although the tone of this piece is mock-heroic, it appears that Jane Austen's support for Mary Stuart was serious. Her *History of England* was written by a very partial historian, prejudiced in favour of the Stuart monarchs. Caroline Austen recalled in later years that her aunt 'always encouraged my youthful beleif in Mary Stuart's perfect innocence of all the crimes with which History has charged her memory'.[43] Caroline's brother James Edward described Jane as a 'vehement defender'[44] and Cassandra's portrait of Mary in *The History of England* stands out as the most flattering of all the monarchs portrayed. The Queen of Scots also influenced one of the names in *Pride and Prejudice*. Jane must have known the link between Anthony Babington, who lost his life through fanatical devotion to Mary's cause, and the real-life Darcy family. The Babington family seat was in Dethick, near Matlock, and Anthony's mother was the daughter of George, Lord Darcy of Aston in South Yorkshire, very close to the Derbyshire border.

The most enthralling aspect of Chatsworth for Johanna Schopenhauer was the room that the Scottish queen called her own during her thirteen-year imprisonment.

On the second floor of the oldest part of the house is the room of the unhappy Mary Stuart, arranged and furnished exactly as it was when she lived there. It is large and high with old tapestries on the walls which give it an appearance of gloom and sadness. A high prie-dieu stands near the window from where the view is not very cheering, looking onto a beautiful but very desolate scene, shut in by hills. The room is furnished with high chairs and oak and walnut tables, all very heavy, reminding us of those dark days which this beautiful and unhappy woman spent here. Her bed with its red velvet curtains, trimmed with silver lace, stands in its old place and one can almost feel the many lonely tears she must have shed there.[45]

The landscape and even the furniture at Chatsworth were freighted with Mary's unhappy fate, but her supporters numbered many more than Jane Austen, Mr Whitaker – author of *Mary Queen of Scots Vindicated* (1787) – Mrs Lefroy of Ashe and Catherine Knight of Godmersham. As Schopenhauer records, 'the name of the unhappy Mary is remembered everywhere with love and pity. Mary's shortcomings are forgotten while her ill luck and charm live on in every heart.'[46]

Just as eighteenth- and nineteenth-century travellers flocked to locations connected with Mary Queen of Scots, so in the twentieth and twenty-first the popularity of the 1995 BBC series of *Pride and Prejudice* has ensured that enthusiasts will make the journey north to Pemberley, in this case Lyme Park in Cheshire. Here is the Palladian mansion, fixed in our minds as Pemberley, whereas in the text the Gardiners are uncertain of its age; here is the lake where the sudden encounter happens ("Miss Bennet!"… "Mr Darcy!"); here is the pond that invokes the infamous wet shirt scene. There is little point venturing inside to look for the staircase, the library and Georgiana's sitting room. The interior shots of Colin Firth's Pemberley were filmed at a different National Trust property, a Jacobean house with the all-important long picture gallery that more modern properties did not usually have. Lucky National Trust. It has benefited handsomely from 'The Pemberley Effect': the 'transformation of a house from an important property, though one relatively unknown to the general public, to a property linked to the "Jane Austen" brand'.[47] In terms of marketing, a page on the Trust's website is dedicated to Austen film and TV locations and the public actively encouraged to imagine themselves in Darcy or Elizabeth's shoes: 'Ever wished to admire "Pemberley" from across the lake? It's easier to follow in the footsteps of Lizzy and Darcy than you might think'.[48]

In the 2005 film, Chatsworth featured as Pemberley House, this location chosen by a director who admitted he had never read the text of *Pride and Prejudice*. If he had, he would have discovered that Elizabeth had already visited the Duke of Devonshire's palatial home when she encounters Mr Darcy in his grounds. In the midst of an embarrassingly awkward silence, Elizabeth has the presence of mind to remember that she had been travelling and 'seen all the principal wonders of the country',[49] among which Chatsworth numbered, 'and they talked of Matlock and Dove Dale with great persever-ance.'[50] Grand, artificial Chatsworth was clearly not the model for Darcy's handsome stone house, with its airy rooms. What jumps off the page of *The Topographer* of September 1789 for any reader familiar with Jane Austen's description of Pemberley is an account of 'Keddleston' – most writers at this time spelled it with a double d – Lord Scarsdale's property on the Matlock Road out of Derby. The house, constructed in 1760, 'is said to be the most perfect in England .... Here is no incongruous mixture of Grecian and Gothic architecture; artificial fountains and natural streams: All is consistent and uniform, and all is in the most elegant style. The house stands on a small elevation, at a small distance from a beautiful stream, in a park abounding with fine trees.'[51]

Having read Gilpin's *Northern Tour*, Jane Austen would have come across another description of Kedleston Hall. Gilpin first admires the setting, the pleasant park, the little stream dammed to create a larger stretch of water, the winding approach to the house itself. The architecture he describes as both elegant and grand, the individual rooms as comfortable and simply decorated. 'Tho every thing was rich;' he comments, 'I do not recollect, that any thing was tawdry, trifling, or affected.'[52] On reading these glowing commendations, Jane Austen may well have thought to herself that to be mistress of *Kedleston* might be something. No property could rival the Pemberley in the novel-ist's head, but it is tempting to believe that Elizabeth Bennet's response to her first view of Darcy's house, 'standing well on rising ground, and backed by a ridge of high woody hills; — and in front, a stream of some natural importance ... swelled into greater, but without any artificial importance ... The rooms ... lofty and handsome, and their furniture ... neither gaudy nor uselessly fine'[53] in part derives from her creator's impression of Kedleston Hall.

Applying to view the house, the Gardiners and their niece are shown around the main apartments by the housekeeper, Mrs Reynolds, whom Elizabeth is surprised to find intelligent, civil and unassuming rather than showy. More similarities to Pemberley surface in James Plumptre's account of his visit to Kedleston in 1793. Of everything the house has to offer, he is most struck with his guide, Mrs Garnett, housekeeper from 1766 to 1809:

> Of all the Housekeepers I ever met with at a Noblemans House, this was the most obliging and intelligent I ever saw. There was a pleasing civility in her manner, which was very ingratiating, she seem'd to take a delight in her business, was willing to answer any questions which were ask'd her, and was studious to shew the best lights for viewing the pictures and setting off the furniture ... [54]

Mrs Reynolds, like Mrs Garnett, is happy to talk about the décor and answer questions, particularly concerning her master. Although a minor character, her role in the novel has a crucial impact on events. Elizabeth encounters several complimentary versions of Darcy on this first visit to Pemberley: she is delighted with the appearance of his tasteful, unostentatious grounds, listens with growing interest to the word picture presented by his aptly-named housekeeper and views a full-length portrait and a miniature, displayed over the mantelpiece in his late father's room. George Wickham's profile features in the collection too, inviting a contrast between the two men's characters – Wickham's lack of moral responsibility, Darcy's good-natured generosity as a master, a landlord, a brother and, implicitly, as a husband. Elizabeth's melting response to Darcy's portrait in the picture gallery – 'as she stood before the canvas ... and fixed his eyes upon herself'[55] – is directly influenced by Mrs Reynolds' energetic praise and foreshadows the dramatic eye-to-eye meeting with the man himself immediately afterwards.

The Revd George Austen had a copy of Boswell's *Life Of Samuel Johnson*,[56] in his library at Steventon, which praised Mrs Garnett as a 'well-drest elderly housekeeper, a most distinct articulator'[57] who impressed both men on their visit in 1777. Jane Austen obviously had no knowledge of James Plumptre's unpublished journal, but perhaps she acquired a fuller account of Kedleston's paragon of a housekeeper from some other quarter. This is all speculation, but what should be a truth universally acknowledged is that Jane Austen knew exactly what she was doing when she sent her liveliest heroine on the road north to Pemberley.

10

Desperate Walkers

B ORN UNDER THE astrological sign of Sagittarius, Jane Austen was destined, according to an early twentieth-century biographer, to become a prodigious walker: 'Sagittarians are very fond of walking: it suits their health and gives them great enjoyment. Jane Austen had this trait herself and bestowed it sympathetically on her heroines.'[1]

The initial indications of Jane's walking prowess were promising. Returning home to Steventon from Bath one summer evening, Cassandra had been met by her father at Andover. The final part of the journey stayed in her memory and in later life she related the details to her niece, Anna Lefroy: 'he brought his Daughter home in a Hack chaise; & almost home they were when they met Jane & Charles, the two little ones of the family, who had got as far as New down to meet the chaise, & have the pleasure of riding home in it'.[2]

This is the earliest mention in family tradition of Jane's escapades as a child; she was probably six and a half, Charles only three.[3] The exact location of 'New down' is unknown, but it was most likely an area of newly enclosed downland near the village. The only place of this name on the Hampshire map is near Micheldever, too far away from Steventon and in the wrong direction for a carriage travelling from Andover.

178

At Steventon Rectory, plenty of opportunities existed for the Austen children to roam about within the confines of the garden. Two walks, bounded by hedgerows, formed Jane's first experiences of walking outdoors. The Wood Walk, with its occasional seats, took in a rustic shrubbery along the southern boundary of the home meadows; Church Walk ran straight up the hill to the parish church, a more taxing trot for a small child. As the years passed, so Jane's walks became more adventurous; most of her letters refer to local journeys made on foot.

Good weather provided an excellent excuse for frequent morning visits to neighbours at Oakley, Dummer and Ashe; Deane Parsonage, two miles away from Steventon, was a favourite destination in all weathers. Martha and Mary Lloyd lived there until James Austen moved in with his first wife Anne in 1792; Mary returned in 1797 as the second Mrs James Austen. Jane frequently braved 'the sloppy lane' that ran between Steventon and Deane, clad in pattens to keep the worst of the liquid mud out of her boots.[4] Some walkers were less intrepid. Mary Russell Mitford, writing to her mother in 1806, complained about a long walk she had been obliged to take with her hosts: 'the scenery, though extremely beautiful, by no means compensated me for all the mud I was forced to wade through. Lady Charles minds it no more than a duck; but I have begged to be excused from such excursions for the future.'[5]

Petticoats six inches deep in dirt were an inescapable reality, but only the very worst conditions kept Jane Austen from her daily walk. One such occasion occurred in early December 1800, when Jane wrote to her sister in despair from the Lloyds' home at Ibthorpe: 'it is too dirty even for such desperate Walkers as Martha & I to get out of doors'.[6]

The miles tramped by James Plumptre during his tours round England, Scotland and Wales between 1790 and 1800 more than earned him the epithet of 'desperate walker'. He walked from Cambridgeshire to North Wales in 1792; through the Peak District in 1793; through Scotland, the Lake District and Derbyshire in 1796; across the West Riding of Yorkshire to the Lakes and North Wales in 1797; to the north-east coast of England, into Scotland, the Lake District and North Wales in 1799. This last mentioned journey was the most ambitious, taking four and a half months and covering 2,236 miles, 1,774 of them on foot. A five-week walk around London, the southern counties and the Isle Of Wight followed in 1800, plus a trip to the source of the River Cam.

For the 1796 tour, Plumptre kept brief notes in leather-bound pocket notebooks. On subsequent tours, he wrote short journals for circulation among his friends and family. He offered the 1799 journal to a publisher, who rejected it on the grounds that it would hold no interest for the public. To a modern reader, Plumptre's travels are fascinating, because they happened at a time when tours were being written up into the kind of travel itineraries we are familiar with today.

Long-distance walking required at the very least a change of clothing and reliable equipment. Committed walkers like Plumptre knew that careful preparation beforehand ensured at the very least the minimum of physical comfort in trying conditions. For his tour with a companion to North Wales in 1792, he notes: 'We had a Knapsack made large enough to hold two shirts, two pair of stockings, neckcloths, pocket Handkerchiefs, shoes, &c … We also took a book, a small bottle covered with wicker and a small drinking can; we had a general plan of our Tour sketched out, and a map …'.[7]

The tour to Scotland in 1799 demanded a greater degree of sartorial elegance, since Plumptre intended to make visits to gentlemen's houses in the course of his journey. A second suit of clothes was called for and more clean shirts than were usually necessary when staying at inns. He hit on the plan of packing everything in a small portmanteau, 'sending it from place to place as occasion served, and when obliged to separate from it, I carried a change of linen, and a few other necessaries in a netted bag, at my back, made like a shooting bag and lined with oilskin.'[8] His servant carried yet another supply of Plumptre's clothes in a knapsack and three pairs of seasoned shoes. Items bought with the lack of packing space in mind included pocket-sized versions of a knife and fork, pistol and drinking horn. A copy of Cowper's poems was squeezed in amongst the more practical clutter.

Dr William Kitchiner's *Traveller's Oracle* gave advice on matters as diverse as personal defence and care of the feet. For protection against human assailants, he designed an umbrella holding a sword; against dangerous dogs, he recommended carrying 'a good tough Black Thorn ... not less than three feet in length'. Marked with feet and inches, this did double duty as a measuring stick.[9] Foot care came high on his list: 'To put the Feet into warm water for a couple of minutes just before going to Bed,' would prove both 'refreshing, and inviting to sleep'.[10] Remedies for blisters were given and a piece of strange advice about shoes: 'I would recommend foot travellers never to wear right and left Shoes — it is bad economy, and indeed serves to cramp the feet.'[11] Stirring songs of Kitchiner's own composition featured throughout, urging hobblers in their ill-fitting shoes along the highways and byways.

At the age of seventeen, Jane Austen had mocked the wearing of unsuitable shoes in her juvenile effusion *A Tour through Wales*. While their mother travels on horseback, her two daughters walk and run alongside, wearing out two pairs of shoes each, despite their being 'capped and heelpeiced at Carmarthen'. Undeterred, they share 'a pair of blue Sattin Slippers' and 'hopped home from Hereford delightfully'.[12] Flimsy footwear invariably caused problems and even 'A Lady of Distinction' thought it politic to publish a 'Recipe for a Corn Plaister' in recognition of the fact that 'the fair' might suffer the indignity of contracting corns.[13] If her outings on foot in and around Bath are anything to go by, Jane Austen covered many miles in a day without much exertion or troublesome corns. She walked for the sheer pleasure of it and not because an enlightened physician had recommended it, for gout or other ailments associated with an indolent lifestyle. One of the Austens' acquaintances was ordered by his doctor 'to walk a great deal, walk till he drops, I believe, Gout or no Gout. It really is to that purpose; I have not exaggerated.'[14]

A sympathetic love of walking endeared Jane Austen to people whom she had previously been determined to dislike: 'I spent friday evening with the Mapletons, & was obliged to submit to being pleased inspite of my inclination. We took a very charming walk from 6 to 8 up Beacon Hill, & across some fields to the Village of Charlcombe, which is sweetly situated in a little green Valley, as a Village with such a name ought to be.'[15]

The author of *A Picturesque Guide to Bath* agreed: 'Charlcombe is one mile and a half north-east of Bath, and is a village of only nine houses and a church, small, but very ancient, and well worth an antiquary's notice. The situation of this diminutive parish is under Lansdown: its views are not extensive, but very pretty. It is almost surrounded with hills adorned with wood and coppices.'[16]

Weston was a favourite destination – Jane's letters record three walking excursions there, the first in June 1799, when she spent a holiday with her brother Edward in Queen Square: 'We walked to Weston one evening last week, & liked it very much. — Liked <u>what</u> very much? Weston? — no — <u>walking</u> to Weston'.[17]

Most of the tourist guides to Bath listed walks and carriage drives in the immediate vicinity. In Mr Austen's library was a copy of Richard Warner's *Excursions from Bath*, published in 1801, with which Jane was familiar.[18] People who travelled to the city usually stayed for at least a month and would be looking for places to visit in the area. *Walks Through Bath*, published in 1819, catered for such needs, providing itineraries and descriptions of notable sites on the way. Walk IV suggests a route from the centre of Bath, passing the waterfall in Weston and returning through Barton's Fields. In addition to the route, the guide gives a full description of Weston and its environs:

> Marlborough-Buildings leads up to Weston-Gate, when the visitor turns on his left into the road. The prospect is now enchanting on all sides … On passing through two fields on the

right of the road, the visitor arrives at the Village of Weston ...
this little retreat ... has altogether a superior appearance ... The
Church is a small erection; but the numerous monuments in its
Burying-Ground are highly attractive and interesting ... [19]

Mrs Chamberlayne, a frequent visitor at Number 1 Paragon
and respected by Jane Austen at first for 'doing her hair well',
became a challenging but welcome walking companion in the
early summer of 1801, allowing Jane some escape from Aunt
Leigh Perrot. One hot day in May, they hiked uphill to Weston
and returned through the fields:

> Our grand walk to Weston ... was accomplished in a very
> striking manner ... in climbing a hill Mrs Chamberlayne is
> very capital; I could with difficulty keep pace with her — yet
> would not flinch for the World. — on plain ground I was quite
> her equal — and so we posted away under a fine hot sun, She
> without any parasol or shade to her hat, stopping for nothing, &
> crossing the Church Yard at Weston with as much expedition as
> if we were afraid of being buried alive. — After seeing what she
> is equal to, I cannot help feeling a regard for her.[20]

At seven years older than Jane Austen, perhaps Mrs
Chamberlayne thought she had something to prove. Having
produced no children, she was physically robust, a quality
she shared with Mrs Croft in *Persuasion* although, unlike Jane
Austen's fictional character, Mrs Chamberlayne was more often
than not encountered without her husband.

A few days after the Weston excursion, on a less strenuous
walk, Mrs Chamberlayne's stamina did not match her companion's, allowing Jane to level the score: 'I walked yesterday
morning with Mrs Chamberlayne to Lyncombe & Widcombe
... Mrs Chamberlayne's pace was not quite so magnificent on
this second trial as in the first; it was nothing more than I could
keep up with, without effort; & for many, many Yards together
... I led the way.'[21]

Four years later, when the Austen ladies were living in lodgings in Gay Street, Jane received a visit from Miss Armstrong, whom she had met the previous year in Lyme. Her visitor had gently taken Jane to task for neglecting the acquaintance, but in such a reasonable manner that Jane had accepted the criticism and made amends by suggesting an evening walk to Weston. Who could resist such an apology?[22]

Not all of Jane's walks in and around Bath were to picturesque villages. She spent a number of days trudging the streets house-hunting and also took an interest in the technological developments of the time. She walked with her Uncle James by the canal in Sydney Gardens and was keen to see an abandoned engineering wonder, Mr Weldon's caisson – Jane calls it 'the Cassoon'[23] – on the road to Combe Hay, about four miles south of Bath, which drew tourists and residents alike. A gigantic watertight coffin-shaped container, fitted into a large cistern, had been constructed for raising and lowering canal boats, a cheaper option than constructing a flight of twenty-two locks on the South Somersetshire Coal Canal. The caisson was completed in 1798, but by 1801 all that remained was a stone-lined hole in the ground. The project was halted when a boat got stuck in May 1799, almost suffocating the passengers before they managed to escape. Despite Mr Leigh Perrot's lameness and need of a stick, he and his niece planned to walk to the site in May 1801, involving a steady, uphill slog; easy for Jane, not so for Uncle James.

Jane's walking activities continued, sometimes with her sister, sometimes with her mother, throughout her stay in Bath. In one respect, this was the best place for women without a carriage, or a man to accompany them. Neither was a necessary accessory in Bath. The Austen ladies carried on their round of visits and outings after Mr Austen's death; they strolled about in front of the Crescent on Sundays and took short walks to local beauty spots. Jane still itched for more strenuous long-distance rambles, although other people's understanding of a long walk invariably fell short of her own. In early April 1805, she went looking for walking companions:

184

I have walked with my Mother to St James Square & Paragon; neither family at home. I have also been with the Cookes trying to fix Mary for a walk this afternoon, but as she was on the point of taking a <u>long walk</u> with some other Lady, there is little chance of her joining us. I should like to know how far they are going; she invited me to go with them [&] when I excused myself as rather tired & mentioned my coming from S^t Ja[mes] Square, she said "that is a long walk indeed."[24]

Walking in Bath often had an entirely different purpose than exercise. Promenading along the crescents and parades on impeccably clean pavements was done with the dual aim of seeing and being seen. Every seaside place and inland spa worth its salt had parades – Tunbridge Wells, Cheltenham, Brighton, Ramsgate, Worthing. Johanna Schopenhauer recorded her impression of promenading in Cheltenham: 'On the main street there are elegant houses, handsome shops, lending libraries and coffee shops, and here the beau monde strolls slowly up and down seeming, as it appeared to us, rather bored. In twos and threes the ladies, with many a yawn, wander slowly from one shop to another'.[25]

She had found this activity rather tedious when she visited Buxton earlier in the year, noting that the whole morning could be taken up with promenading in the Crescent, the pump room and baths, which provided a smart backdrop against which to preen and posture. A covered, colonnaded walkway afforded protection from inclement weather. The main promenade in Cheltenham, a broad, straight, shady walk, some 900 feet long, led to the springs. Here, strolling under the leafy elm trees, young women ensured that they were dressed to impress: 'The special charm of English women in their morning outfits is well known, and here in the green half-light the nymph-like figures in white are shown off to great advantage.'[26]

Before the nymphs could appear in public, they had to acquire fashionable attire, but the sort of outfit designed for promenading was not at all practical for anywhere other than

185

a mud-free urban setting. Camilla Stanley, in *Catharine, or the Bower*, swoons over the description of such finery in a letter from a London correspondent: '"She sends me a long account of the new Regency walking dress ... and it is so beautiful that I am quite dieing with envy for it."'[27]

Lord Osborne in *The Watsons* has female display and male appreciation in mind rather than muddy reality when he recommends nankin half-boots to Emma Watson: '"Nothing sets off a neat ancle more than a half-boot; nankin galoshed with black looks very well."'[28] Nankin was a yellow reinforced cotton, completely impractical for walking in the dirty lanes around Stanton village, but highly fashionable and eminently suitable for promenading.

Of all Jane Austen's characters who parade in public, Isabella Thorpe is the promenader *par excellence*. A naïve Catherine Morland is dragged along in her wake, completely unconscious of her friend's determination to hunt down a rich husband. Isabella knows how to attract the gaze of onlookers, with 'the graceful spirit of her walk, the fashionable air of her figure and dress'.[29] She makes the most of what she has by way of physical charms. From Edgar's Buildings to the Assembly Rooms and all the locations between, Isabella flaunts her smart outfits and stylish deportment; then, believing she has secured Captain Tilney's attention, she declares it 'odious to parade about the Pump Room'.[30] Only a month before, she had indulged in the pleasurable activity of flirting with two young men at the same time, in the same spot, pursuing them from thence into Cheap Street.

Lucy and Anne Steele, Augusta Hawkins, Mary Crawford, Julia and Maria Bertram, Lydia and Kitty Bennet would all be drawn to promenading and it is safe to presume that Elizabeth Elliot parades around Bath, while affecting to disdain such an activity. Ogling men have certainly spotted her out and about and 'are all wild after Miss Elliot'.[31] Her father parades, arm in arm with Colonel Wallis, and is a critical spectator too. From a shop in Bond Street one frosty morning, Sir Walter counts eighty-seven unappealing women walking by. Add John Thorpe, Admiral Crawford, John Willoughby, Captain Tilney and Mr Elton to the list of gentlemen voyeurs in Bath and Jane Austen's opinion of the pursuit is clear.

Bath was a relatively safe environment where females could walk unattended by men. Only relatively, however; Bath is where Willoughby seduces Colonel Brandon's susceptible young ward, out on the streets unsupervised. Catherine's protectors in Bath, the Allens, take better care of her, yet she is free to walk between their lodgings in Great Pulteney Street and Edgar's Buildings, where the Thorpes are staying, and to Milsom Street to visit the Tilneys. Mr Allen trusts Catherine's moral sense of what is right and wrong behaviour. She has been brought up very differently to Isabella. Catherine herself draws a distinction between walking in Bath and walking at home: '"I walk about here, and so I do there; — but here I see a variety of people in every street, and there I can only go and call on Mrs. Allen."'[32]

Henry Tilney is reassured by Catherine's eagerness to take a country walk. He discovers that she is not like Isabella, always wishing to be in the social whirl of an urban setting. In Milsom Street, Catherine is openly admired by scheming General Tilney for 'the elasticity of her walk', when all she is doing is walking downstairs. Her endearing lack of personal vanity is shown as she makes her way back to the Allens, 'with great elasticity, though she had never thought of it before.'[33]

Beechen Cliff is the destination chosen for the walk, described in the *Picturesque Guide to Bath* as: 'covered with a beautiful coppice-wood ... more than four hundred feet above the surface of the Avon, and affords from its summit, a very singular view of the city and the vale from Bath-Ford to Kelston.'[34] This is the 'singular view' Catherine rejects as unworthy of making a picture following Henry's lecture on picturesque principles. Although this is entertaining, it proves that Catherine is willing to admit her ignorance and capable of listening and learning, all qualities appealing to Henry and all revealed on a walk. Yet her mind is also capable of making huge leaps into the blue, as Henry discovers. Catherine's suspicions are aroused by the General's daily habit of taking an early ramble in the Abbey grounds, also his avoidance of his dead wife's favourite walk among damp and gloomy fir trees.

Walking, but not parading, in an urban environment held attractions for Jane Austen. From Henry's London house in Sloane Street, she walked out to the shops and to Kensington Gardens. Elinor and Marianne Dashwood do the same on their winter stay in Berkeley Street with Mrs Jennings. On her visit to London, Johanna Schopenhauer noted the never-ending surge of pedestrians and quickly realized that there were rules to be followed and practical courtesies to be appreciated:

> The custom of the English, when they meet people, always to give way to those on their right, greatly eases walking about and does away with much pushing and jostling. Ladies ... are always permitted to walk along the house side of the pavements, irrespective of whether this is on the right or the left. To begin with, a strange lady finds it odd when he who guides her through London, lets go of her arm the moment they have crossed the street, and passes behind her to change sides. Quite soon, however, one becomes convinced of the usefulness of this national courtesy.[35]

Walking conditions in and around Chawton, where the widowed Mrs Austen and her two daughters moved in 1809, suited Jane very well. The cottage shrubbery and orchard, protected by a row of beech and quickset hedging must have reminded them of the old familiar walks at Steventon Rectory. Jane's delight is palpable: 'You cannot imagine — it is not in Human Nature to imagine what a nice walk we have round the Orchard'[36] she wrote to Cassandra in May 1811. Their nephew, James Edward, remembered the garden in his *Memoir*: 'a high wooden fence and hornbeam hedge shut out the Winchester road, which skirted the little domain. Trees were planted each side to form a shrubbery walk, carried round the enclosure, which gave sufficient space for ladies' exercise.'[37]

This space had to serve in winter, when the weather and the state of the roads prevented exercise farther afield but, given the chance, Jane and Cassandra preferred to take longer walks, around Edward's estate, to Alton and to Anna and Ben Lefroy's house at Wyards. James Edward makes no mention of his aunt's great love of striding out in the 'Character and Tastes' chapter of his *Memoir*, choosing instead to present an image of a lady making more refined progress around a shrubbery. Yet his younger sister Caroline remembered Jane's relish for walking:

> After luncheon, my Aunts generally walked out — sometimes they went to Alton for shopping — Often, one or other of them, to the Great House … when a brother was inhabiting it, to make a visit — or if the house were standing empty they liked to stroll about the grounds — sometimes to Chawton Park — a noble beech wood, just within a walk.[38]

It appears that Chawton was drier underfoot than Steventon. In the winter of 1813, Jane replied in a teasing tone to a letter from Cassandra: '"A very sloppy lane" last friday! — What an odd sort of country you must be in! I cannot at all understand it! It was just greasy here on friday, in consequence of the little snow that had fallen in the night … Upon the whole, the Weather for Winter-weather is delightful, the walking excellent. — I cannot imagine what sort of a place Steventon can be!'[39]

In February, she described walking to Alton and back, delightful exercise despite the dirt.[40] Most of Jane Austen's heroines are determined walkers – only Fanny Price droops after a quarter of a mile – and they are rarely thwarted by bad weather. Marianne and Elinor Dashwood derive great pleasure from their walks at Barton. They frequently cover the half mile between the cottage and the Park and are keen to explore the local area. The hills tempt the sisters to breathe in the bracing air as they climb to the summits and provide them with an alternative to the muddy valleys in the wetter months. Marianne, as desperate a walker as Jane Austen herself, insists on striding out whatever the weather, which is how she comes to miss her footing and fall for Willoughby. When he leaves for London, Marianne wilfully isolates herself: 'If her sisters intended to walk on the downs, she directly stole away towards the lanes; if they talked of the valleys, she was as speedy in climbing the hills, and could never be found when the others set off.'[41]

Solitary walking in this instance gives pain to her sisters and mother and is a selfish activity. Following Willoughby's marriage to the heiress Miss Grey, Marianne indulges her wounded sensibilities still further by exhibiting a total disregard for her health. At Cleveland her walking habits take on a worrying degree of desperation. She seeks seclusion in long walks around the grounds. Two twilight rambles through the shrubbery and into the wildest, wettest parts of the garden, two evenings sitting in wet shoes and stockings, bring on the feverish symptoms that almost kill her. Yet walking is part of her redemptive therapy too; during her convalescence, she and Elinor pace the lane alongside Barton Cottage and talk Willoughby out of her system. Walking is a key feature in Marianne's programme of improvement: '"we will take long walks together every day. We will walk to the farm at the edge of the down ... we will walk to Sir John's new plantations at Barton-Cross, and the Abbeyland; and we will often go to the old ruins of the Priory"'.[42]

Of all Jane Austen's walking heroines, Elizabeth Bennet is the most energetic. She regularly walks from Longbourn to visit Charlotte at Lucas Lodge and three or four times a week covers the mile to Meryton with her sisters, tempted by the milliner's shop, Aunt Philips' news and, later, the regiment of officers who are quartered there for the winter. Only a prolonged spell of constant rain can keep the Bennet girls away from the town, as it does before the Netherfield ball on 26 November. Fear of catching cold, the problem of cleaning muddy clothes and shoes and the state of the road would all play their part in confining the sisters indoors. Through January, the girls' walks to Meryton are described as 'sometimes dirty and sometimes cold',[43] as were the author's own walks between Chawton and Alton at this time of year.

Two days after her twenty-third birthday, Jane Austen experienced the enjoyment of walking alone on a frosty winter's day to Deane. 'I do not know that I ever did such a thing in my life before' she wrote to her sister in some surprise.[44] She grants 20-year-old Elizabeth Bennet this liberty in the early chapters of *Pride and Prejudice*. Three miles to Netherfield is nothing, she claims, and despite Mrs Bennet's argument that she will not be fit to be seen when she arrives, Elizabeth insists on going. Her physical and mental energy are both irresistibly tangible, as she crosses 'field after field at a quick pace, jumping over stiles and springing over puddles with impatient activity ... [her] face glowing with the warmth of exercise.'[45]

In this way, Jane Austen gets Elizabeth to Netherfield, to spend a prolonged time with the Bingleys, attract the admiration of Mr Darcy and the opprobrium of Bingley's sisters: 'That she should have walked three miles so early in the day, in such dirty weather, and by herself, was almost incredible to Mrs Hurst and Miss Bingley; and Elizabeth was convinced that they held her in contempt for it.'[46]

Their criticism of Elizabeth's unconventional – they would argue unladylike – behaviour, underscores their need to establish social superiority. They have wealth and polished, metropolitan manners, but their fortune has come from trade, hence their concerted attack on the 'wild' exhibition of female independence shown by the daughter of a gentleman. Caroline has the added motive of seeking to damn Elizabeth in Mr Darcy's eyes: '"what could she mean by it? It seems to me to shew an abominable sort of conceited independence, a most country town indifference to decorum."'[47]

John Gregory, author of *A Father's Legacy to his Daughters*, recommended exercise for women, 'such as walking, and riding on horseback', but cautioned against showing 'too much spirit' by strenuous physical activity.[48] Bingley's sisters confine themselves to walking sedately around the shrubbery. Darcy's response is equivocal. He will not descend to petty criticism and refuses to give Caroline Bingley the satisfaction of agreeing with her catty remarks on Elizabeth's appearance – her complexion, he says, was brightened by the exercise – yet he doubts the occasion's warranting such a long walk completely alone. He certainly would prevent his sister following Elizabeth's example, but we discover later *why* he would not want Georgiana out and about on her own.

Caroline Bingley's list of essential female accomplishments includes 'a certain something in her air and manner of walking'[49] and many conduct manuals of the time stressed the importance of deportment: 'She must enter a room either with the buoyant step of a young nymph, if youth is her passport to sportiveness; or, if she is advanced nearer the meridian of life, she then may glide in, with that ease of manner which gives play to all the graceful motions of her elegantly undulating form.'[50] Caroline's transparent ploy to gain Darcy's notice by drifting elegantly but aimlessly around the drawing room at Netherfield has no effect at all.

At Rosings, a convenient half mile from Hunsford Parsonage, Elizabeth walks through the grounds for exercise and for privacy. She favours one particular route, 'where there was a nice sheltered path, which no one seemed to value but herself, and where she felt beyond the reach of Lady Catherine's curiosity.'[51] For two weeks, she has this path to herself, but as soon as Darcy discovers where she prefers to ramble, he joins her, believing that his company is being sought: 'More than once did Elizabeth in her ramble within the Park, unexpectedly meet Mr. Darcy … and to prevent its ever happening again, took care to inform him at first, that it was a favourite haunt of hers. — How it could occur a second time therefore was very odd! — Yet it did, and even a third … he actually thought it necessary to turn back and walk with her.'[52]

This kind of 'encouragement' brings on Darcy's first proposal of marriage, after which Elizabeth finds her daily walk even more necessary. Solitude is needed for reflection and very soon she walks herself into a better understanding of her family's culpability in Bingley's departure from Netherfield and a clearer appraisal of both Wickham and Darcy's characters. It is fitting that Darcy's second proposal is accepted as he and Elizabeth lag behind Bingley and Jane on a long ramble in the fields and lanes around Longbourn. In this instance, the characters are forgiven for an ignorance of their surroundings: 'They walked on, without knowing in what direction. There was too much to be thought, and felt, and said, for attention to any other objects.'[53]

Walking brings on proposals of marriage in other novels too. Edward Ferrars 'walked himself into the proper resolution'[54] between Barton Cottage and the village before proposing to Elinor; Edmund and Fanny drift around the grounds of Mansfield Park for the whole summer; Emma accepts Mr Knightley as they walk in the Hartfield shrubbery; Anne and Captain Wentworth renew their engagement as they pace the streets of Bath and Henry Tilney asks Catherine to marry him on their way to the Allens' house.

Mary Crawford is the great walker in Mansfield Park. Sitting still fatigues her, she claims; she must always be moving. What a contrast to Fanny Price, who is soon 'knocked up' by any kind of exercise beyond a sedate ride. Walking at all times of the day is a habitual form of exercise at Mansfield Park, for some, if not for others. Fanny and Lady Bertram are notable exceptions. Mrs Norris 'who was walking all day' and 'thinking every body ought to walk as much'[55] exerts her power over Fanny in Edmund's absence, sending her a quarter of a mile across the Park to the White House twice in the course of a sweateringly hot day. The author of *The Mirror of the Graces* warned in melodramatic terms of a terrible fate awaiting those who exposed themselves to the night air, even in summer: 'when the imperceptible damps, saturating the thinly-clad limbs, sends the wanderer home infected with the disease that is to lay her, ere a returning spring, in the silent tomb!'[56] but evening strolls become part of the daily routine after the Crawfords are welcomed into the family circle, Edmund escorting Mary and Mrs

Grant back to the Parsonage and Henry Crawford attending the Bertram sisters home. Edmund and Julia return on foot from dinner with the Grants, 'eager in their praise of the night and their remarks on the stars'.[57] One of Jane Austen's earliest surviving letters to Cassandra describes a delightful walk home in the early autumn from Goodnestone to her brother Edward's home at Rowling: 'We supped there, & walked home at night under the shade of two Umbrellas.'[58]

Fanny's physical weakness enables Edmund to leave her behind on a shady bench at Sotherton, while he is drawn deeper into the wood by Mary Crawford. In contrast to Fanny, Mary exhibits all the signs of good health and her liveliness has the added appeal of novelty for Edmund. Her teasing assertions about times and distances are very attractive to him and to the reader. He leaves Fanny behind with a sense of release and walks off joyfully for a whole hour's tête-à-tête with an engagingly argumentative companion. His admiration of Mary's is expressed in terms of her physicality, how she 'tripped off' with a 'light and graceful tread'. '"How well she walks!"' he exclaims aloud to Fanny.[59]

The freedom allowed by walking at Sotherton is altogether a bad thing. Everyone's moral compass goes awry on this visit, except Fanny's. She is the still spectator of their various comings and goings. This scene possesses a high degree of spatial management – all of the characters are viewed in relation to each other's movements and their hidden motivations foreshadowed at a deeper level. Henry Crawford tempts a willing Maria to make an illicit escape through the locked gate to the knoll. On the other side they deliberately take a circuitous path, where they cannot be seen. An irritated Julia pursues them, having passed Mr Rushworth 'posting away' through the heat of the afternoon to fetch the key.[60] The day ends on an uncertain note, with everyone's spirits exhausted: 'their ramble did not appear to have been more than partially agreeable, or at all productive of any thing useful'.[61] Nothing has been achieved by way of improvement to the Rushworth estate and the subject is never raised again, but much future mischief has been instigated.

The activity of walking in *Mansfield Park* is rarely a comfortable one. In the Parsonage shrubbery, Fanny is forced to listen to Miss Crawford's hopes of a future life with Edmund; in the Park shrubbery, Edmund attempts to persuade her to marry Henry Crawford, as they take what he calls 'a comfortable walk together'.[62] Fanny frequently retreats to the cold East Room to walk herself into composure. It happens after she has refused to take part in the theatricals and again immediately after Henry Crawford's proposal. In her father's cramped and disorderly house in Portsmouth she does not have the luxury of space in which to walk and think. She is confined from Monday to Saturday and her health suffers from lack of fresh air and exercise. Henry Crawford is sensitive enough to recognize the deprivation and, while he is in Portsmouth, ensures that Fanny takes the air. He has a double motive, of course, but his consideration for Fanny's well-being does appear genuine. He protects her and her sister in the bustling, shoving streets of the town and is successful in persuading her to take his arm as they walk on the ramparts for two hours after church.

Finally, walking does achieve a beneficial outcome. As in *Sense and Sensibility*, the activity effects a cure for disappointed love: 'After wandering about and sitting under trees with Fanny all the summer evenings, [Edmund] had so well talked his mind into submission, as to be very tolerably cheerful again.'[63] The therapy is so successful that Edmund convinces himself that mild light eyes are every bit as attractive as sparkling dark ones, proposes to Fanny and marries her.

Visiting and social interaction are predominant in *Emma*, which calls for plenty of walking between the various houses in the locality. Emma prides herself on being hospitable on her father's account, the Westons enjoy company, Miss Bates and her mother love to be called on, the Coles are sociable and looking to increase their circle of acquaintance; everyone lives within the range of a short walk. Mr Knightley tramps the three miles between Donwell and Hartfield most days, to spend time with

Emma and relieve her of the burden of entertaining her father. Unlike Mr Woodhouse, who never ventures on foot beyond the shrubbery, Mr Knightley is robust, healthy and fond of exercise. Even snow does not deter him. No sitting in front of the fire for him. At the Crown Inn ball, Emma appraises Mr Knightley's 'tall, firm, upright figure', an obvious benefit of regular exercise.[64] The habit runs in the family: over the Christmas period, John Knightley takes his two boys on daily walks to Donwell. They return from their six-mile round trip with glowing faces and healthy appetites. In the spring, they are out walking again when they encounter Jane Fairfax on her way to the Post Office in the rain. Through the ensuing argument over who should collect the Bates' mail, Emma thinks she detects the real reason for Jane's choice of destination. Mr Dixon, she suspects, has written from Ireland. In this way, the everyday activity of walking advances and complicates the narrative. On subsequent readings, we realize that Jane's 'glow both of complexion and spirits'[65] has little to do with exercise, nothing at all to do with Mr Dixon and everything to do with Frank Churchill's imminent return to Highbury.

Everyone walks for a purpose in *Emma*. Harriet and the Martins take walks in the moonlight, Robert Martin accompanies his sisters on shopping expeditions in the town. Emma and Harriet pay a charitable visit on foot to a poor family in Vicarage Lane and meet Mr Elton setting out on the same mission. Harriet walks between the school and Hartfield and provides useful company for Emma on the half-mile walk to Randalls. Walking grants opportunities for romantic meetings: Miss Taylor and Mr Weston begin their courtship through an encounter in the rain, Mr Weston showing his interest by gallantly dashing off to a nearby farmhouse to borrow umbrellas. Robert Martin collects walnuts and goes on foot along the Donwell road into Highbury, hoping to meet up with Harriet, and Mr Elton is more than happy to walk from his parsonage to Hartfield, where he enjoys looking at Emma and paying heavy compliments, little suspecting the match she has in mind for him. Mr Knightley encourages Mr Woodhouse to take his short winter walk so that he can be left alone to tell Emma of Robert Martin's proposal. On this occasion, they argue, but at the resolution of the novel, walking brings on a spur-of-the-moment proposal, as Emma and Mr Knightley take several turns in the garden.

As soon as Frank Churchill arrives in Highbury, he is understandably keen to get out and about in the locality. His first questions on meeting Emma are linked to his secret determination to see Jane Fairfax as often as possible: '"Was she a horse-woman? — Pleasant rides? — Pleasant walks?"'[66] On his very first morning, Frank chooses the walk that he and his stepmother will take. He specifies Highbury, which Mrs Weston interprets as Hartfield. He is forced to spend an hour there, before they turn their steps towards the village, where he walks up and down, ostensibly trying to identify the cottage where his old nurse lived, but all the while hoping that Jane Fairfax will see him through the window of the Bates' house.

On the occasions when walking brings characters together as a group, they are divided by the undertow of secrecy and concealment. Jane Austen has two such parties meet on their after-dinner walk – Mr Knightley, Emma and Harriet; Mr and Mrs Weston, Frank, Jane Fairfax and Miss Bates – when Frank makes his famous blunder concerning Mr Perry's carriage. The word game at Hartfield immediately afterwards arouses Mr Knightley's suspicions, but his observations to Emma are so confidently brushed aside that he becomes convinced of an attachment between her and Frank. Irritated, he walks away from the emotionally overheated atmosphere of Hartfield to 'the coolness and solitude' of his own house.[67]

The same dislocation is experienced on the strawberry-picking day at Donwell Abbey. The invited party wander in the sun-scorched gardens in a scattered, desultory manner. The 'Dixon' jibe is still disturbing the air around Jane Fairfax and Frank, Harriet sticks like glue to Mr Knightley, Emma, presuming Mrs Elton to be at the front, walks apart with Mr

Weston behind everyone else. For Emma, the best part of the day is spent walking with Mr Knightley, through the grounds that she will one day enjoy as mistress of Donwell. Finally, in a delicious touch, Mr Elton receives his well-deserved comeuppance for humiliating Harriet by refusing to dance with her at the Crown ball, after advertising his liberty by sauntering about in front of her. Having walked all the way to Donwell to meet Mr Knightley, Mr Elton finds that his visit has been overlooked: '"Such a dreadful broiling morning! — I went over the fields too — (speaking in a tone of great ill usage,) Which made it so much the worse ... And no apology left, no message for me."'[68]

For the heroine of *Persuasion*, walking is, more often than not, a form of escape. Most days Anne walks to Lady Russell's lodge on the Kellynch estate, for exercise and to get away from her father and elder sister. Some respite from daily irritations is possible; escape from past pain is not so easy. Early in the novel, she retreats to a favourite part of the grounds to cool her flushed cheeks as she imagines Captain Wentworth walking there once more, but daily contact with Wentworth at Uppercross renders any thought of release from her emotions futile. On the long November walk to Winthrop, she witnesses the flirtation between her former lover and Louisa Musgrove and her sense of fading youth, beauty and love colours the scene: 'Anne's *pleasure* in the walk must arise from the exercise and the day, from the view and the last smiles of the year upon the tawny leaves and withered hedges'.[69]

Avoidance of Wentworth is impossible, given the habits of the two Musgrove families. Only a quarter of a mile separates Uppercross Cottage from the Great House and everyone runs about at all hours between the two. Mary constantly whines about her delicate state of health, but when her Musgrove sisters-in-law try to exclude her and escape to Winthrop, stating that it is to be a *long* walk, Mary replies in a piqued tone, '"I should like to join you very much, I am very fond of a long walk".'[70] Henrietta aims to meet Charles Hayter strolling in the vicinity of Winthrop and, in this novel, as in others, walking is a means of contact with the opposite sex. Louisa and Wentworth walk side by side across the fields, disturbing Anne's poetic reveries, but the walk home to Uppercross is a mix of divided and united couples: Charles Musgrove shows his displeasure with Mary by continually dropping her arm, Charles Hayter walks companionably with Henrietta. Captain Wentworth accompanies Louisa, but with Anne on his mind. He is aware of her fatigue and helps her quietly but firmly into Admiral Croft's carriage. This long walk, which promised Anne little gratification beyond the faded autumn landscape grants her a more emotionally complex experience, 'so compounded of pleasure and pain, that she knew not which prevailed'.[71]

Anne is granted more pleasure than pain at Lyme and strolling by the sea restores her bloom and confidence. She walks with Captain Wentworth's naval friends along the Cobb, discusses Byron's poetry with Captain Benwick and attracts the admiration of Mr Elliot. In Bath, walking again becomes a means of escape from Sir Walter and Elizabeth while, in Lyme, Wentworth takes to the hills to distance himself from Louisa. Bath provides the ideal location for Anne and Wentworth to meet, it is a pedestrian's paradise, yet they are denied the opportunity until they make their way along Union Street in the final chapters of the novel. From there they dawdle along Gravel Walk, oblivious to everyone and everything around them as they take the long way back to Camden Place.

Jane Austen finished writing *Persuasion* in the summer of 1816, by which time, her walking days were almost over. In December of that year, she wrote to James Edward, telling him that Ben Lefroy had invited her to Wyards, 'but I was forced to decline it, the walk is beyond my strength'.[72] By January, she felt more optimistic and wrote to her friend Alethea Bigg at Manydown, 'I feel myself getting stronger than I was half a year ago, & can so perfectly well walk to Alton, or back again, without the slightest fatigue that I hope to be able to do both when Summer comes.'[73] Contrary to her cheerful expectations, the early summer took her to lodgings in College Street,

Winchester, where physical activity became severely curtailed: 'I live chiefly on the sofa, but am allowed to walk from one room to the other' she wrote, in her very last letter.[74] At twenty-four, Jane Austen had described herself as a 'desperate walker'; at forty-one, she was just desperate.

11

At Home, Quiet, Confined

WITH THE EXCEPTION of Emma Woodhouse, none of Jane Austen's heroines is pinned down in the kind of country village Jane recommended to her niece Anna as the ideal location for the '3 or 4 Families'[1] featured in her novel-in-progress. Catherine Morland leaves Fullerton for her adventures in Bath and Gloucestershire after the first chapter and only returns temporarily for the final three. Elizabeth Bennet escapes from Meryton into Kent and Derbyshire. The Dashwoods and Anne Elliot live in houses detached from their communities and are uprooted against their will, as is Fanny Price, yet despite the initial trauma of upheaval, these women learn to evaluate the world beyond the familiar and, more crucially, assess their own thoughts and emotional desires. Mobility in this sense is a force for change, a force for good. Living 'at home, quiet, confined,'[2] does no one any favours initially, but at the resolution of each novel we imagine the main protagonists breathing a sigh of relief as they settle into comfortably uneventful lives.

Emma is the only heroine who remains in one place and although the three or four families in the neighbourhood swell to five or six, her self-awareness suffers as a consequence. Home is her comfort zone, where she is doted on by her father and acknowledged as the first lady in the locality. A lack of experience outside the immediate community leads to an exaggerated sense of superiority and unwarrantable interference in the lives of others. She has a stable family home, but financial and domestic certainties make her complacent and limited in her view of the world. While Emma's imagination roams far and wide in the realms of romantic possibilities, almost everyone else in her circle is physically on the move. Her sister Isabella, despite her imagined frailties, has travelled as far as Cromer and makes frequent journeys between London and Highbury. Jane Fairfax, a local girl with knowledge of the world beyond, has moved around with the Campbells since her childhood and has no experience of comfort zones. In Highbury her dependent state and uncertain prospects are clear to everyone, but so are her poise and maturity. Mrs Elton has a narrower experience of life than Jane Fairfax, but she has lived in Bristol and Bath and taken carriage excursions into the countryside around Maple Grove, which gives her an advantage over her rival. Emma is dismissive of Mrs Elton's assumed superiority but, even so, she feels her previously unassailable position within the first rank of Highbury society to be under attack. Even Harriet Smith goes where Emma cannot – albeit under pressure – to London, where she is cured of her teenage crush on Mr Knightley as well as her toothache. Harriet also has the advantage over Emma in having spent time away from home at Abbey Mill Farm, learning the ways of a different family. On her marriage, Emma's travel prospects open up with a honeymoon on the coast, the modest origin, perhaps, of an annual escape from Mr Woodhouse and a widening of her narrow perspective.

A rational urge to experience the world beyond home territory – Emma's longing for the sea, Elizabeth's enthusiasm for the Lakes, Catherine's joy at the prospect of spending a few weeks in Bath – is quietly applauded. In marked contrast are Lydia Bennet's determination to take Brighton by storm, the hankering for London of Mary Crawford, Maria Bertram and Lady Susan, and even 'the young people ... all wild to see Lyme',[3] which comprehends more of wilful Louisa Musgrove than restrained

Anne Elliot in its urgency. One of Jane Austen's earliest heroines takes to the roads of London on a jaunt from Bond Street
to Hampstead. The lack of a travelling purse is no deterrent,
neither is the want of a companion. The 'beautifull' Cassandra
sets off alone, at first on foot, then in a hackney carriage. Unable
to pay the coachman in cash, she hands over a stolen bonnet and
returns home after 'a day well spent'.[4] Other girls with a thirst
for getting out and about follow hot on her heels: Eliza Harcourt,
Laura and Sophia, Elizabeth and Fanny Johnson.[5] The exploits
of the peripatetic pair in *Love and Freindship*, who skitter around
the country causing mayhem wherever they go, are dedicated to
Eliza de Feuillide, who led by her own admission 'a racketing
life'.[6] She easily exceeded the miles covered by Laura and Sophia,
having travelled from India to England, on to France, then back
to London, from where she sallied out to the homes of friends
and relations and to various watering places. Jane might have
been fascinated by her cousin's wanderings, but she allowed only
one female character from her six published novels to venture
beyond English shores. For Mrs Croft the unpredictable has a
strong appeal – '"We none of us expect to be in smooth water
all our days."'[7] – but of greater strength is the companionship
she shares with the Admiral. Wherever he is, she is happy; she is
equally at home at Kellynch and on-board ship.

At its extreme, the 'rage of rambling',[8] warned the Revd
Thomas Gisborne in *An Enquiry Into The Duties Of The Female
Sex*, was a female sin of the most pernicious kind, promoted and
facilitated by improvements in turnpike roads, carriages and
coaching inns. Had Mr Collins chosen to deliver a sermon on
the subject, he would have found more material in Gisborne's
text than in Dr James Fordyce's *Sermons to Young Women*,
published in 1766. Greater opportunities for short- and long-
distance travel existed by the time the *Enquiry* came out thirty
years later, when women were no longer heeding, if they ever
had, St Paul's admonition to be 'keepers at home'. Gisborne was
happy to countenance charitable calls on afflicted neighbours
and longer journeys taken for health reasons, but he voiced

the suspicion that motives of health were used too often as an excuse for indulging 'whim and folly'[9] at seaside resorts and spa towns. He laid the blame on women's restless desire for novelty – 'it happens much more frequently that the husband is led away from home in accommodation to the humours of his wife, than that the latter is dragged away by the determination of her husband'.[10]

Jane Austen was no stranger to this kind of attack on female dissatisfaction with the monotony of life, but she recognized that censure could be fairly equally apportioned between the sexes. In an early piece of juvenilia, she depicted a married couple wrangling over whose fault it was that they were holidaying in cramped lodgings in town, when they owned 'a most commodious House situated in a most delightfull Country and surrounded by a most agreable Neighbourhood'.[11] They are unable to decide where the responsibility lies, so they end the quarrel and return home with a degree of joy that warrants the ringing of the church bells. In *Mansfield Park* the male and female characters who crave escape from a quiet country existence do so from a range of more complex motivations and there is no celebratory return for any of them. Jane Austen steers her heroines along the middle course she adopted for herself; all are keen to see new places, not one is wild for perpetual roving, all recognize the value of a settled home. Mrs Morland's sound advice to her eldest daughter rings true for everyone: '"Wherever you are you should always be contented, but especially at home, because there you must spend the most of your time."'[12]

The Revd Gisborne fretted that a continual round of visiting and excursions disrupted domestic routine and weakened neighbourhood ties, but only the rich and well connected possessed the wherewithal for uninterrupted travel solely for pleasure. The Countess of Bessborough spent almost eighteen months, from the summer of 1807 to the winter of 1808, travelling around the country with a retinue of servants, including a lady's maid, governess, secretary and family doctor. She stayed on the large estates of her friends and relations in the north of England, at Bolton, Wentworth, Howick, Castle Howard and Alnwick. She wintered in Cornwall, returned to London for the season, spent summer in Bognor and the autumn at Petworth House, Chatsworth, Hardwick and Woburn.[13] There were few women of the Austens' acquaintance who could, or who wished to, indulge themselves to this extent. Reality for them comprised one seaside holiday a year, if they were lucky, a short stay in Bath, Cheltenham, or Tunbridge Wells if they or a member of the family needed to take the waters, and duty visits to relations. Many were tied to the home year after year by children and pregnancy. Jane Austen herself experienced the pleasures and benefits of venturing beyond familiar territory and she envied the wives of soldiers and sailors who travelled more than most – Mrs Croft, robust, self-assured, shrewd and business-like, was created out of admiration for such women – but deprived of peace and stability, her writing and her spirits suffered.

Gisborne's strictures reflect the anxieties raised by the growing number of women who possessed the urge to see and learn new things, about the world and about themselves, in a variety of unfamiliar environments. '"I have travelled so little,"' confesses Anne Elliot, '"that every fresh place would be of interest to me"'[14] and education in its broadest sense was one undoubted benefit that conduct writers could not ignore; travel widened the mind and Gisborne recognized as much:

By a more extensive communication with the world, knowledge, liberality of sentiment, and refinement of manners, have been widely diffused. Rational curiosity has gladly availed itself of the ease and convenience with which the pleasure that attends the inspection of celebrated works of art, and of grand and beautiful scenes of nature, may be enjoyed. Occasional journies undertaken for such purposes, though neither the improvement of health, nor any other urgent call of duty, should be among the motives which give birth to them, are at suitable times not only innocent but commendable.[15]

Girls who had the benefit of a governess, formal schooling or a parent with a good grasp of the subject, received instruction in geography. Agnes Porter, governess to two generations of the Earl of Ilchester's family between 1784 and 1806, took her pupils outdoors to study features of the landscape as well as poring over maps indoors.[16] Among the books she mentions in her letters and diaries are Maria and Richard Edgeworth's *Practical Education* (1798) and Carl Moritz's *Travels, Chiefly on Foot, through Several Parts of England, in 1782*. Less fortunate girls were subjected to texts such as *Mrs Brook's Dialogue*, a study 'Designed for Young Ladies and Schools', which seemed specifically aimed at suppressing for life any nascent enthusiasm for travelling. The title page alone is enough to induce narcolepsy: *'A Dialogue Between A Lady And Her Pupils, Describing A Journey through England and Wales; In Which Detail Of The Different Arts And Manufactures Of Each City And Town Is Accurately Given; Interspersed With Observations And Descriptions In Natural History'.*

In the Chawton House Library copy, Frances Wright, a former reader, has scrawled several versions of her signature on the reverse of the title page, suggesting boredom and indifference rather than proud possession. Mrs Brook does not advocate travel for pleasure – journeys hardly feature and enjoyment is an alien concept – but for knowledge of the dustiest kind. This is not a book to whet Catherine Morland's interest in travel literature, nor indulge Marianne Dashwood's love of picturesque landscapes. William Gilpin, had he been occupying it at the time, would have turned in his grave. Even Fanny Price might rebel against the prospect of being marched through the major manufacturing towns of the kingdom. The author states her intentions in the preface:

> She has often remarked, that in most books of travels, where any mention is made of manufactures, it is in a manner so slight, as hardly to leave a permanent impression on the reader's mind ... As the Author hath for some years past made the education of young ladies her study, she perceived a book

206

of this kind was much wanted, and thought, that by arranging it in the form of a *tour* it was the most likely to make a lasting impression on the memory of youth, and also give them a geographical knowledge of the places noted for any branch of manufacture.[17]

The characters taking part in this edifying 'dialogue' are a know-it-all aunt and her two nieces, Maria and Louisa. As early as the second page, Maria, rather improbably, requests her aunt to 'give us an account of the places that are noted for any different branch of manufacture, and also the manner of working them.' Like Maria and Julia Bertram, this Maria and her sister Louisa, 'know the map of England' and will be only too happy to 'point out every town on it while you mention to us the different trades in which the inhabitants are employed.' 'It will be a great pleasure to me,' continues Maria, 'to go over my maps again, as you know that geography is my favourite study.'[18] This is a static activity of rote learning, a diatribe rather than a dialogue. Both girls ask unlikely questions, such as 'I often hear mention made of malt, and know that it is used in brewing, but wish to be informed in what manner it is made.'[19] Their self-appointed tutor needs no prompting. Off she goes on a two-page disquisition on brewing.

The educating aunt talks herself dry through all of the English and Welsh counties, pontificating at length on subjects as diverse as pickling herrings, gathering saffron and making silk. Tom Bertram, had he ever delved into such a book, which is not likely, would have been pleased to discover that this female compendium of knowledge recognized Northampton as 'the most considerable horse market in the kingdom' and Daventry as famous for its whips.[20] In the section on Surrey, there is no mention of its Garden of England status, nor is there in the passages on Kent. Charcoal-burning and the mineral salt of Epsom occupy the aunt's attention. Emma's respect and love for Miss Taylor would not have survived doses of knowledge administered from this source. In the Dashwoods' Sussex,

Brighton is touched upon as 'a place of fashionable resort for bathing, and drinking the waters' but the nieces unbelievably ask no questions and the aunt proceeds to iron furnaces and needle-making. How Lydia Bennet would have yawned at the mere mention of Brighton had she been exposed to Mrs Brook's account in her formative years.

What does the aunt glean from Jane Austen's Hampshire? Petersfield, Alresford, Alton and Odiham are lumped together as containing 'nothing to attract our curiosity.' The Hospital of the Holy Cross in Winchester is thought worthy of mention and Portsmouth is described as a rope-making centre. Dorset is galloped through in unseemly haste, with a passing reference to sheep and stone; in Wiltshire, Stonehenge is given a sentence, Wilton carpet manufacture two pages. In Somerset, Bath is awarded two sentences. Bristol on the other hand is packed with trades of all descriptions – glass-making takes up six pages and our instructress gets so carried away that she promises her nieces a visit to a glass factory to see the men at work, but 'in the mean time we will continue our journey on our maps; and don't you think it a very pleasing way of travelling, without fatigueing ourselves?'[21] Neither girl's response is recorded.

Devon is reduced to woollen cloth, lace, porcelain and carpet manufacture, fishing and herring-curing. There is no mention of dramatic cliffs or rugged moorland, nothing to create a wild desire to leap into a carriage and head for the south west. Instead, the girls' weary fingers trace the roads into Monmouthshire, where Louisa decides that she has had enough: 'I am quite tired to see so many towns that afford nothing new, nor diverting; I shall grow quite grave for want of something to amuse me.' Her aunt's remedy is a lengthy description of 'japan ware' and a timely warning of the consequences of inattention and reluctance to learn.[22] Never once is it explained how this tedious information will be of use in the future, but goody-two-shoes Maria is happy to take it on trust: 'I am so far from being tired of the accounts that you have given us, that I am quite delighted with our imaginary journey; and perceive, since you have been so good as to describe every thing to us, that there is nothing but may be made a source of entertainment; shall we not proceed on then?'[23] At the end of the exhaustive and exhausting tour through England and Wales their tedious travels end in London with soap, starch and wallpaper.

Susanna Watts' *A Visit to London*, published in 1805, educated her young readers in a far more entertaining way in a story accompanied by illustrations. This little book, featuring the Sandby family on holiday in the capital, is light and entertaining. Both parents introduce moral reflection into their observations of the sights, the institutions and the people, but they are not dry instructors. They joke with their son and daughter and listen to their opinions; this young pair enjoy themselves in London far more than Mrs Brook's pupils and not a soap manufactory to be seen. The children visit the docks, the Guildhall, the Tower, the East India Docks, the royal palaces and parks, Westminster Abbey and the principal shopping streets. Mr Sandby carries a map of the city in his pocket and frequently points out to the youngsters where they are. At the end of the visit, he acknowledges London to be a very special place and there must have been few young readers who disagreed with him: '"We will allow that there are charms peculiar to the country, and you may prefer them, and welcome; but let us do London the justice to acknowledge, that for many advantages and conveniences, there is not such a place in the world."'[24]

The nation's profitable commercial output promoted a feeling of pride and guidebooks to manufacturing towns began to appear on publishers' lists in response to the increasing number of tourists passing through these urban centres on their excursions of pleasure to more appealing locations. The writer's personal experience made for a more interesting read than Mrs Brook's relentless slog through manufacturing processes. Two of the earliest were written by women – Miss Jane Harvey's *A Sentimental Tour through Newcastle. By a Young Lady* published in 1794, followed in 1804 by *A Walk through Leicester*, by *A Visit to London* author Susanna Watts. The latter is a clear, practical guide, filled with opinions, theories and common sense, designed for those 'who *travel* with a POCKET CICERONE', but also 'those who are at home'.[25] The guide's author remained anonymous in the first two editions and the target audience was primarily 'the curious and intelligent' male, as specified by the male editor: 'We now request our good-humoured stranger to accept of such our guidance; whether he be the tourist, whose object of enquiry is general information — or the man of reflection, who, wherever he goes, whether in crouded towns or solitary fields, finds something to engage his meditation'.[26]

The author, however, cannot have intended to rule out women from her readership. Her area of interest is diverse, extending well beyond manufacturing to antiquarian sites, canals, church architecture, schools, jails, asylums, tea gardens, bowling greens, booksellers and theatres. The German traveller Johanna Schopenhauer rhapsodized over moors, glens, mountains and English parkland but she also visited industrial sites in the early years of the nineteenth century and recorded a heartfelt response to what she witnessed:

> Wherever we went we saw the poor man working to make the rich man even richer, while he himself laboured and scraped a bare living. It is a wonderful picture of human diligence but alas not seen from a very pleasing angle ... Sad is the sight of the pale and dirty miner who has to burrow like a mole deep into the earth, and then does not live beyond a few working years. A deep feeling of pity overcame us at the sight of it all, a feeling we experienced often and long on many occasions.[27]

This was an education indeed. Schopenhauer's journals, first published in Germany, gained immediate acclaim, yet in the second edition she thought it necessary to reiterate the following apology: 'I repeat my request to the reader, not to take up this book with too great expectation. It contains a woman's simple tales of what she has seen and observed, written to entertain pleasingly, not to instruct deeply.'[28]

Mrs Morgan considered superfluous any apology for the intellectual value of her observations in *A Tour To Milford Haven*. 'As a female,' she asserts in the preface, 'I have certainly no occasion to excuse my temerity; so many of my sex have shewn they are capable of the most admirable compositions on the most important subjects.'[29] She skewered with her pen those travel writers who, like Colonel Byng, judged places by the state of the principal inn, listed bills of fare, noted the waiters' manners and commented on the comfort or otherwise of the beds. This kind of commentary, she said, was 'a very dull, not to say vulgar, way of filling up time and paper.'[30] Yet she was anxious to divert impending criticism, both of her writing and of a gender-driven 'rage for rambling', first by appearing to belittle her production, then by challenging those who claimed that travel was antithetical to female virtue and domesticity. She pronounced herself unafraid 'of being accused of going out of my sphere in publishing this trifling Work' and continued –

> To those who think a woman cannot find leisure to write, without neglecting either her person or some part of her family duty, I say nothing. They must believe, that the sex is formed merely to dress and be admired, or for domestic drudgery. Those notions have long ago been exploded by people of polite manners and liberal education.[31]

Not for her were the frippery fashion magazines extolling the latest must-have outfit for carriage wear. *Ackermanns Repository*, *La Belle Assemblée*, the *Women's Monthly Museum*, *Heideloff's Gallery of Fashion* and *Costumes Parisien* regularly featured walking and carriage costumes, all hopelessly inadequate for the kind of road journeys undertaken by more adventurous women, or by Jane Austen and the majority of her female characters. Flimsy shoes and expensive fabrics would hardly survive rural mud and rutted lanes. Apart from Anne Elliot's thick boots, Catherine Morland's travelling habit and Elizabeth

Bennet's muddy petticoat, Jane says nothing in her novels of women's outdoor dress. The 'beautifull' Cassandra steals the best bonnet from her mother's millinery shop for her jaunt in a London hackney carriage, but Fanny Knight chose a more conventional method of acquiring fashionable headgear from a milliner in the capital. In a letter of 1813, Jane described the article: 'My Cap is come home & I like it very much, Fanny has one also; hers is white Sarsenet & Lace, of a different shape from mine, more fit for morning, Carriage wear — which is what it is intended for — & is ... shaped around the face ... & a round crown inserted behind.'[32]

Hats were key in promoting a fashionable appearance on any journey, but did not necessarily attract male attention. Ankles did and carriages provided a means of displaying them to advantage. 'The Ladies' Eton', a school for girls in Bloomsbury, kept an old coach propped up in a back room for pupils to practise climbing in and out in an elegant manner.[33] The author of *The Mirror of the Graces* affected to inveigh against overt finery, but made an exception for 'attractive and fancy articles' of carriage dress.[34] Special attention is awarded to stockings and footwear, given that 'there are ladies in England with feet and ancles of so delicate a symmetry, that there is nothing in modelling or in marble to excel their perfection.'[35] 'To exhibit such physical charms, the finest rounded ancles are most effectually shown by wearing a silk stocking *without any clock*. The eye then slides easily over the unbroken line, and takes in all its beauties.' For those with less than perfect lower limbs, remedies are at hand: 'when the ancle is rather large, or square, then a pretty unobtrusive net clock, of the same colour as the stocking, will be a useful division, and induce the beholder to believe the perfect symmetry of the parts.' But no hope is held out to those of stouter build: 'A very thick leg cannot be amended; and in this case I can only recommend absolute neatness in the dressing of the limb, and petticoats so long that there is hardly a chance of its ever being seen.'[36]

John Thorpe, his eye well practised in sliding over exposed

parts of female anatomy, refuses to take one of his sisters to Clifton because her ankles are not slender enough. In addition to flashing a well-turned ankle and dressing in the height of fashion, ladies were advised to maintain their delicate complexions by avoiding extremes of temperature. The author of *The Mirror of the Graces* warned her readers against open carriages. Coarsely textured skin, weathering and sunburn were the consequences attached to journeys made 'unveiled, and frequently without bonnets, in the open air. The head and face have then no defence against the attacks of the surrounding atmosphere, and the effects are obvious. The barouche, for this reason, and the more consequential one of subjecting its inmates to dangerous chills, is a fatal addition to the variety of English equipages.'[37]

Travelling into Wales in 1791, Mary Morgan found that she could protect herself very effectively in an open carriage against the cold, 'but I cannot guard myself against the sun and air, which have such an effect upon my face, and heat it so violently, that I am ashamed to be seen. Besides that my skin is so parched, as to be extremely painful; and I cannot sleep for the uneasiness it occasions.'[38]

The Mirror of the Graces supplied two cosmetic recipes for unsightly tanning of the skin and chapped lips:

Crême de l'Enclos
[This is an excellent wash, to be used night and morning for the removal of tan.]
Take half a pint of milk, with the juice of a lemon, and a spoonful of white brandy, boil the whole, and skim it clear from all skum. When cool, it is ready for use.

Baume à l'Antique
[This is a very fine cure for chopped lips.]
Take four ounces of the oil of roses, half an ounce of white wax, and half an ounce of spermaceti; melt them in a glass vessel, and stir them with a wooden spoon, pour it out into glass-cups for use.[39]

Elizabeth Bennet does not seem concerned or even aware of her tanned appearance at Pemberley, the consequence of driving through the Derbyshire countryside minus protective head-wear in an open carriage. For Mary Russell Mitford, nothing could equal the wild pleasure of being 'whirled along fast, fast, fast, by a blood horse in a gig; this, under a bright sun, with a brisk wind full in my face',[40] despite the ruinous effects on her complexion. Roughened and reddened by sea air, Mrs Croft looks older than her thirty-eight years, but what she has lost in complexion she has gained in character. She is sure of herself, articulate and vigorous.

With so much advice regarding what to wear and so many warnings against the ravages of the weather and the deleterious effect of travelling on domestic duty and virtue, it is a wonder that women ever ventured beyond the shrubbery, but serious female travellers had other matters to concern them than male opposition, cosmetic remedies or the niceties of dress. Those who aimed to publish their journals attempted to present a different view of the home tour from their male counterparts, but they had to be careful to avoid stepping on any toes. While Johanna Schopenhauer was thrilled to cross the Channel to England, Mary Wollstonecraft could not wait to escape in the opposite direction. Only in revolutionary Europe, she claimed, could she breathe the fresh air of freedom: 'In France or Italy, have women confined themselves to domestic life? No!'[41] Mary Berry, who had travelled on the Continent in the 1780s before the war with France closed it down, felt intellectually stifled in England and neither a city nor a rural existence alleviated her frustration. She professed herself sorry for her countrywomen who believed that travelling from London to country estates was the route to happiness: 'All English women think it nec-essary to profess loving the country, and to long to be in the country, altho' their minds are often neither sufficiently opened, nor their pursuits sufficiently interesting, to make such a taste rational.'[42]

She found London equally restricting: 'The whole world

to me, that is to say the whole circle of my ideas, begins to be confined between N. Audley-Street and Twickenham.'[43] Women like Mary Wollstonecraft who craved excitement but voiced unpatriotic views in this age of European conflict did not win many friends and others who left these shores were solicitous to avoid similar opprobrium. Ann Radcliffe, aware of the prevailing political and social criticism of women who took themselves off on a European tour, was careful to stress that her husband had accompanied her and contributed to her published account of a journey made in 1794 to Holland and Germany, culminating in a tour of the English Lakes. She stresses their relief at arriving back on English soil and their sense of English superiority: 'we landed in England under impressions of delight more varied and strong than can be conceived, without referring to the joy of an escape from districts where there was scarcely an home for the natives, and to the love of our own country, greatly enhanced by all that had been seen of others.'[44]

Women travelling entirely alone within the British Isles, for whatever reason, attracted as much censure as those who ventured to foreign locations. Jane Austen's teenage creations, the 'beautifull' Cassandra, Eliza Harcourt and Laura and Sophia travel where and when they please, unhampered by current strictures on female movement, but none of the later heroines travels at her own instigation. The Musgrove girls might be wild for Lyme, but only under their brother's supervision can they get there. It was not respectable for females to go anywhere without a male servant or relative, especially if they were young and unmarried. Lady Catherine, a firm believer in young women being 'properly guarded and attended, according to their situation in life', had issued directives that her niece Georgiana, as the daughter of a rich landowner and his titled wife, be accompanied to Ramsgate by *two* male servants. Elizabeth and the reader later learn that such 'protection' has not prevented Mr Wickham's designs on the heiress. On hearing of Elizabeth and Maria's return to Hertfordshire from Hunsford, Lady Catherine has, predictably, something to say on the occasion: '"Mrs Collins, you must send a servant with them ... I cannot bear the idea of two young women travelling post by themselves. It is highly improper"'.[45] Her pronouncement is entirely superfluous; the Gardiners are one step ahead and with the minimum of fuss have already arranged for their manservant to join the girls in the hired chaise.

In 1808, at the age of forty and single, Elizabeth Isabella Spence chose to go on a summer tour with only a servant, 'without any interruption from company ... that I might travel from place to place as fancy prompted.'[46] She avoided staying at inns, however, preferring to rent private cottages or rely on friends for accommodation. Mrs Sherwood took a greater risk, travelling completely alone in a public coach at night in October 1803 in order to meet her husband's regiment in Sunderland. She left home in the afternoon and reached her destination some hours after midnight on the second day. At twenty-eight and the only female, she was an object of interest to several 'strange jockey-like men' who occupied the carriage. Fortunately, whenever the passengers alighted for the horses to be changed and the men to drink, she was looked after by an elderly farmer, 'and this he did punctually through the whole night, and very sorry I was when a change of coach at Leeds brought me into other company.' The next coach carried a Scottish lady, her brother, two male Quakers and an impudent young officer. In Durham, at an inn where Mrs Sherwood hoped to spend the night, the Quakers stated their intention of going on to Sunderland and the only other female passenger left in another coach with her brother. Sensing the opportunity for an easy conquest, the officer made his move: 'He turned to me and said, "You, madam, will not, I trust, deny me your company." He spoke as if he meant to insult me, and did not care how I took it; he was perfectly aware that I was alone.'[47]

As far as he was concerned, Mrs Sherwood was advertising her availability by travelling without protection. A woman's reputation could easily be ruined, in public and private coaches alike. Mr Allen alerts Catherine Morland to the impropriety of

216

being seen in John Thorpe's gig – '"it has an odd appearance, if young ladies are frequently driven about ... by young men, to whom they are not even related."[48] Mrs Percival, every inch as inflexible as Lady Catherine, colours with anger and berates her niece for daring to travel in a carriage to a ball with young Mr Stanley and without a chaperone.[49] Some young ladies behaved extremely badly in carriages with young men who were not their relatives – it is impossible not to imagine Lydia Bennet flinging herself at Wickham once the doors of the chaise were closed on them; Nancy Steele with Dr Davis at her mercy might do the same. The famous courtesan Harriette Wilson often waited for Lord Ponsonby in a carriage outside the House of Lords so that she could savour the 'pleasure' of a clandestine drive through the dark streets[50] and often drove out of London and back on sexual assignations. Thomas Rowlandson's explicit cartoons of the period depict what young women could get up to in carriages,[51] but few questioned a man's right to climb into a coach and travel where he liked, alone, or with whom he pleased.

Jane Austen's male characters are all able to go wherever, whenever, on a whim, on business, on horseback or in carriages, the steady as well as the flighty – Colonel Brandon, Edward Ferrars, Willoughby, Bingley, Darcy, Wickham, Henry Tilney, Tom Bertram, Henry Crawford. Mr Knightley, who rides off to London or into Kingston when he pleases, recognizes '"that a man of three or four-and-twenty"' – Frank Churchill in this case – possesses '"liberty of mind [and] limb"'[52] to travel where he chooses. Male mobility contrasts with female lack of it, as the Austen brothers' freedom to travel highlighted the constraints on their sisters. Jane made short local journeys in carriages with female relatives and friends easily enough, to Basingstoke from Deane with James Austen's wife driving the chair,[53] for instance. A letter to Cassandra in 1800 mentions a projected trip with Martha Lloyd from Whitchurch to Steventon, on which occasion Jane imagined them behaving in a disreputable manner in a post chaise, 'one upon the other, our heads hanging out at one door, & our feet at the opposite.'[54] Maybe Jane stretched a similar joke beyond its limits in a letter to her elder sister from Bath in 1801. It would appear that Cassandra replied, questioning the propriety of her 25-year-old sister accepting the offer of a seat in Mr Evelyn's phaeton. Jane attempted to allay her fears, while stating her own determination to go ahead with the scheme: 'There is now something like an engagement between us & the Phaeton, which to confess my frailty I have a great desire to go out in. I really beleive he is very harmless; people do not seem to be afraid of him here, and he gets Groundsel for his birds & all that.'[55]

Mr Evelyn was a married man, but did he have a reputation for philandering? Or was he a foolhardy coachman? Jane had described him as 'a Yahoo' in a previous letter,[56] so perhaps his brash, noisy behaviour attracted embarrassing attention. Whatever the truth of it, Jane thoroughly enjoyed her trip out of Bath with him: 'I am just returned from my Airing in the very bewitching Phaeton & four, for which I was prepared by a note from Mr E. soon after breakfast: We went to the top of Kingsdown — & had a very pleasant drive'.[57]

Too often, Jane's travelling arrangements were obstructed by her brothers. On longer journeys, both she and Cassandra had very often to rely on an unreliable Henry. From Rowling in September 1796, Jane wrote in frustration to her sister that a sudden decision to visit his dentist in Yarmouth would prevent Henry taking her home to Steventon as promised – 'my absence seems likely to be lengthened still farther. I am sorry for it, but what can I do?'[58] Speculating that if Henry's plans to move on to the Knights' estate at Godmersham for three weeks' shooting were realized she would be stranded in Kent until mid-October, she asked Frank to accompany her instead. Eighteen days later, Henry had still not materialized, but Frank had agreed to take her as far as London: 'as for Henry's coming into Kent again,' she wrote ruefully, 'the time of its taking place is so very uncertain, that I should be waiting for Deadmen's Shoes.'[59] Jane could be as wild as she liked about travelling home – and she frequently *was* desperate to return to peace and normality – nothing could move Henry when he chose to be fickle. Cassandra also found herself stranded in Kent from time to time, or waiting at home to be transported to London, usually as a consequence of Henry's uncertain movements. Writing from Henrietta Street in mid-September 1813, Jane had to disappoint her sister's expectation of Henry's arrival in Chawton: 'Henry's plans are not what one could wish. He does not mean to be at Chawton till ye 29.... His plan is to get a couple of days of Pheasant Shooting ... his wish was to bring you back with him.'

Henry's changed arrangements threw into disarray Cassandra's plan to visit Adlestrop and also caused accommodation problems at the cottage, since Elizabeth Heathcote and her sister Alethea would be staying there at the same time as Henry. Later the same day, Henry came up with another idea – he would visit Chawton the following Saturday.[60] The uncertainty did not end there. After dinner, Jane found herself writing yet another letter to her sister, explaining that Henry 'has lately recollected something of an engagement ... which perhaps may delay his visit. — He seems determined to come to you soon however.'[61] Jane's next communication, from Godmersham, reveals that Henry had not gone to Chawton after all: 'I wonder Henry did not go down on Saturday; — he does not in general fall <u>within</u> a doubtful Intention.'[62]

Comparisons between Henry Austen and Henry Crawford have frequently been drawn: their mercurial personalities, their propensity to fly around the country at will; but where transport responsibilities are concerned, Mary's brother proves more considerate than Jane and Cassandra's. He collects her harp in his barouche – admittedly when all other means have failed – and 'escorted her, with the utmost kindness, into Northamptonshire, and as readily engaged to fetch her away again at half an hour's notice, whenever she were weary of the place.'[63] It is true that he delays his sister's arrival in London by more than a fortnight, but Mary is not averse to a deferment that enables her to see Edmund on his return from Peterborough. She is also apprised of her brother's reasons for staying longer at Mansfield Parsonage; he consults and confides in her, unlike Henry Austen, whose unwillingness to divulge his travel plans to *his* sisters meant that on at least one occasion Jane had to resort to eavesdropping: 'By a little convenient Listening, I now know that Henry wishes to go to G^m for a few days before Easter, & has indeed promised to do it. — This being the case, there can be no time for your remaining in London after your return from Adlestrop ... It is a great comfort to have got at the truth.'[64]

Henry's illness at the end of 1815 kept Jane in Hans Place for almost two months and even during that time he prevaricated over where he wanted to be, leaving his sisters unsure of their own arrangements. He stated that he had no plans for leaving London before 18 December 'when he thinks of going to Oxford for a few days; — today indeed, his feelings are for continuing where he is, through the next two months. One knows the uncertainty of all this, but should it be so, we must think the best & hope the best & do the best'.[65]

With the proofs of *Emma* corrected and progressing through the printing presses, a telling phrase Jane had recently checked must have come into her mind: '"A young *woman*, if she fall into bad hands, may be teazed, and kept at a distance from those she wants to be with; but one cannot comprehend a young *man's* being under such restraint"'.[66]

12

Off We Drove, Drove, Drove

JANE AUSTEN'S JOURNEYS took her into more English counties than any of her heroines visited. By the age of twenty-one, she had travelled from Hampshire to Oxfordshire, Berkshire, Gloucestershire, Kent and Middlesex (now Greater London). At this stage in their lives, Elinor and Marianne Dashwood had moved from Sussex into Devon and Dorset, with a brief stay in London; Wiltshire-born Catherine Morland had taken a holiday in Somerset and settled in Gloucestershire; Elizabeth Bennet had visited Kent, London and Derbyshire; Fanny Price removed from Portsmouth to Northamptonshire twice and Emma ventured nowhere outside Surrey – there is nothing to suggest that she had ever seen her sister's house in Brunswick Square. Anne Elliot's geographical scope is almost as narrow. At thirteen she was sent to school in Bath, in the same county as Kellynch; the greatest distance she had covered at the age of twenty-seven was the seventeen miles to Lyme, by which age Jane Austen had added Wiltshire, Somerset, Surrey and Devon to her list. Dorset followed the year after that, Sussex in her twenty-ninth year, Staffordshire and Warwickshire in her thirtieth.

A summer journey in 1796 from Steventon to London was the first Jane described in any extant letter. Accompanied by Edward and Frank in a chaise from Hartford Bridge, ten miles on the mail road east of Basingstoke, she crossed Bagshot Heath and slept overnight at Staines. At seven the following morning, they set off for Hounslow Heath '& had a very pleasant Drive' in cloudy, cool weather to Cork Street. This short account of a carriage journey sets the tone for Jane Austen's subsequent letters about travelling. She knew that the complaints and anxious predictions made by the generality of travellers were neither edifying nor entertaining – she had survived this trip, she joked to Cassandra, 'without suffering so much from the Heat as I had hoped to do'.[1] Mary Russell Mitford was equally dismissive of querulous correspondents:

> If they tell you of a journey, you must expect to hear of "moving accidents by flood and field." The weather is always bad; if there be but a cloud as big as a pin's head, it descends in the form of a shower the moment they have opened their carriage. They are always overset in the dirtiest ways, and benighted in the most dangerous places; their horses are always restive and their postilions always drunken. The inns are dirty, the chambermaid awkward, and the sheets damp …[2]

Jane Austen suffered a number of discomforts on long-distance journeys, but she always derived some kind of humour from real, imagined or narrowly averted mishaps. Returning with her parents to Steventon following a visit to Godmersham in the autumn of 1798, she wrote a lengthy letter to her sister from the Bull and George Inn at Dartford. Edward's coachman, Daniel, had taken them as far as Sittingbourne, from where they hired a post chaise, drawn by 'a famous pair of horses', spurred on in record time to Rochester by a postilion 'determined to show my mother that Kentish drivers were not always tedious'. She made a slight reference to the roads being 'heavy' on the next leg of the journey and the horses 'very indifferent', but of greater significance was her mother's good health. Travel sickness was Mrs Austen's old friend and she practised various ways of keeping it at bay: 'My mother took some of her bitters at Ospringe, and some more at Rochester, and she ate some bread several times'[3]. She also tucked into steak and boiled chicken at the inn. Mrs Austen's well-being was of prime importance to Jane on this journey, since mother and daughter shared a double-bedded room at the Bull and George, while Mr Austen bagged the single.

Jane was plagued with anxiety enough when she almost lost her writing box, containing 'all my worldly wealth', and her clothes trunk, mistakenly packed onto a chaise with other luggage bound for Gravesend and the West Indies. She tells the story entertainingly, with none of the exaggerated whining Miss Mitford so disdained. Mr Nottley, the landlord, had sent a rider after the carriage 'and in half an hour's time I had the pleasure of being as rich as ever'. Her day's journey, she reported, 'has been pleasanter in every respect than I expected. I have been very little crowded and by no means unhappy'. In a phrase that recalls Lady Catherine de Bourgh determining the following day's weather at Rosings, Jane thanked Cassandra for her 'watchfulness with regard to the weather on our accounts', which had proved 'very effectual'. She ended the letter with humorous speculation on the likelihood of the inn landlord, 'decidedly for Clapham and Battersea', allowing them to avoid London on the next stage of their journey by taking the alternative road through Croydon and Kingston.[4]

Whichever route they eventually decided on, Staines was the overnight stop on the second evening. Here, Jane did not enjoy an undisturbed sleep. Her mother began to feel the effects of the lengthy journey and spent the night suffering from 'that particular kind of evacuation which has generally preceded her Illnesses',[5] presumably vomiting or diarrhoea.

The following day's carriage journey must have been something of an ordeal for all concerned, but at Basingstoke Mrs Austen cheered up considerably at the sight of Dr Lyford and a dish of broth. Twelve drops of laudanum and dandelion tea were prescribed, but neither prevented Mrs Austen taking to her bed for five weeks, during which time Jane had to nurse her and take on responsibility for the household. The poem Mrs Austen wrote in 1805 on her recovery from illness in Bath hints at how her husband and daughters contributed to her escape from death's clutches: while Mr Austen offered up prayers, Cassandra and Jane took on the more onerous burden of practical care.[6] During what must have seemed an endless five weeks of running up and down the stairs to her mother's room, giving orders in the kitchen and dealing with letters of concern and enquiry, Jane surely envied her father his peaceful library. One thing is for sure, she would have lived in constant apprehension of other lengthy journeys with her mother.

Mr Woodhouse's alarms concerning the risk to health faced on any journey are disproportionate, but illnesses associated with travelling caused understandable anxieties. Motion sickness from carriage travel was common enough for Mary Musgrove to feign indisposition as a consequence of overcrowding, for Kitty Bennet to be sick because she could not see out of the windows and for one of Mrs Leigh Perrot's servants to suffer from it. Jane detected a tendency in her aunt to make the worst of any situation and reported sardonically to Cassandra: 'She ... looks about with great diligence & success for Inconvenience & Evil — among which she ingeniously places the danger of her new Housemaids catching cold on the outside of the Coach, when she goes down to Bath — for a carriage makes her sick.'[7]

Colonel Byng sallied forth on his tour to the west of England well stocked with medicines, in particular 'James's powder; so shou'd a fever overtake me, I will hope that by taking some of his doses and being well wrap'd up in blankets I shall chase away sickness, without consulting the medical country blockheads, who kill, or cure, by chance.'[8] Dr Kitchiner made a number of precautionary recommendations to carriage travellers, which are just as applicable to today's airline passengers:

it is very beneficial occasionally to change our position; that is, to sit sometimes toward one side, and sometimes to the other, and sometimes to recline, &c. ...

Travellers in Carriages are very liable to have their Legs swelled; in order to prevent which, wear easy and thick Shoes, rather than light and Thin Boots, — untie your Garters, loose your Girdle, and alight and walk as often as opportunity permits, in order to excite circulation.[9]

The best remedy for travel sickness he could suggest was to suck strong peppermint lozenges, 'excellent Stomach warmers, and very comforting companions in Cold Weather; — they will often stop Sea-sickness, and will fortify your Stomach when you have to fast longer than usual.'[10] Elizabeth Raffald, author of *The Experienced English Housekeeper*, which ran to many editions throughout the eighteenth and nineteenth centuries, provided instructions for making peppermint drops 'to carry in the Pocket':

TAKE one pound of treble refined sugar, beat it fine and sift it through a lawn sieve, then mix it with the whites of two eggs, beat it to a thick froth, then add sixty drops of the oil of pep-permint and beat them all well together, then with a tea-spoon drop it upon fine cap paper, the size of half a nutmeg, and put them upon the hearth to dry, the next day take them off, and they are fit for use.[11]

Her *'Portable Soup for Travellers'*, an eighteenth-century version of Pot Noodles, sounds perfect for soothing Mrs Austen's dis-ordered stomach. It was made from beef, veal, ham, anchovies, celery and carrots, boiled together in a cauldron for four hours, sieved, reduced in a clean pan to a quarter of its volume 'till it looks thick like glue', seasoned with cayenne pepper, poured into shallow dishes and allowed to set, then cut into small rounds and stored in a tin, 'with writing paper betwixt every cake'. A pint of boiling water added to each dried disc made a 'good bason of broth'.[12]

Despite her travel discomforts, Mrs Austen continued to

endure long-distance journeys, to Bath and back with Jane in May and June 1799, and to Adlestrop, Bookham and Harpsden in the summer of the same year with both daughters and her husband. To Jane's great relief, the forty-one-mile carriage ride from Steventon to Devizes and twenty-one miles from Devizes to Bath produced no ill effects: 'My Mother does not seem at all the worse for her Journey' she wrote to Cassandra from their lodgings at 13 Queen Square. With the prospect of a holiday in her favourite town ahead of her, Mrs Austen had tackled the two flights of stairs to her bedroom without turning a hair. Nothing problematical had occurred on the journey, so, aware that a travel correspondent was duty-bound to anticipate some frustration or other and knowing that Cassandra would enjoy the fabrication, Jane claimed:

> I have some hopes of being plagued about my Trunk; — I <u>had</u> more a few hours ago, for it was too heavy to go by the Coach which brought Thomas & Rebecca from Devizes ... & for a long time we could hear of no Waggon to convey it. — At last however, we unluckily discovered that one was just on the point of setting out for this place — but at any rate, the Trunk cannot be here until tomorrow — so far we are safe — & who knows what may not happen to procure a farther delay.[13]

No records exist of the journey back to Steventon, nor the summer visits to Gloucestershire, Surrey and Oxfordshire, but the next carriage drive to Bath happened in May 1801. On this occasion, Jane and her mother were there house-hunting and, again, Mrs Austen had suffered no indisposition on the road. On their arrival at the Leigh Perrots' house in Paragon, Jane sat down to contact Cassandra, taking up part of the first two pages with an account of the journey from the Lloyds' house at Ibthorpe. The information follows the usual course – nothing of note happened, apart from the accidental breaking in two of Cassandra's drawing ruler, leaving only the obvious to be detailed as entertainingly as possible: 'we changed Horses at the end of every stage, & paid at almost every Turnpike; — we had charming weather, hardly any Dust, & were exceedingly agreable, as we did not speak above once in three miles.'[14]

They stopped to eat on the road between Ludgershall and Everleigh[15] but not at an inn. Neither *Cary's New Itinerary* nor *Paterson's Roads* lists a coaching house on this stretch, so their 'grand Meal' of beef, cucumber and probably other delights was most likely a picnic provided by Martha Lloyd.[16] At Devizes they hired 'a very neat chaise', but despite its genteel appearance the journey from there to Bath had taken over three hours to accomplish. Jane Austen had completed *Susan* (*Northanger Abbey*) two years previously but she was still making additions to update it; roads, distances and journey times in the Bath area were uppermost in her mind. John Thorpe's boastful claim of covering the twenty-five miles from Tetbury in two and a half hours must have made her laugh afresh as she compared that to twenty-one miles travelled in more than three. If something had raised a smile, she might have been distracted for a while from feelings of near despair. Jane, like Anne Elliot, had no idea when, or if, she would ever escape from Bath and her description of the city from the approach road echoes her emotional state: 'The first veiw of Bath in fine weather does not answer my expectations; I think I see more distinctly thro' Rain. — The Sun was got behind everything, and the appearance of the place from the top of Kingsdown, was all vapour, shadow, smoke & confusion.'[17]

That summer, the Austens visited Devon while they waited to move into 4 Sydney Place. A letter from Henry's wife Eliza to cousin Phylly in October confirms that they spent some time there,[18] perhaps with Mr Austen's former pupil Richard Buller. From Colyton Rectory, only three miles inland, they could have driven through the pretty lanes to a number of seaside places. Jane had previously expressed her delight at 'the prospect of spending future summers by the Sea'[19] when the idea of moving from Steventon was first mooted and shortly after wrote to Cassandra, 'Sidmouth is now talked of as our Summer abode'.[20]

She admired the travelling urge in others and began to see a way of tasting its pleasures herself. 'For a time', she wrote, 'we shall now possess some of the advantages which I have often thought of with Envy in the wives of Sailors or Soldiers.'[21] A less predictable existence perhaps held an appeal for Jane Austen. While it is true that she produced nothing new by way of publishable material in the unsettled years between 1801 and 1809, the journeys she made on foot in and around Bath and carriage trips into unfamiliar territory enriched the imaginative genius that later produced *Mansfield Park*, *Emma* and *Persuasion*.

Roads from Bath to the south west were thronged with coaches and chaises heading for the Devonshire seaside resorts. The Austens joined them every autumn or summer for the next three years. En route to Dawlish in 1802, a journey of a hundred miles, they would have stopped every twelve miles or so to change horses, with an overnight stay at Bridgwater – *Cary's New Itinerary* lists the George Inn – or Taunton, which had a greater choice of accommodation (the Castle, the George, the London Inn and the White Hart).[22] Few details are given in *Sense and Sensibility* of the Dashwoods' return to Barton from Cleveland along part of the same route, but they also took two days to reach their destination. The Austens must have spared a thought for Mrs Leigh Perrot's ordeal three years previously at the Assize Court as they passed through Taunton, but apart from that depressing interlude, the rest of the time would surely have been spent admiring the scenery.

William Gilpin, whose picturesque tours Jane Austen loved reading, travelled a section of the road west from Wells to Bridgwater before turning off to Exmoor and North Devon. He described various places in his *Observations On The Western Parts of England*, published in 1798, of which she would have taken note before she set out. Perhaps she carried a copy with her in the carriage, so that she *would* know where she had been and *would* recollect what she had seen. Gilpin found Wells 'a pleasant town' and the cathedral 'a beautiful pile', despite the Saxon 'heaviness' of its architecture. He travelled to Glastonbury on the same road as the Austens but said nothing of the scenery, beyond commenting on the flat meadows around the abbey. Two sketches of the ruin accompany his lengthy discourse on its history and picturesque merits. He disliked the tower on the Tor, but thought the view from its summit 'glorious'. He was more forthcoming on the subject of landscape on the road from Glastonbury to Bridgwater, 'a very fine country' he called it. Just beyond Piper's Inn, on what is now the A39, the coach passed over the Polden Hills, where Gilpin caught a glimpse of ample woods, the Mendips, Sedgemoor and the sea. He identified several landmarks that Jane Austen would also have seen: Lord Chatham's obelisk, designed by Capability Brown in 1765, Sir Charles Tynte's Halswell House, the spire of Bridgwater's great church. In Bridgwater itself, Gilpin asserted, 'There is very little … worth a traveller's attention'.[23] If the Austens stayed the night at the George Inn, they probably made an early start on the road south west to Dawlish next morning. Gilpin's road from Bridgwater took him west over the Quantock Hills to Minehead and the North Devon coast.

By the time *Sense and Sensibility* was published in 1811, Dawlish had developed into a fashionable seaside resort – it is the only place in Devon Robert Ferrars can name – 'esteemed equally salutary for invalids' and pleasure-seekers alike. When the Austens were there in 1802, 'it was resorted to by those who wished for more retirement than they could enjoy at well-frequented places.'[24] The best Jane Austen could say of it twelve years later was that it had a wretched library.[25] Elegant lodging houses for people of quality soon began to change the nature of the resort and Jane's decision to make it Robert and Lucy's honeymoon destination was probably reinforced when she saw for herself what it would inevitably become. She could certainly picture the route they would take to Dawlish from Exeter's New London Inn, running alongside the Exe estuary past Powderham Castle and through Starcross. Austen family tradition states that a visit was also made to Teignmouth in 1802;[26] the 1810 *Guide to All The Watering and Sea-Bathing Places* mentions that it is within an easy carriage ride of Dawlish. The *Guide* suggests several circular rides, one of which takes in Luscombe Castle, owned by Charles Hoare and only recently completed when the Austens visited the area. The Austens patronized Hoares' Bank in London and might have called in to see the new building and grounds, designed by John Nash and Humphry Repton in a rare collaboration. The *Guide* recommends making a special detour to visit it, so by 1810 it was open for viewing by genteel tourists.

The Austens did not return to Devon in 1803, but travelled to Dorset instead. They were at Lyme in November when a fire broke out. Their journey took the same route out of Bath as the previous year, but turned off the main mail road at Stratton to follow the old Roman Fosse Way through Shepton Mallet to Ilchester, then down to Crewkerne and on to Lyme. This is the road Mr Elliot follows in the opposite direction, after admiring Anne Elliot on the seashore and spending the night at the resort's principal inn. In 1804 the Austens were impressed enough to return to Lyme and Jane's only surviving letter from this year was written from lodgings there on 14 September. She said nothing of journeys into the surrounding countryside, but her knowledge of the locality feeds into *Persuasion*, where she steps out of the narrative to give an affectionate guide to the places she loved, all within walking distance and well worth the effort of toiling uphill east, north and west out of the town. None of the characters at this point in the novel sits 'in unwearied contemplation' of the low rocks and the flowing of the tide in Charmouth's 'sweet retired bay'; visits 'the woody varieties of the cheerful village of Up Lyme', or is charmed by Pinny's 'green chasms between romantic rocks',[27] but these are the locations Captain Wentworth comes to value as he ponders his fate after Louisa's accident. '"The country around Lyme is very fine ... the more I saw, the more I found to admire"' he states, and Anne Elliot's response echoes her creator's: '"So much novelty and beauty! ... there is real beauty at Lyme".'[28] None of the three novels written after Jane Austen's journeys to coastal resorts in the south west is free from the influence of the sea, but at Lyme she began the eleven-year mental journey towards the beauties of *Persuasion*.

This was Mr Austen's last holiday. He died in January 1805 and with him went Jane's hopes of returning to the Devon or Dorset coast in summers to come. With a reduced annual income, the Austen ladies would be reliant on their relatives for hospitality away from Bath, a narrowing of travel opportunities that Henry and James took for granted. 'They will not only suffer no personal deprivation, but will be able to pay occasional visits of health and pleasure to their friends', a sanguine Henry wrote to Frank only a few days after their father's death. James expressed the same sentiment – his mother's summers would 'be spent in the country amongst her Relations & chiefly I trust among her children — the winters she will pass in comfortable Lodgings in Bath.'[29] It was a pity that none of those relations lived in Devon or Dorset. Travel from now on for the widow and her spinster daughters would be a means of reducing household expenses and Jane knew it: 'I think we are just the kind of people & party to be treated about among our relations; — we cannot be supposed to be very rich.'[30]

Thankfully, Edward came up with a plan in April for taking his mother and sisters to the sea later in the year. Jane found the prospect 'desirable & delightful', especially since Henry would be of the party.[31] At the end of July, Mrs Austen left Godmersham for Worthing, but from June to September Jane and Cassandra stayed in Kent with Edward. They spent a week each with the Bridges family at Goodnestone Farm in August and another together at Sandling Park, with Elizabeth's sister and husband. The extended family were also becoming involved in the 'treating about'. Jane and Cassandra stayed at Sandling while Edward, Elizabeth and Fanny visited Henry and Eliza in London, a visit that worried Jane initially, since she believed it would wreck her chances of going to the sea. In the event it did not, but what is apparent is the sisters' increasing subjection to the travelling arrangements made by their brothers. Jane Austen was no stranger to Fanny Price's sense of powerlessness as she waited in Portsmouth for someone to collect her. Writing from Goodnestone to Godmersham, Jane confided to Cassandra: 'It would be inconvenient to me to stay ... longer than the beginning of next week, on account of my clothes, and therefore I trust it will suit Edward to fetch or send for me on Monday, or Tuesday if Monday should be wet ... The purport of Elizabeth's letter makes me anxious to hear more of what we are to do and not to do'.[32]

At last, on 17 September, Edward's holiday plan came into operation, with the party setting out on a journey of eighty-five miles to the Sussex resort of Worthing. They arrived the following day, having travelled on turnpike roads through Battle, Horsebridge and Brighton.[33] This was to be a long holiday of three or even four months in lodgings – cheaper than those in Bath over the main tourist season – during which time Jane and Anne Sharp, the Godmersham governess, became good friends.

James Austen accommodated his mother and sisters in their old home at Steventon Rectory over January 1806. Cassandra and Jane spent three weeks at Manydown in February, then returned to Steventon until mid-March before rejoining their mother in Bath. In the summer of 1806, the Austen women moved to Southampton, by way of Clifton, Adlestrop, Stoneleigh and Hamstall Ridware. Only a poem of Jane's exists for this year, no letters to her brothers or her niece Fanny, describing the long journeys into Gloucestershire, Warwickshire and Staffordshire, but in July 1808 Jane reminded her sister of their 'happy feelings of Escape' from Bath two years previously.[34] Catherine Morland was surely in Jane's mind as she closed the carriage door and 'caught the last view of Bath without any regret'.[35] The first part of the journey from Clifton to Adlestrop, passing through Bristol, Old Sodbury and Petty France was familiar, but beyond there, the road presented fresh scenes. In Henry Tilney's open curricle, Catherine Morland has the opportunity to admire 'as much of the countryside as possible' between Petty France and Northanger Abbey, although on this journey she is more engrossed by her handsome companion.[36]

On the agreeable drive of twenty miles from the Abbey to Woodston, she notices little until the pretty village is reached. Despite the General's apology for the flatness of the terrain, Catherine admires the neat houses and shops, all of golden Cotswold stone. Jane Austen would have seen the same style of architecture as she passed through Tetbury, Cirencester, Northleach and Stow-on-the-Wold on her way to Adlestrop. If she had consulted her copy of Richard Warner's *Excursions From Bath*, she would have read the author's description of the landscape around Cirencester. He calls it 'a tame scene ... nothing occurs to interest the mind' and complains about 'the tiresomeness of dull uniformity'. Between there and Tetbury, he mentions the source of the Thames – disappointing in its sparsity – and, like General Tilney, comments on the 'extensive flatness for many miles.' His spirits revive a little in Tetbury, where from higher ground he can see Lansdown Hill in Bath and the Welsh mountains. He calls in at a woollen mill on the edge of the town, owned by a Mr Austin, then makes his way back to Bath past numerous dairy farms.[37]

Adlestrop Park and Rectory in 1806 presented an improved face to the world. Humphry Repton had been at work here since Jane's last visit in 1799, enclosing the village green, planting a screen to hide the cottages, incorporating the grounds of Parsonage and Park and adding to the flower garden a stream that rippled downhill over rocky ledges into a lake.[38] The theme of improvements comes into *Mansfield Park* and Repton is mentioned by name as the best man to effect changes at Sotherton for a fee of five guineas a day. This was to be a shorter visit than expected – Mrs Austen's cousin, the Revd Thomas Leigh, transported his guests almost immediately to Stoneleigh Abbey, where the vexed question of inheritance had to be settled. He had waited for his cousin and her daughters to arrive at Adlestrop before he left, so that he could take them 'so far on their road to Mr Cooper's whom they are going to visit at Hamstall.'[39]

The journey of thirty-five miles north along the Fosse Way was easily accomplished in a day and the travellers arrived to a late, but sumptuous supper: 'Fish Venison and all manner of good things' reported Mrs Austen to one of her daughters-in-law.[40] The kitchen gardens at the Abbey were as extensive as General Tilney's and the grounds supplied fish, venison, pigeons, rabbits and many kinds of poultry. A brewery and bakery operated all day every day and a dairy produced butter, cheese and cream. Mrs Austen was as impressed as Mr Collins at Rosings with the number of windows, staircases and bedrooms. Jane might have discovered a prototype Miss Bates here, in the person of Lady Saye and Sele, whom Mrs Austen found 'rather tormenting … she fatigues me sadly on the whole', she said, although she 'affords Jane many a good laugh'.[41] Perhaps Jane also based the featureless chapel at Sotherton on the one at Stoneleigh; the present administrators Stoneleigh Abbey Ltd certainly think so: 'In *Mansfield Park*: During the Bertrams' visit to Sotherton Court Fanny Price notices the *"crimson velvet cushions on the ledge of the family gallery in the chapel"*. Those velvet cushions can still be found in the chapel at Stoneleigh.'[42]

From Stoneleigh, the Austens continued their journey to Edward Cooper's rectory at Hamstall Ridware, following the Gardiners' road as far as Lichfield, then branching off on the road north and travelling another eight miles. The journey back to Hampshire at the beginning of October after a five-week stay was the longest Jane Austen would ever undertake, covering over 140 miles through Kenilworth, Banbury, Woodstock, Oxford, Abingdon and Newbury. The ladies stayed at Steventon for a week, then moved on to Southampton to live with Frank and his wife. In the summer of 1807 they visited Edward and his family at Chawton Great House. It was the first time they had seen this estate and little suspected that they would be living in the village within two years. Jane recorded at the end of December an expenditure of £1.2s.10d on a journey, perhaps this one to Chawton.[43]

The year 1808 saw Jane at Steventon and Kintbury, in London and in Kent. The letter she sent to Cassandra about the carriage drive from London to Godmersham in June recalls previous

descriptions of journeys, detailing the weather, timings and the
lack of incident. She had been staying with Henry and Eliza in
Brompton and set off from the Arlington Hotel in Bath Street
with Mary, James Edward and Caroline in her brother James'
new carriage. She found the countryside through which they
passed 'very beautiful', but with a 'fidgety' 3-year-old niece and
a nephew not quite ten, the hours spent in an enclosed space
cannot have been entirely comfortable. Jane admits to being
'rather crowded'. James travelled to Kent by stage coach; there
would not have been enough room for him in the carriage as
well. 'Our first eight miles were hot,' Jane reported,

> Deptford Hill brought to my mind our hot journey into Kent
> fourteen years ago; but after Blackheath we suffered nothing,
> and as the day advanced it grew quite cool. At Dartford, which
> we reached within the two hours and three-quarters, we went
> to the Bull, the same inn at which we breakfasted in that said
> journey, and on the present occasion had about the same bad
> butter. At half-past ten we were again off, and, travelling
> on without any adventure reached Sittingbourne by three.
> Daniel was watching for us at the door of the George ... A few
> minutes, of course, did for Sittingbourne; and so off we drove,
> drove, drove, and by six o'clock were at Godmersham.[44]

As early as the following day, straight after breakfast, Edward
made arrangements for Jane's return to Hampshire: 'he wanted
to know James's plans and mine, and from what his own now
are I think it already nearly certain that I shall return when they
do, though not with them.'[45] Edward stated his intention of going
to Alton on business and collecting his eldest son from there at
the same time. He would not be taking young Edward back to
school in Winchester at the beginning of the autumn term, so,
although Jane had expected to stay at Godmersham longer than
three weeks, she had to travel at her brother's convenience. From
Alton, she would have to 'get on afterwards somehow or other'
to Southampton. Added to the disappointment was the distress

of considering herself a burden: 'I shall at any rate be glad not to be obliged to be an incumbrance on those who have brought me here, for, as James has no horse, I must feel in their carriage that I am taking his place.'[46]

Edward pushed the point more forcibly by informing her that Mrs Cooke had invited James and Mary to Great Bookham on their way home, an invitation they were keen to accept but would have to refuse if Jane travelled back in their carriage, 'the nature of the road affording no conveyance to James'. Although Edward's initial inquiry regarding Jane's own plans had all the appearance of offering her a choice, in reality she had none. 'I shall therefore make them all easy on that head as soon as I can', she assured her Cassandra.[47] Three days later, Edward had second thoughts about leaving his sister stranded in Alton and apprised her of his 'kind intention' of taking her all the way home to Southampton, where he and Edward Junior would spend a day with them and stay overnight. Within a few days the plan changed again: Henry made one of his vague offers to take Jane home 'some time in September', but her friends Alethea and Catherine Bigg were now expected at Southampton in July and Jane was keen to see them. On this occasion, she was not overruled.[48]

How much Jane contributed to transport costs when her brothers' carriages were involved is not known, but she commented that 'A Legacy' would be necessary to enable her mother, sister and herself to accompany young Edward from Winchester to Godmersham at Christmas, as her sister-in-law Elizabeth had suggested. Her visit to Canterbury, she reported to Cassandra, was 'very agreable' and 'without cost'; perhaps generous Mrs Knight, with whom she was staying, paid Jane's portion of the expenses. Towards the end of the same letter, Jane expressed her desire to call in on relations on the road home, but Edward had his own agenda which put visiting out of the reckoning: 'till I have a travelling purse of my own,' she wrote, 'I must submit to such things'.[49]

Plans for moving to Chawton from Southampton were in

full swing the following January. The date set for travelling to Godmersham, where they would stay for the summer, was 3 April. Jane, Cassandra and their mother intended to sleep at Alton that night, then take the Guildford road to Great Bookham, to stay with the Cookes for almost a week. On 11 April, they hoped to be in Kent. Jane made it plain that the weather could alter these plans but, in the event, Mrs Austen's poor health kept them in Alton for three whole weeks. They did not make the journey to Godmersham until after 20 April and arrived there on 15 May, via which road and which relations is not known. Jane and her mother left Edward's on 30 June and Cassandra followed with her brother a week later; on 7 July, they took possession of their final home in Chawton.

Journeys to London and to friends and relations at no great distance were carried on as usual through the next three years, but Jane's mind was ranging far and wide, from Sussex to Devonshire and from Hertfordshire to Derbyshire, as she revised *Sense and Sensibility* and *Pride and Prejudice* ready for publication. Her imagination travelled beyond England's shores when she began *Mansfield Park*, probably in the spring of 1812,[50] aided by Sir John Carr's *Travels in Spain* and Sir Charles William Pasley's *Essay on the Military Policy and Institutions of the British Empire*. For knowledge of Northamptonshire, she made enquiries of Martha Lloyd and Henry; as for Portsmouth, the chances are that she had seen it for herself.

Happiest for Jane Austen were the journeys she made with her brother Henry, when he could be relied upon to be in the right place at the right time. With him she could relax and indulge her love of travelling. On a trip to London in May 1813, she was so impressed by the landscape that she sent a glowing account to Cassandra, together with the usual details about the weather and journey times. From Chawton they took the road to Farnham, along a narrow ridge called the Hog's Back to Guildford, then on to Ripley, Esher and Kingston. Jane's enjoyment of the whole excursion shines through the most extensive description of countryside she had ever given in a letter:

How lucky we were in our weather yesterday! ... We had no rain of any consequence; the head of the Curricle was put half-up three or four times, but our share of the Showers was very trifling, though they seemed heavy all round us, when we were on the Hog's-back ... Three hours & a q^r took us to Guildford, where we staid barely two hours, & had only just time enough for all we had to do there, that is, eating a long comfortable Breakfast, watching the Carriages ... & taking a little stroll afterwards. From some veiws which that stroll gave us, I think most highly of the situation of Guildford ... I was very much pleased with the Country in general — ; — between Guildford & Ripley I thought it particularly pretty, also about Painshill & every where else; & from a Mr Spicer's Grounds at Esher which we walked into before our dinner, the veiws were beautiful. I cannot say what we did *not* see, but I should think there could not be a Wood or a Meadow or a Palace or a remarkable spot in England that was not spread out before us, on one side or the other ... Upon the whole it was an excellent Journey & very thoroughly enjoyed by me ... [51]

Esher Place is mentioned in *Paterson's Roads*, but no description is given.[52] Mr Spicer was a stockbroker who set about rebuilding the house between 1805 and 1821 to his own taste, although he kept the fifteenth-century Wayneflete Tower. The cost of reconstructing the house was estimated at £12,800, of which £450 was assigned to the Doric portico. A staggering £22,924 spent on other buildings included £854 for a new vinery and garden walls, £1,506 for new stables and £3,037 for further additions to the front of the house. In 1813 when Jane and Henry saw the estate, Mr Spicer's project was half-completed. Jane also mentioned that Claremont Park, across the road from Esher Place, was going to be sold yet again; 'it is a house that never seems to have prospered', she remarked.[53] A succession of owners and tenants had occupied it for short periods after Lord Clive had demolished the previous house but died before the new one was finished. It became the home of Prince Leopold of Saxe-Coburg and Princess Charlotte on their marriage in 1816. In March of that year, following Jane's visit to Carlton House the previous November, the Prince Regent's librarian invited Jane to write a historical romance and dedicate it to Prince Leopold, an invitation she declined. She might have smiled had she passed Claremont on future occasions, but after 1815 she took neither that road nor any road to London.

Jane's last visit to Godmersham was made in the autumn of 1813. She stayed for two months and Edward's 12-year-old daughter Marianne later recalled how her aunt would sit silently sewing, then suddenly laugh out loud, write something down, then return to her needlework.[54] Back on her favourite road to London in March 1814, Jane tested her new novel, *Mansfield Park*, on Henry. They began reading, perhaps aloud, at Bentley Green, halfway between Alton and Farnham, and got as far as Maria's marriage to Mr Rushworth before reaching their destination. At home in Henrietta Street, over the next few days, Henry praised the characters and the storyline. Jane said nothing of Henry's response to the geographical locations, but she was gratified after publication by Admiral Foote's surprise 'that I had the power of drawing the Portsmouth-Scenes so well.'[55] James Austen and 'Mr B.L.' also admired her accurate depiction of the town.

In June 1814, Jane was invited to Great Bookham by the Cookes. She began worrying immediately about the cost of travelling post from Hampshire to Surrey, but was perhaps compensated by an excursion to Box Hill and a useful reacquaintance with other places. She had travelled through Kingston and was already familiar with Leatherhead, probably Mickleham and Dorking too and her local knowledge helped to create Emma's Highbury. Gilpin considered Box Hill to be of picturesque value, with its 'downy back and precipitous sides', its 'great variety of pleasing views into the lower parts of Surrey' and its 'hillocks, every where interspersed with the mellow verdure of box'.[56] He noted the proliferation of elegant houses, built high on the downs to take advantage of the breathtaking scenery. 'The whole county indeed from Leatherhead almost to Guildford,' he enthused, 'is thus richly adorned'.[57] Journeys around Hampshire to stay with friends and family followed later in the year and early into the next. Sisters Elizabeth Heathcote and Alethea Bigg welcomed Jane and Cassandra to their house in Winchester, Mary and James Austen accommodated them for a fortnight at Steventon, during which time visits to old friends and neighbours in the area were made.

The longest journey Jane Austen made in the final two years of her life was to Cheltenham, in the late spring of 1816. Accompanied by Cassandra, she travelled the seventy-seven miles from Chawton, via Steventon, into Gloucestershire, following a route familiar to her since childhood. Various unpleasant health disorders had begun to manifest themselves – stomach upsets, back pain, general weakness and weight loss – and it is not known whether she enjoyed this particular travelling experience. For one accustomed to pleasurable carriage drives and a constitution strong enough to withstand sickness on the road, any physical discomfort must have been both worrying and irritating. After a fortnight drinking the waters in the spa town, the sisters travelled back to Hampshire by way of the Fowles at Kintbury, where Jane's failing health was noticed. She never travelled that road again. It is sadly ironic that she was working on *Persuasion* at this time, introducing characters who had sailed the oceans and opening up travel opportunities for Anne Elliot as her own were closing down.

One year later, before she left Chawton for Winchester to be within reach of Mr Lyford the physician, Jane wrote to her friend Anne Sharp, outlining the travelling arrangements. She would make the sixteen-mile journey with Cassandra in her elder brother's carriage, she explained. Despite her anxieties she was still able to see humour in her situation: 'On Sat^y next, I am actually going thither … And as this is only two days off you will be convinced that I am now really a very genteel, portable sort of an Invalid'.[58] Installed in lodgings in College Street, she wrote to her nephew James Edward and revealed a little about

Saturday's journey. Cassandra's attempt to hold off the rain had failed on this occasion and Jane had suffered some distress at seeing her brother Henry and nephew William Knight getting wet as they rode beside the carriage, but she underplayed any personal discomfort: 'my Journey hither ... was performed with very little fatigue, & had it been a fine day I think I shd have felt none'.[59]

Cassandra's pen recorded Jane's final journey on 24 July 1817 from the door of 8 College Street into the Cathedral precincts. 'Every thing was conducted with the greatest tranquility,' she wrote to Fanny Knight, '& but that I was determined I would see the last & was therefore upon the listen, I should not have known when they left the House. I watched the little mournful procession the length of the Street & when it turned from my sight & I had lost her for ever — even then I was not overpowered ...'.[60]

Notes

The idiosyncratic spelling, grammar and punctuation found in extracts from primary sources have been retained for the sake of contemporary colour and flavour, with deviations from modern usage indicated only where the sense is compromised.

ABBREVIATIONS

GENERAL

A Lady Travels	Michaelis, Ruth and Merson, Jena and Willy (trans.) (1988), *A Lady Travels: The Diaries of Johanna Schopenhauer*, London: Routledge.
Espriella's Letters	Southey, Robert (1807), *Letters From England By Don Manuel Alvarez Espriella* (2nd American edn 1808). New York: David Longworth.
Folio Byng	Byng, Colonel John (1996), *Rides Round Britain*. London: Folio Society.
FR	Le Faye, Deirdre (2004), *Jane Austen: A Family Record*. Oxford: Oxford University Press.
Letters	Le Faye, Deirdre (ed.) (2011), *Jane Austen's Letters*. Oxford: Oxford University Press.
Memoir	Sutherland, Kathryn (ed.) (2002), *A Memoir of Jane Austen: J.E. Austen-Leigh*. Oxford: Oxford University Press.
Outlandish Cousin	Le Faye, Deirdre (2002), *Jane Austen's 'Outlandish Cousin': The Life and Letters of Eliza de Feuillide*. London: The British Library.
Reminiscences	Le Faye, Deirdre (1986), *Reminiscences of Caroline Austen*. Chawton: The Jane Austen Society.
Traveller's Oracle	Kitchiner, Dr William, M.D. (1827), *The Traveller's Oracle Or, Maxims For Locomotion*. London: Henry Colburn.

WORKS BY JANE AUSTEN

The Cambridge Edition of the Works of Jane Austen

Sense and Sensibility (S&S)	Ed. Peter Copeland (2006)
Pride and Prejudice (P&P)	Ed. Pat Rogers (2006)
Mansfield Park (MP)	Ed. John Wiltshire (2005)
Emma (E)	Eds. Richard Cronin and Dorothy McMillan (2005)
Northanger Abbey (NA)	Eds. Barbara M. Benedict and Deirdre le Faye (2006)
Persuasion (P)	Eds. Janet Todd and Antje Blank (2006)
Juvenilia	Ed. Peter Sabor (2006)
Later Manuscripts (LM)	Eds. Janet Todd and Linda Bree (2008)

INSTITUTIONS

BL   The British Library
HRO   Hampshire Record Office
JASNA Jane Austen Society North America

1. A Laudable Thirst For Travelling

1. *Letters* 39, 14 September 1804, p.97.
2. *NA*, Vol. I, Ch. 1.
3. *P&P*, Vol. II, Ch. 8.
4. Simond, Louis (1817) *Journal of a Tour and Residence in Great Britain During the Years 1810 and 1811 By A French Traveller*. Edinburgh: James Ballantyne & Company, Vol. II, p.130.
5. *Outlandish Cousin*, p.60.
6. *E*, Vol. I, Ch. 18.
7. *Letters* 90, 25 September 1813, p.238.
8. *E*, Vol. III, Ch. 6.
9. *Letters* 150(C), 24 January 1817, p.342.
10. *Ibid.* 159, 27 May 1817, p.357.
11. *Ibid.* 86, 3–6 July 1813, p.223.
12. Selwyn, David (ed.) (1996), *Jane Austen: Collected Poems and Verse of the Austen Family*. Manchester: Carcanet Press, p.12.
13. *NA*, Vol. II, Ch. 10.
14. Mogg, Edward (1826), *Paterson's Roads* (18th edn). London: Longman, Rees, Orme, Brown, and Green, p.50.
15. *Espriella's Letters*, p.19.
16. *P&P*, Vol. II, Ch. 9.
17. Combe, William and Rowlandson, Thomas (1815), *The Tour of Doctor Syntax In Search of the Picturesque* (6th Edition). London: R. Ackermann, p.206.
18. *S&S*, Vol. I, Ch. 18.

2. A Tolerable Proficient In Geography

1. *Juvenilia: Catharine, or the Bower*, pp.250–51.
2. Watts, Susanna (1805), *A Visit to London, Containing A Description of the Principal Curiosities In The British Metropolis*. London. Printed by J. Adlard, Duke-street, Smithfield, For Tabart and Co., p.107.
3. *P&P*, Vol. II, Ch. 4.

4. *Traveller's Oracle*, Part 1, p.26.
5. *Juvenilia: Love & Freindship*, pp.108, 109.
6. *LM*: 'See they come'. pp.245–6 and notes, pp.711–13.
7. Le Faye, Deirdre (1999), *Another book owned by Mr Austen*. Chawton: Jane Austen Society Report, p.27.
8. Le Faye, Deirdre (2002) *Jane Austen: The World of Her Novels*. London: Frances Lincoln, p.161.
9. *Juvenilia: Edgar and Emma*, pp.33–7.
10. *Letters* 107, 9–18 September 1814, p.288.
11. *Ibid*. 113, 30 November 1814, p.296.
12. *Ibid*. 104, 10–18 August 1814, p.281.
13. *Ibid*. pp.280–81.
14. Grey, J. David (ed.) (1986), *The Jane Austen Handbook*. London: The Athlone Press, p.380.
15. Mitford, Mary Russell (1982), *Our Village*. Oxford: Oxford University Press, p.1.
16. Oliphant, Margaret (1870), *Miss Austen and Miss Mitford*. Blackwood's Edinburgh Magazine, p.107; cited in Sutherland, Kathryn (2005), *Jane Austen's Textual Lives*. Oxford: Oxford University Press, p.69.
17. Jennings, Paul (date unknown), extract from *Jane in Vain*, London: *The Observer*.
18. Barchas, Janine (2012), *Matters of Fact in Jane Austen*. Baltimore: The Johns Hopkins University Press, p.73.
19. *New Bath Guide* (1790). Bath: Richard Cruttwell, p.54.
20. *NA*, Vol. I, Ch. 4.
21. Lane, Maggie (1996), *A Charming Place: Bath in the Life and Novels of Jane Austen*. Bath: Millstream Books, p.38.
22. *P*, Vol. II, Ch. 11.
23. *MP*, Vol. II, Ch. 11.
24. *P&P*, Vol. III, Ch. 16.
25. *E*, Vol. III, Ch. 16.
26. *P*, Vol. II, Ch. 11.
27. *Letters* 86, 3–6 July 1813, p.224.
28. *S&S, Vol*. II, Ch. 10.
29. *MP*, Vol. III, Ch. 14.
30. *Ibid*., Vol. III, Ch. 17.
31. *E*, Vol. II, Ch. 9.
32. *Ibid*., Vol. II, Ch. 5.
33. *Ibid*., Vol. III, Ch. 6.
34. *Ibid*., Vol. III, Ch. 12.
35. *P*, Vol. I, Ch. 11.
36. *Ibid*., Vol. II, Ch. 6.
37. *Ibid*., Vol. II, Ch. 5.

3. Fifty Miles Of Good Road

1. *S&S*, Vol. I, Ch. 10.
2. *P*, Vol. II, Ch. 3.
3. *S&S*, Vol. I, Ch. 16.
4. *Ibid*., Vol. I, Ch. 9.
5. Bennett, Francis (2007), *The Roads of Devon and Cornwall*. Exeter: The Short Run Press, p.100.
6. Warner, the Revd Richard of Bath (1800), *A Walk Through Some of the Western Counties of England*. Bath: Richard Cruttwell, p.123.
7. Climenson, Emily J. (1899), *Passages From The Diaries Of Mrs. Philip Lybbe Powys*. London: Longmans, Green, and Co., p.157.

8. Lefroy, Helen and Turner, Gavin (eds.) (2007), *The Letters of Mrs Lefroy*. Chawton: The Jane Austen Society, p.57.
9. *Letters* 10, 27–8 October 1798, p.17.
10. *A Lady Travels*, p.129.
11. Tristram, W. Outram (1893), *Coaching Days and Coaching Ways*. London: Macmillan, p.10.
12. Day, Malcolm (2006), *Voices from the World of Jane Austen*. Newton Abbot: David & Charles, p.128.
13. Beresford, John (ed.) (1968), *The Revd James Woodforde*. Oxford: Oxford University Press, pp.171–2.
14. Austen-Leigh, R.A. (ed.) (1942), *Austen Papers 1704–1856*. London: Spottiswoode, Ballantyne & Co., p.190.
15. *E*, Vol. I, Ch. 15.
16. *P*, Vol. II, Ch. 6.
17. Simons, Paul (9 October 2002), 'Weather Eye', *The Times*, p.30.
18. *Reminiscences*, p.31.
19. *MP*, Vol. III, Ch. 7.
20. *Letters* 97, Wednesday 2 to Thursday 3 March 1814, p.266.
21. Young, Arthur, *Northern Tour* (1770) and *Six Weeks Tour* (1768), cited in Moir, Esther (1964), *The Discovery of Britain*. London: Routledge & Kegan Paul, p.10.
22. *NA*, Vol. I, Ch. 13.
23. *LM: The Watsons*, p.79.
24. *Ibid.* p.120.
25. Mingay, Gordon (1981), *Mrs Hurst Dancing & Other Scenes From Regency Life 1812–1823*. London: Victor Gollancz, p.25.
26. *MP*, Vol. I, Ch. 8.
27. *Ibid.*, Vol. I, Ch. 8.
28. *Ibid.*, Vol. I, Ch. 4.
29. *Ibid.*, Vol. II, Ch. 2.
30. *Traveller's Oracle*, Part 1, p.125.
31. *Espriella's Letters*, p.14.
32. Austen-Leigh, R.A. (ed.) (1942), *op. cit.*, p.245.
33. *NA*, Vol. I, Ch. 7.
34. Ibbetson, Laporte and Hassell, J., Mess. (1793), *A Picturesque Guide to Bath, Bristol Hot-Wells, the River Avon, and the Adjacent Country*. London: Hookham and Carpenter, Bond-Street, pp.148–51.
35. *MP*, Vol. II, Ch. 7.
36. Folio Byng, 'Tour to the North 1792', pp.284, 289.
37. Beardsley, Martyn and Bennett, Nicholas (eds.) (2007), *Gratefull to Providence: The Diary and Accounts of Matthew Flinders, Surgeon, Apothecary and Man-Midwife 1775–1802*. Woodbridge: The Boydell Press, Vol. I, p.38.
38. *S&S*, Vol. II, Ch. 8.
39. Cobbett, William (2010), *Rural Rides (1763–1835)*. London: Folio Society, p.12.
40. *Memoir*, Ch 1, p.14.
41. Souden, David (ed.) (1991), *Byng's Tours: The Journals of the Hon. John Byng 1781–1792*. London: Century, p.16.
42. Ousby, Ian (ed.) (1992), *James Plumptre's Britain: The Journals of a Tourist in the 1790s*. London: Hutchinson, p.168.
43. Spence, Elizabeth Isabella (1809), *Summer Excursions, Through Parts Of Oxfordshire, Gloucestershire, Warwickshire, Staffordshire, Herefordshire, Derbyshire, And South Wales*. London: Longman, Hurst, Rees, And Orme, Vol. I, pp.4, 43.
44. Morgan, Mrs Mary (1795), *A Tour To Milford Haven, In the Year 1791*. London: Printed for John Stockdale, in Piccadilly, pp.120–21.
45. *LM: The Watsons*, p.87.

46. *P*, Vol. II, Ch. 2.
47. *Letters* 29, 3–5 January 1801, p.71.
48. Climenson, Emily J. (1899) *op. cit.*, p.157.
49. Arnold, Hilary (1998), 'Mrs Margaret Graves and Her Letters From Bath, 1793–1807', in *Bath History VII*. Bath: Millstream Books, p.79.
50. *S&S*, Vol. I, Ch. 5.
51. *Espriella's Letters*, p.200.
52. Beresford, John (ed.) (1968), *op. cit.*, Vol. V, p.240.
53. *S&S*, Vol. I, Ch. 7.
54. *The Times*, 23 May 1803, p.4.
55. Watts, Susanna (1805), *A Visit to London, Containing A Description of the Principal Curiosities In The British Metropolis*. London. Printed by J. Adlard, Duke-street, Smithfield, For Tabart and Co., p.41.
56. *Outlandish Cousin*, pp.123–4.
57. *Reading Mercury*, 19 August 1793, p.3, col. 5.
58. Bramston Archive, HRO 3A00W/A3/11.
59. Vick, Robin (1996), 'Rural Crime', *The Jane Austen Society Report*. Chawton: Jane Austen Society, pp.40–41.
60. *Reading Mercury*, 22 July 1793, p.3, cited in Vick, Robin (1996), *op. cit.*, p.41.
61. *E*, Vol. III, Ch. 3.
62. *Hampshire Chronicle*, 16 December 1805, p.4, col. 4.
63. *The Times*, 29 October and 13 November 1811, cited in *Emma*, p.584, Note 1.
64. Brander, Michael (1973), *The Georgian Gentleman*. London: Saxon House, p.164.
65. *Outlandish Cousin*, p.25.
66. *Ibid*. p.89.
67. Folio Byng, 'Tour to the North 1792', p.363.
68. *The Times*, 1 January 1798, p.3, cited in Vick, Robin (1996), 'Rural Crime', *The Jane Austen Society Report*. Chawton: Jane Austen Society, p.40.
69. *Reading Mercury*, 29 October 1798, p.3; *Ibid*. p.40.
70. Fullerton, Susannah (2005), *Jane Austen & Crime*. Sydney: Jane Austen Society of Australia Inc. pp.45–6.
71. *Ibid*. p.47.
72. Hewitt, Rachel (2010), *Map of a Nation*. London: Granta Books, p.183.
73. *LM: Sanditon*, p.137.
74. *P&P*, Vol. II, Ch. 9.
75. Cited in Bennett, Francis (2007). *op. cit.*, p.110.
76. *Letters* 19, 17 May 1799, p.41.
77. *Ibid*. 84, 20 May 1813, pp.219–20.
78. *P&P*, Vol. I, Ch. 3.

4. An Animal Made For Speed

1. *Letters* 22, 19 June 1799, pp.48–9.
2. Johnson, R. Brimley (1925), *The Letters of Mary Russell Mitford*. London: John Lane The Bodley Head, pp.33–4.
3. *LM: Sanditon*, p.149.
4. *Juvenilia: The Memoirs of Mr Clifford*, p.51.
5. *Letters* 96, 6–7 November 1813, p.263.
6. *E*, Vol. II, Ch 5.
7. *NA*, Vol. I, Ch. 8.
8. *LM: The Watsons*, p.115.
9. Sambrook, Pamela (2003), *A Country House At Work*. London: National Trust, p.58.
10. *S&S*, Vol. I, Ch. 12.
11. *MP*, Vol. I, Ch. 7.

12. *Ibid.*, Vol. I, Ch. 7.
13. *Ibid.*, Vol. I, Ch. 7.
14. Birtwistle, Sue and Conklin, Susie (1995), *The Making of Pride and Prejudice*. London: Penguin, p.3.
15. See portraits by George Stubbs, Joshua Reynolds, Henry Raeburn and Daniel Gardner.
16. Williams, Charles (pre-1806), *An Enquiry after Stretchit in Gloucestershire or the Sailor's Reply*. London: National Maritime Museum.
17. Rowlandson, Thomas, *The Gallop*.
18. Gregory, Dr John (1808), *A Father's Legacy to his Daughters*. A New Edition. London: T. Cadell and W. Davies, pp.56–7.
19. Johnson, R. Brimley (1925), *op. cit.*, p.142.
20. *P&P*, Vol. I, Ch. 7.
21. Buchan, William MD (1798), *Domestic Medicine: or, A Treatise on the Prevention and Cure of Diseases by Regimen and Simple Medicines*, (16th edn). London: A. Strachan, T. Cadell Jun. and W. Davies, pp.86, 84.
22. Folio Byng, 'A Ride Taken in July 1785', p.61.
23. *Reminiscences*, pp.24–5.
24. *FR*, p.43.
25. *Ibid*. p.48.
26. *Letters* 27, 20–21 November 1800, p.63.
27. *FR*, p.263.
28. *New Bath Guide* (1790). Bath: Richard Cruttwell, pp.38–9.
29. *Letters* 43, 8–11 April 1805, p.103.
30. *New Bath Guide* (1800). Bath: Richard Cruttwell, p.39.
31. *A Lady Travels*, p.35.
32. Anonymous (1810), *Guide to all the Seabathing Places*. London: Printed for Richard Phillips, p.87.
33. Bamford, Francis (ed.) (1936), *Dear Miss Heber*. London: Constable and Company, p.183.
34. Mingay, Gordon (1981), *Mrs Hurst Dancing & Other Scenes From Regency Life 1812–1823*. London: Victor Gollancz, pp.15, 18, 23.
35. *Letters* 14, 18–19 December 1798, p.28.
36. *S&S*, Vol. I, Ch. 9.
37. *Letters* 25, 8–9 November 1800, p.59.
38. Tomalin, Claire (1997), *Jane Austen: A Life*. London: Viking, p.93.
39. *MP*, Vol. II, Ch. 6.
40. *Reminiscences*, p.6.
41. *Ibid*. p.41.
42. *Letters* 23, 25–7 October 1800, p.52; *Ibid*. 63, 27–8 December 1808, p.167; *Ibid*. 30, 8–9 January 1801, p.74.
43. *Ibid*. 104, 10–18 August 1814, p.280.
44. *Reminiscences*, pp.51–4.
45. Selwyn, David (ed.) (1996), *Jane Austen: Collected Poems and Verse of the Austen Family*. Manchester: Carcanet Press, p.44.
46. Austen-Leigh, R.A. (ed.) (1942), *Austen Papers 1704–1856*. London: Spottiswoode, Ballantyne, & Co., p.260.
47. *Ibid*. p.293.
48. Rochefoucauld, François de la and Scarfe, Norman (2011), *A Frenchman's Year in Suffolk, 1784*. The Boydell Press, p.5.
49. *Ibid*. p.52.
50. Folio Byng, 'A Ride into the West 1782', pp.9–10.
51. *Ibid*. p.31.
52. Rochefoucauld, François de la and Scarfe, Norman (2011), *op. cit.*, p.52.

53. *A Lady Travels*, p.100.
54. *MP*, Vol. I, Ch. 12.
55. *Juvenilia: Memoirs of Mr Clifford*, p.51.
56. *NA*, Vol. 1, Ch. 7.
57. *S&S*, Vol. III, Ch. 8.
58. *E*, Vol. I, Ch. 1.
59. *Ibid.*, Vol. II, Ch. 11.
60. *LM: The Watsons*, p.108.
61. *NA*, Vol. I, Ch. 7.
62. *Espriella's Letters*, p.21.
63. *Traveller's Oracle*, Part 1, p.149.
64. *Ibid.* pp.132, 133.
65. *Ibid.* pp.138–9.
66. *A Lady Travels*, p.20.
67. *Ibid.* p.138.
68. Lefroy, Helen and Turner, Gavin (eds.) (2007), *The Letters of Mrs Lefroy*. Chawton: The Jane Austen Society, 16 November 1802, p.92; 23 January 1803, p.101; 29 January 1803, p.102.
69. *Ibid.* September 1803, p.132.
70. *Letters* 150(C), 24 January 1817, p.341.
71. *Ibid.* 153, 13 March 1817, p.348; *Ibid.* 155, 23–25 March 1817, pp.351, 352.
72. *E*, Vol. III, Ch. 6.

5. Determined On A Curricle

1. Felton, William (1794), *A Treatise On Carriages*. London: J. Debrett, Vol. I, p.vii.
2. Hibbert, Christopher (ed.) (1991), *Captain Gronnow: His Reminiscences of Regency and Victorian Life, 1810–60*. London: Kyle Cathie, pp.74–5.
3. Murray, Venetia (1998), *High Society: A Social History of the Regency Period, 1788–1830*. London: Viking, p.110.
4. Lord Brabourne, Edward (1884), *Letters of Jane Austen*. London: Richard Bentley & Son, Vol. I, pp.35–6.
5. *Outlandish Cousin*, p.152.
6. *Ibid.* p.129.
7. *Ibid.* p.150.
8. *P&P*, Vol. III, Ch. 17.
9. Felton, William (1794), *op. cit.*, Vol. I, p.114.
10. *Letters* 78, 24 January 1813, p.207.
11. *Ibid.* 95, 3 November 1813, p.257.
12. *LM: The Watsons*, p.79.
13. *E*, Vol. I, Ch. 11.
14. Ackermann, Rudolf (1815), *The Repository of Arts, Literature, Commerce, Manufactures, Fashions and Politics*. London: R. Ackermann, p.366.
15. *Traveller's Oracle*, Part 2, p.30.
16. Murray, Venetia (1998), *op. cit.*, p.68.
17. *Traveller's Oracle*, Part 2, pp.124–5.
18. Murray, Venetia (1998), *op. cit.*, pp.110–11.
19. *NA*, Vol. I, Ch. 7.
20. *Ibid.*, Vol. I, Ch. 9.
21. Felton, William (1796), *A Treatise On Carriages*. London: J. Debrett, Vol. II, p.107.
22. *Ibid.*, p.3.
23. *LM: Sanditon*, p.172.
24. *P*, Vol. I, Ch. 10.
25. Felton, William (1796), *op. cit.*, Vol. II, p.95.

26. Lefroy, Helen and Turner, Gavin (eds.) (2007), *The Letters of Mrs Lefroy*. Chawton: The Jane Austen Society, 17 June 1801, p.35; 20 June 1801, p.36; 14 March 1802, p.63; 7 April 1803, p.110.
27. *NA*, Vol. II, Ch. 5.
28. *LM: The Watsons*, p.106.
29. *Letters* 95, 3 November 1813, p.260; *Ibid.* 96, 6–7 Nov 1813, p.264.
30. *MP*, Vol. II, Ch. 3.
31. Vick, Robin (1999), 'Mr Austen's Carriage', *The Jane Austen Society Report*. Chawton: Jane Austen Society, p.23.
32. *FR*, p.96.
33. *Letters* 11, 17–18 November 1798, p.20.
34. Vick, Robin (1999), *op. cit.*, p.23.
35. Felton, William (1796), *op. cit.*, Vol. II, p.51.
36. Folio Byng, 'A Tour Into Sussex 1788', p.131.
37. *NA*, Vol. II, Ch. 5.
38. *P*, Vol. I, Ch. 1.
39. Ackermann, Rudolf (1816), 'Description of The Military Carriage Of Napoleon Bonaparte, Taken After The Battle Of Waterloo, And Now Exhibiting At The London Museum, Piccadilly', *Repository of Arts, Literature, Fashions &c*, new series. London: R. Ackermann, pp.99–103.
40. Murray, Venetia (1998) *op. cit.*, p.283.
41. *P*, Vol. II, Ch. 12.
42. Felton, William (1796), *op. cit.*, Vol. II, p.68.
43. *P&P*, Vol. III, Ch. 10.
44. *Memoir*, p.66.
45. *Juvenilia: Love & Freindship*, p.129.
46. *Letters* 17, 8–9 January 1799, p.34.
47. *FR*, p.107.
48. Lefroy, Helen and Turner, Gavin (eds.) (2007), *op. cit.*, pp.42, 87, 191.
49. *NA*, Vol. I, Ch. 2.
50. *LM: Sanditon*, p.163; *MP*, Vol. II, Ch. 2.
51. *E*, Vol. I, Ch. 15.
52. Day, Malcolm (2006), *Voices from the World of Jane Austen*. Newton Abbot: David & Charles, pp.135–6.
53. *E*, Vol. II, Ch. 14.
54. *Ibid.*, Note 7, p.575.
55. *Letters* 64, 10–11 January 1809, p.171.
56. *FR*, p.246.
57. *Letters* 73, 29 May 1811, p.195.
58. *Ibid.* 85, 24 May 1813, p.222.
59. *Ibid.* 5, 5 September 1796, p.8.
60. *P&P*, Vol. II, Ch. 5; Vol. II, Ch. 14; Vol. III, Ch. 14.
61. *Juvenilia: Collection of Letters*, pp.197–202.
62. *S&S*, Vol. I, Ch. 2.
63. *E*, Vol. III, Ch. 2.
64. *Ibid.*, Vol. II, Ch. 5.
65. *Juvenilia: The Three Sisters*, pp.74–89.
66. *S&S*, Vol. III, Ch. 11.
67. *MP*, Vol. II, Ch. 5.

6. Regularity And Dispatch

1. *Letters* 94, 26 October 1813, p.255.
2. *Traveller's Oracle*, Part 1, p.155.

3. Rochefoucauld, François de la and Scarfe, Norman (2011), *A Frenchman's Year in Suffolk, 1784*. London: The Boydell Press, p.96.
4. Lichtenberg, G.C. (1776–78), *Visits to England*, cited in Gatrell, Vic (2006), *City of Laughter Sex and Satire in Eighteenth-Century London*. London: Atlantic Books, p.27.
5. Lewis, W.S. (ed.) (1937), *Horace Walpole, Correspondence* (42 vols). Oxford: Oxford University Press, p.249.
6. Brennan, Flora (trans.) (1987), *Puckler's Progress: The Adventures of Prince Puckler-Muskau in England, Wales and Ireland as Told in Letters to His Former Wife – 1826–9*. London: Collins, p.27.
7. Cary, John (1798), *Cary's Itinerary* (8th edn, 1819) [first ed. 1798]. London: Printed for J. Cary No. 181 Strand. pp.105, 258, 574–612.
8. *Letters* 52, 15–17 June 1808, p.130.
9. BL Additional MSS 27828, *Place Papers* (unpublished), Vol. 4, fos 7–9.
10. *A Lady Travels*, p.143.
11. Swift, Andrew and Elliott, Kirsten (2012), *Literary Walks in Bath*. Bath: Akeman Press, p.1.
12. *New Bath Guide* (1790), Bath: Richard Cruttwell, pp.72–4.
13. Martin, Joanna (ed.) (1998), *A Governess in the Age of Jane Austen, The Journals and Letters of Agnes Porter*, Letter 77, July 1811. London: The Hambledon Press, p.313.
14. BL Add. MSS 27828, *op. cit.*
15. Irving, Washington (1820–21), *The Sketch Book of Geoffrey Crayon, Gent.* (section entitled The Stage-Coach) www.gutenberg.org.
16. *Letters* 6, 18 September 1796, p.11.
17. *Outlandish Cousin*, pp.123–4.
18. Folio Byng, 'Tour into South Wales 1787', p.127.
19. Murray, Venetia (1998), *High Society: A Social History of the Regency Period, 1788–1830*. London: Viking, p.283.
20. *Traveller's Oracle*, Part 1, p.74.
21. *Letters* 60, 24–5 October 1808, p.156.
22. *Reminiscences*, p.54.
23. *Espriella's Letters*, p.163.
24. *Juvenilia: Love & Freindship*, pp.133–4.
25. *Letters* 105, 23–4 August 1814, pp.281–2.
26. Lord Brabourne, Edward (1884), *Letters of Jane Austen*. London: Richard Bentley & Son, Vol. II, p.365.
27. Harman, Claire (2009), *Jane's Fame*. London: Canongate, p.60.
28. Austen, Caroline (1991), *My Aunt Jane Austen*. Chawton: The Jane Austen Society, p.4.
29. *Letters* 76(C), 29–31 October 1812, pp.203–4 and Note 6, p.417.
30. Hurst, Jane (2008), *A History of Alton 1800–1850*. Hampshire: privately printed, p.8.
31. Andrews, Cyril Bruyn (ed.) (no date), *Clouds and Sunshine by An English Tourist of The Eighteenth Century Part I of the Tour of 1789 from the Torrington Diaries by The Hon. John Byng (1743–1813)*. Marlow, Bucks: Roy Patrick Smith, p.15.
32. *A Lady Travels*, p.103.
33. Rochefoucauld, François de la and Scarfe, Norman (2011), *op. cit.*, p.5.
34. *Traveller's Oracle*, Part 1, p.146.
35. *S&S*, Vol. II, Ch. 10.
36. Selwyn, David (ed.) (1996), *Jane Austen: Collected Poems and Verse of the Austen Family*. Manchester: Carcanet Press, p.5.
37. *Letters* 101, 14 June 1814, p.275.
38. *NA*, Vol. II, Ch. 14.
39. *Letters* 43, 8–11 April 1805, p.104.
40. *A Lady Travels*, p.136.
41. *Ibid.*, pp.137–8.

42. *Letters* 157, 6 April 1817, p.354.
43. *A Lady Travels*, pp.123–4.
44. *New Bath Guide* (1790), *op. cit.*, pp.48–52.
45. *NA*, Vol. I, Ch. 10.
46. *P*, Vol. II, Ch. 11.
47. *Bath Chronicle*, 16 September 1785.
48. *New Bath Guide* (1790), *op. cit.*, pp.72–4.
49. Folio Byng, 'Tour into South Wales 1787', p.85.
50. Hurst, Jane (2008), *op. cit.*, pp.22–3.
51. Raffael, Michael (2006), *Bath Curiosities*. Edinburgh: Birlinn, p.73.
52. Murray, Venetia (1998), *op. cit.*, p.10.
53. *Letters* 29, 3–5 January 1801, p.69.
54. *E*, Vol. II, Ch. 9.
55. *Espriella's Letters*, p. 67.
56. Johnson, R. Brimley (1925), *The Letters of Mary Russell Mitford*. London: John Lane The Bodley Head Ltd., p.71.
57. *P&P*, Vol. III, Ch. 4; *MP*, Vol. III, Ch. 13; *E*, Vol. III, Ch. 9.
58. *MP*, Vol. I, Ch. 4.
59. *E*, Vol. II, Ch. 16.
60. *Ibid.*, Vol. II, Ch. 16.
61. *Ibid.*, Vol. III, Ch. 14.
62. *P&P*, Vol. III, Ch. 4.
63. *LM: Lady Susan*, p.75.

7. Mention My Name At The Bell

1. *The Traveller's Oracle*, Part 1, p.110.
2. *Ibid.*, p.37.
3. Folio Byng, 'A Ride into the West 1782', p.31.
4. Andrews, Cyril Bruyn (ed.) (no date), *op. cit.*, p.137.
5. Folio Byng, 'Tour of 1792', p.288.
6. *A Lady Travels*, p.46.
7. *P&P*, Vol. II, Ch. 16. The notes mention two inns called The George near Ware, p.510.
8. *Ibid.*, Vol. II, Ch. 16.
9 *FR*, p.52.
10. *Letters* 9, 24 October 1798, p.15.
11. *Ibid.*, 19, 17 May 1799, p.41.
12. Mogg, Edward (1826), *Paterson's Roads* (18th edn). London: Longman, Rees, Orme, Brown, and Green, p.32.
13. *Letters* 97, 2–3 March 1814, p.266.
14. Gilpin, William (1798), *Observations on the Western Parts of England, Relative Chiefly To Picturesque Beauty*. London: T. Cadell Jun. and W. Davies, p.256.
15. Morgan, Mrs Mary (1795), *A Tour To Milford Haven, In the Year 1791*. London: Printed for John Stockdale, in Piccadilly, p.12.
16. *Letters* 87, 15–16 September 1813, p.230.
17. Folio Byng, 'Tour in 1782', pp.10, 14; 'Tour in 1785', p.52; 'Tour in 1787', p.72; 'Tour in 1788', p.154; 'Tour in 1790', p.215.
18. *E*, Vol. II, Ch. 18.
19. Folio Byng, 'Tour in 1787', p.68.
20. *Ibid.*, 'Tour in 1792', p.283.
21. Lefroy, Helen and Turner, Gavin (eds.) (2007), *The Letters of Mrs Lefroy*. Chawton: The Jane Austen Society, 5 January 1803, pp.97–8.
22. *Traveller's Oracle*, Part 1, pp.107–8.
23. *Ibid.*, pp.45, 105.

24. Murray, Venetia (1998), *High Society: A Social History of the Regency Period, 1788–1830*. London: Viking, p.284.
25. *A Lady Travels*, p.45.
26. Anonymous (1810), *A Guide To All The Watering And Sea-Bathing Places*. London: Richard Phillips, p.283.
27. Lane, Maggie (2003), *Jane Austen and Lyme Regis*. Hampshire: The Jane Austen Society, p.42.
28. *P*, Vol. I, Ch. 12.
29. *New Bath Guide* (1790), p.72.
30. Murray, Venetia (1998), *op. cit.*, p.174.
31. *Ibid.*, p.175.
32. *A Lady Travels*, p.135.
33. Trusler, John (1790), *The London Adviser and Guide: Containing every Instruction and Information useful and necessary to persons living in London and coming to reside there*, p.170.
34. *LM: Sanditon*, p.154.
35. *Ibid.* p.207.
36. *S&S*, Vol. III, Ch. 11.
37. *Espriella's Letters*, p.17.
38. *NA*, Vol. I, Ch. 7.
39. Swift, Andrew and Elliott, Kirsten (2012), *op. cit.*, p.7.
40. *A Lady Travels*, p.130.
41. *E*, Vol. II, Ch. 6.
42. *Ibid.*, Vol. I, Ch. 15.
43. *LM: The Watsons*, p.91.
44. *Letters*, Topographical Index, p.589.
45. *E*, Vol. II, Ch. 6.
46. *Ibid.*, Vol. III, Ch. 2.
47. Hurst, Jane (2008), *A History of Alton 1800 to 1850*. Hampshire: Jane Hurst, p.12.
48. *Letters*, Topographical Index, p.616.
49. *Ibid.*, p.590.
50. *Ibid.*, 15, 24–26 December 1798, p.31 and *FR*, p.109.
51. *Letters* 45, 24 August 1808, p.113.
52. *Ibid.*, 92, 14–15 October 1813, p.247.

8. Excursions Of Pleasure

1. *P&P*, Vol. I, Ch. 9.
2. *S&S*, Vol. I, Ch. 12.
3. *Reminiscences*, pp.22–3.
4. *Letters* 55, 30 June–1 July 1808, p.143.
5. *Ibid.*, p.142.
6. *Ibid.*, 60, 24–5 October 1808, p.158.
7. Johnson, R. Brimley (1925), *The Letters of Mary Russell Mitford*. London: John Lane The Bodley Head, p.37.
8. Climenson, Emily J. (ed.) (1899), *Passages From The Diaries of Mrs. Philip Lybbe Powys of Hardwick House. Oxon. A.D. 1756 to 1808*. London: Longmans, Green, and Co., p.163.
9. *Ibid.* p.174.
10. Folio Byng, 'Tour into South Wales 1787', p.98.
11. *E*, Vol. III, Ch. 6.
12. Warner, Rev. Richard (1801), *Excursions From Bath*. Bath: Richard Cruttwell, pp.279–80.
13. *E*, Vol. III, Ch. 6.

14. Folio Byng, 'Tour into South Wales 1787', pp.95, 97; 'Tour to the North 1792', p.323.
15. *NA*, Vol. II, Ch. 5.
16. Johnson, R. Brimley (1925), *op. cit.*, p.39.
17. Climenson, Emily J. (1899), *op. cit.*, p.167.
18. Folio Byng, 'Tour into South Wales 1787', p.71; 'A Ride Taken in July 1785', p.59.
19. Simond, Louis (1815), *Journal of a Tour and Residence in Great Britain During the Years 1810 and 1811 by A French Traveller*. Edinburgh: George Ramsay and Company, Vol. I, p.7.
20. Folio Byng, 'A Tour into Kent 1790', pp.261–2.
21. *Letters* 45, 24 August 1805, pp.111, 113.
22. Austen-Leigh, R.A. (ed.) (1942), *Austen Papers 1704–1856*. London: Spottiswoode, Ballantyne & Co., p.247.
23. Kenyon Jones, Christine (2010), 'Portraying ambiguous cousinship: *Mansfield Park* and the family of the real Lord Mansfield', *Persuasions* Online. USA: JASNA.
24. *Letters* 85, 24 May 1813, p.221.
25. Lewis, W.S. (ed.) (1937), *Horace Walpole, Correspondence*, (42 vols). Oxford: Oxford University Press, Vol. XXV, p.423.
26. Tinniswood, Adrian (1998), *The Polite Tourist: A History of Country House Visiting*. London: National Trust, back cover.
27. Moir, Esther (1964), *The Discovery of Britain*. London: Routledge & Kegan Paul, p.86.
28. Climenson, Emily J. (1899), *op. cit.*, p.165.
29. Moir, Esther (1964), *op. cit.*, p.96.
30. *S&S*, Vol. II, Ch. 12.
31. Lewis, W.S. (ed.) (1937), *op. cit.*, Vol. XXXIII, p.411.
32. *A Lady Travels*, p.26.
33. *MP*, Vol. I, Ch. 9.
34. *Ibid.*, Vol. I, Ch. 9.
35. *P&P*, Vol. III, Ch. 14.
36. *NA*, Vol. II, Ch. 7.
37. *MP*, Vol. I, Ch. 9.
38. Morgan, Mrs Mary (1795), *A Tour To Milford Haven, In the Year 1791*. London: Printed for John Stockdale, in Piccadilly, pp.87–8.
39. *Ibid.*, pp.113–14.
40. Felton, William (1796), *op. cit.*, Vol. II, Appendix 6.
41. *E*, Vol. III, Ch. 7.
42. *Ibid.*, Vol. III, Ch. 6.
43. *Ibid.* Vol. I, Ch. 18.
44. Gisborne, Thomas (1810), *An Enquiry Into The Duties Of The Female Sex*, 9th edn. London: T. Cadell and W. Davies, p.309.
45. Sullivan, R.J. (1780), *Observations made during a Tour through parts of England, Scotland and Wales in a series of Letters*. London: T. Becket, p.199.
46. Ousby, Ian (ed.) (1992), *James Plumptre's Britain*. London: Hutchinson, p.70.
47. *Ibid.*, p.99.
48. Spence, Elizabeth Isabella (1809), *Summer Excursions, Through Parts Of Oxfordshire, Gloucestershire, Warwickshire, Staffordshire, Herefordshire, Derbyshire, And South Wales*. London: Longman, Hurst, Rees, And Orme, Vol. II, p.111.
49. *A Lady Travels*, pp.39, 40, 43.
50. *Ibid.*, pp.64–5.
51. Morgan, Mrs Mary (1795), *op. cit.*, pp.228–9.
52. *Letters* 95, 3 November 1813, p.258.
53. Rollins, Hyder Edward (ed.) (1958), *Letters of John Keats*. Cambridge, MA: Harvard University Press, Vol. I, pp.298–309.
54. Gilpin, William (1792), *Observations Relative Chiefly To Picturesque Beauty, Made in the Year 1772, On Several Parts of England; Particularly The Mountains and Lakes of*

Cumberland, and Westmoreland, 3rd edn. London: R. Blamire, Vol. II, p.68.

55. Budworth, Joseph (1792), *A Fortnight's Ramble to the Lakes in Westmoreland, Lancashire, and Cumberland, By a Rambler*, 1st edn. London: J. Nichols, p.xii.

56. *Letters* 90, 25 September 1813, p.240.

57. Andrews, Malcolm (1989), *The Search for the Picturesque*. California: Stanford University Press, p.154.

58. Spence, Elizabeth Isabella (1809), *op. cit.*, Vol. I, pp.162–3.

59. Lockhart, John Gibson (1837), *Memoirs of the Life of Sir Walter Scott* (7 vols), Edinburgh, Vol. II, p.292.

60. *Letters* 108, 28 September 1814, p.289.

61. Richardson, Lady (ed.) (1875), *Autobiography of Mrs Elizabeth Fletcher, 1770–1858*. Edinburgh: Publisher unknown, p.299. Cited in *FR*, p.275.

62. *Memoir*, p.91.

63. *Selling Jane Austen to Hampshire Tourists*, 3 June 2010, www.news.bbc.co.uk/local/hampshire.

64. Hill, Constance and Ellen G. (1902), *Jane Austen: Her Homes and Her Friends*. London and New York: John Lane, p.v.

65. *Ibid.*, p.4.

66. *Ibid.*, p.7.

67. *Memoir*, p.69.

68. Hill, Constance and Ellen G. (1902), *op. cit.*, p.178.

69. *Ibid.*, p.254.

70. Sutherland, Kathryn (2005), *Textual Lives*, Oxford: Oxford University Press, p.68.

71. Tennyson, Lord Hallam (1897), *Alfred Lord Tennyson: A Memoir by His Son*. London: Macmillan, Vol. II, p.47.

72. Hill, Constance and Ellen G. (1902), *op. cit.*, pp.137–8.

9. North To Pemberley

1. Anonymous (September 1789), 'Journal of a Tour from Oxford thro' the Peak of Derbyshire, etc.', *The Topographer*. London: Robson and Clarke, Vol. I, No. VI, Article II, pp.314–22.

2. Climenson, Emily J. (ed.) (1899), *Passages from the Diaries of Mrs. Philip Lybbe Powys of Hardwick House, Oxon, AD 1756 to 1808*. London: Longmans, Green, and Co., p.338.

3. *P&P*, Vol. II, Ch. 19.

4. *Ibid.*, Vol. II, Ch. 19.

5. Ousby, Ian (ed.) (1992), *James Plumptre's Britain: The Journals of a Tourist in the 1790s*. London: Hutchinson, p.59.

6. *Letters* 79, 29 January 1813, p.210.

7. Brook, Mrs (1795), *A Dialogue Between A Lady And Her Pupils, Describing A Journey through England and Wales* ... London: Printed for and sold by Thomas Clio Rickman, pp.181–3.

8. *A Lady Travels*, p.32.

9. *Ibid.*, p.33–4.

10. *Juvenilia: Letter from Sophia Sentiment*, p.361.

11. *Outlandish Cousin*, p.88.

12. Simond, Louis (1817), *Journal of a Tour and Residence in Great Britain During the Years 1810 and 1811 By A French Traveller*. Edinburgh: James Ballantyne & Company, Vol. II, pp.140–41.

13. *Outlandish Cousin*, p.89.

14. Simond, Louis (1817), *op. cit.*, p.140.

15. Morgan, Mrs Mary (1795), *A Tour To Milford Haven, In the Year 1791*. Printed for John Stockdale, in Piccadilly, p.73. Tournay was the site of the Duke of Marlborough's victory over the French in 1704.

16. *A Lady Travels*, p.12.
17. *Ibid.*, p.12.
18. *Ibid.*, p.16.
19. Gilpin, William (1792), *Observations Relative Chiefly to Picturesque Beauty. Made in the Year 1772, On several Parts of England; Particularly The Mountains and Lakes of Cumberland and Westmoreland*, 3rd edn. London: Printed for R. Blamire, Vol. I, pp.38–45.
20. Andrews, Cyril Bruyn (ed.) (1954), *The Torrington Diaries*. London: Eyre & Spottiswoode, p.102.
21. Spence, Elizabeth Isabella (1809), *Summer Excursions, Through Parts Of Oxfordshire, Gloucestershire, Warwickshire, Staffordshire, Herefordshire, Derbyshire, And South Wales*. London: Longman, Hurst, Rees, And Orme. pp.101, 102.
22. Austen-Leigh, R.A. (ed.) (1942), *Austen Papers 1704–1856*. London: Spottiswoode and Ballantyne, p.247.
23. Gilpin, William (1792) *op. cit.*, Vol. II, p.122.
24. Austen, Jane, *The History of England*. London: BL, 1993, p.xix.
25. Gilpin, William (1792), *op. cit.*, Vol. I, p.45.
26. *Ibid.*, p.47.
27. *Ibid.*, p.74.
28. Simond, Louis (1817), *op. cit.*, Vol. II, p.120.
29. *A Lady Travels*, pp.17–18.
30. *E*, Vol. II, Ch. 18.
31. Ousby, Ian (ed.) (1992), *op. cit.*, p.74.
32. *P&P*, Vol. II, Ch. 19.
33. *A Lady Travels*, p.22.
34. Spence, Elizabeth Isabella (1809), *op. cit.*, Vol. I, pp.155–7.
35. Andrews, C. Bruyn (ed.) (1954), *op. cit.*, p.251.
36. *A Lady Travels*, p.21.
37. Gilpin, William (1792), *op. cit.*, Vol. II, p.224.
38. Ousby, Ian (ed.) (1992), *op. cit.*, p.63.
39. Gilpin, William (1792), *op. cit.*, Vol. II, p.217.
40. Ousby, Ian (ed.) (1992), *op. cit.*, p.72.
41. Simond, Louis (1817), *op. cit.*, Vol. II, pp.109–12.
42. Austen, Jane, *The History of England*. London: BL, 1993, p.xxii.
43. Austen, Caroline (1991), *op. cit.*, p.9.
44. *Memoir*, p.71.
45. *A Lady Travels*, p.27.
46. *Ibid.*, p.11.
47. Parry, Sarah (2008), 'The Pemberley Effect', *Persuasions*, No. 30. USA: JASNA, p.113.
48. *Ibid.*, p.121.
49. *P&P*, Vol. II, Ch. 19.
50. *Ibid.*, Vol. III, Ch. 1.
51. *The Topographer* (September 1789), *op. cit.*, p.317.
52. Gilpin, William (1792), *op. cit.*, Vol. II, p.237.
53. *P&P*, Vol. III, Ch. 1.
54. Gilpin, William (1792), *op. cit.*, p.62.
55. *P&P*, Vol. III, Ch. 1.
56. *Letters* 12, 25 November 1798, p.23.
57. Hill, George Birkbeck (ed.) (1934), *Boswell's Life of Johnson*. Oxford: Clarendon Press, Vol. 3, p.161.

10. Desperate Walkers

1. Jenkins, Elizabeth (1959), '16th December. Sagittarius', *Jane Austen Society Collected Reports*. Chawton: The Jane Austen Society, p.154.
2. *Memoir*, p.16.
3. Le Faye, Deirdre (2006), *A Chronology of Jane Austen*. Cambridge: Cambridge University Press, p.89.
4. *Memoir*, p.157.
5. Johnson, R. Brimley (1925), *The Letters of Mary Russell Mitford*. London: John Lane The Bodley Head, p.35.
6. *Letters* 28, 30 November–1 December 1800, pp.66–7.
7. Ousby, Ian (ed.) (1992), *James Plumptre's Britain: The Journals of a Tourist in the 1790s*. London: Hutchinson, p.33.
8. *Ibid.*, p.88.
9. *Traveller's Oracle*, Part 1, pp.53–4.
10. *Ibid.*, p.14.
11. *Ibid.*, p.252.
12. *Juvenilia: A Tour through Wales — in a Letter from a young Lady*, p.224.
13. A Lady of Distinction (1811), *Regency Etiquette: The Mirror of Graces*, facsimile edition, Mendocino: R.L. Shep (1997), pp.233–4. 'Take one ounce of turpentine, half an ounce of red lead, one ounce of frankincense, half a pound of white rosin, one pint of Florence oil; boil these ingredients in a pipkin, and keep stirring them over a slow fire with an elder stick until it turns black; then turn it out to harden for use. It must be applied by spreading it on a piece of leather oiled all over, and then put to the corn. Wearing it constantly for some time will effectually eradicate the corn.'
14. *Letters* 87, 15–16 September 1813, p.231.
15. *Ibid.*, 20, 2 June 1799, p.44.
16. Ibbetson, Laporte, and J. Hassell, Mess. (1793), *A Picturesque Guide to Bath*. London: Hookham and Carpenter, p.139.
17. *Letters* 21, 11 June 1799, p.47.
18. Le Faye, Deirdre (2006), *op. cit.* p.335.
19. Egan, Pierce (1819), *Walks Through Bath*. Bath: Meyler and Son, pp.185–6.
20. *Letters* 37, 21–2 May 1801, p.91.
21. *Ibid.*, 38, 26–7 May 1801, p.93.
22. *Ibid.*, 44, 21–3 April 1805, p.108.
23. *Ibid.*, 36, 12–13 May 1801, pp.89–90.
24. *Ibid.*, 43, 8–11 April 1805, p.105.
25. *A Lady Travels*, p.105.
26. *Ibid.*, p.106.
27. *Juvenilia: Catharine, or the Bower*, p.263.
28. *LM: The Watsons*, p.115.
29. *NA*, Vol. I, Ch. 3.
30. *Ibid.*, Vol. II, Ch. 3.
31. *P*, Vol. II, Ch. 7.
32. *NA*, Vol. I, Ch. 10.
33. *Ibid.*, Vol. I, Ch. 13.
34. Ibbetson, Laporte, and J. Hassell, Mess. (1793), *op. cit.*, p.142.
35. *A Lady Travels*, pp.136–7.
36. *Letters* 74, 31 May 1811, p.200.
37. *Memoir*, p.68.
38. Austen, Caroline (1991), *op. cit.*, p.7.
39. *Letters* 78, 24 January 1813, p.209.
40. *Ibid.*, 80, 4 February 1813, p.212.
41. *S&S*, Vol. I, Ch. 16.

42. *Ibid.*, Vol. III, Ch. 10.
43. *P&P*, Vol. II, Ch. 4.
44. *Letters* 14, 18–19 December 1798, p.27.
45. *P&P*, Vol. I, Ch. 7.
46. *Ibid.*, Vol. I, Ch. 7.
47. *Ibid.*, Vol. I, Ch. 8.
48. Gregory, Dr John (1808), *A Father's Legacy to his Daughters*, new edn. London: T. Cadell and W. Davies, pp.48, 58.
49. *P&P*, Vol. I, Ch. 8.
50. A Lady of Distinction (1811), *op. cit.*, p.155.
51. *P&P*, Vol. II, Ch. 7.
52. *Ibid.*, Vol. II, Ch. 10.
53. *Ibid.*, Vol. III, Ch. 16.
54. *S&S*, Vol. III, Ch. 13.
55. *MP*, Vol. I, Ch. 4.
56. A Lady of Distinction (1811), *op. cit.*, p.38.
57. *Ibid.*, Vol. I, Ch. 7, p.83.
58. *Letters* 5, 5 September 1796, p.8.
59. *MP*, Vol. I, Ch. 11.
60. *Ibid.*, Vol. I, Ch. 10.
61. *Ibid.*, Vol. I, Ch. 10.
62. *Ibid.*, Vol. III, Ch. 4.
63. *Ibid.*, Vol. III, Ch. 17.
64. *E*, Vol. III, Ch. 2.
65. *Ibid.*, Vol. II, Ch. 16.
66. *Ibid.*, Vol. II, Ch. 5.
67. *Ibid.*, Vol. III, Ch. 5.
68. *Ibid.*, Vol. III, Ch. 16.
69. *P*, Vol. I, Ch. 10.
70. *Ibid.*, Vol. I, Ch. 10.
71. *Ibid.*, Vol. I, Ch. 10.
72. *Letters* 146, 16–17 December 1816, p.337.
73. *Ibid.*, 149, 23 January 1817, p.340.
74. *Ibid.*, 161(C), 28–9 May 1817, p.358.

11. At Home, Quiet, Confined

1. *Letters* 107, 9–18 September 1814, p.287.
2. *P*, Vol. II, Ch. 11.
3. *Ibid.*, Vol. I, Ch. 11.
4. *Juvenilia: The beautifull Cassandra*, pp.54–6.
5. *Juvenilia: Henry and Eliza*, pp.38–45; *Love and Freindship*, pp.103–41; *A Tour Through Wales*, p.224.
6. *Outlandish Cousin*, p.54.
7. *P*, Vol. I, Ch. 8.
8. Gisborne, Thomas (1810), *An Enquiry Into The Duties Of The Female Sex*, 9th edn. London: T. Cadell and W. Davies, p.309.
9. *Ibid.*, pp.300, 299.
10. *Ibid.*, p.310.
11. *Juvenilia: Edgar and Emma*, pp.33–4.
12. *NA*, Vol. II, Ch. 15.
13. Murray, Venetia (1998), *High Society: A Social History of the Regency Period, 1788–1830*. London: Viking, pp.230–31

14. *P*, Vol. II, Ch. 8.
15. Gisborne, Thomas (1810), *op. cit.*, p.303.
16. Martin, Joanna (1998), *A Governess in the Age of Jane Austen*. London: The Hambledon Press, p.63.
17. Brook, Mrs (1795), *op. cit.*, pp.ii–iii.
18. *Ibid.*, p.2.
19. *Ibid.*, p.4.
20. *Ibid.*, p.164.
21. *Ibid.*, p.102.
22. *Ibid.*, pp.128–31.
23. *Ibid.*, p.137.
24. Watts, Susanna (1805), *A Visit to London, Containing A Description of the Principal Curiosities In The British Metropolis*. London: Printed by J. Adlard, Duke-street, Smithfield, For Tabart and Co., pp.190–91.
25. Watts, Susanna (1804), *A Walk Through Leicester*. London: Thomas Combe. (Facsimile edition (1967). Brussels: Leicester University Press, extract taken from the Address.)
26. *Ibid.*, pp.1–2.
27. *A Lady Travels*, pp.41–2.
28. *Ibid.*, p.xi.
29. Morgan, Mary (1795), *A Tour To Milford Haven, In the Year 1791*. London: Printed for John Stockdale, in Piccadilly, p.ix.
30. *Ibid.*, pp.2–3.
31. *Ibid.*, p.ix.
32. *Letters* 88, 16 September 1813, p.232.
33. *FR*, p.70.
34. A Lady of Distinction (1811), *op. cit.*, p.112.
35. *Ibid.*, p.132.
36. *Ibid.*, pp.134–5. A clock is an embroidered or lace decoration running from ankle to calf.
37. *Ibid.*, pp.45–6.
38. Morgan, Mary (1795), *op. cit.*, p.143.
39. A Lady of Distinction (1811), *op. cit.*, pp.222, 223.
40. Johnson, R. Brimley (1925), *The Letters of Mary Russell Mitford*. London: John Lane The Bodley Head, p.142.
41. Dolan, Brian (2002), *Ladies of the Grand Tour*. London: Flamingo, p.4.
42. Lewis, Lady Theresa (ed.) (1865), *Journals and Correspondence of Miss Berry 1783 to 1852*. London: Longmans, Green, and Co., p.313.
43. Dolan, Brian (2002), *op. cit.*, p.4.
44. Radcliffe, Ann (1795), *A Journey Made In The Summer of 1794, Through Holland and the Western Frontier of Germany, with a Return Down the Rhine: To Which Are Added, Observations During A Tour To The Lakes Of Lancashire, Westmoreland, and Cumberland*. Dublin: Printed by William Porter, p.370.
45. *P&P*, Vol. II, Ch. 14.
46. Spence, E.I. (1809), *Summer Excursions*. London: Longman, Hurst, Rees, And Orme, p.2.
47. Darton, F.J. Harvey (ed.) (no date), *The Life and Times of Mrs Sherwood*. London: Wells Gardner, Darton & Co., pp.209, 210.
48. *NA*, Vol. I, Ch. 13.
49. *Juvenilia: Catharine, or the Bower*, p.274.
50. Laver, James (1930), *Harriette Wilson's Memoirs*, 2nd edn. Plymouth: Peter Davies, p.145.
51. Rowlandson, Thomas (c.1800), *Rural Felicity, or Love in a Chaise*. London: British Museum. *Carriages and Riders at Full Speed Across Open Grassland*, London: UCL Art Museum.

52. *E*, Vol. I, Ch. 18.
53. *Letters* 25, 8–9 November 1800, p.58.
54. *Ibid.*, 28, 30 November–1 December 1800, p.68.
55. *Ibid.*, 38, 26–7 May 1801, pp.94–5.
56. *Ibid.*, 22, 19 June 1799, pp.48–9.
57. *Ibid.*, 38, 26–7 May 1801, pp.94–5.
58. *Ibid.*, 4, 1 September 1796, pp.5–6.
59. *Ibid.*, 7, 18 September 1796, p.12.
60. *Ibid.*, 87, 15–16 September 1813, pp.228–9.
61. *Ibid.*, 88, 16 September 1813, p.231.
62. *Ibid.*, 89, 23–4 September 1813, p.236.
63. *MP*, Vol. I, Ch. 4.
64. *Letters* 98, 5–8 March 1814, pp.270–71.
65. *Ibid.*, 128, 26 November 1815, p.314.
66. *E*, Vol. I, Ch. 14.

12. Off We Drove, Drove, Drove

1. *Letters* 3, 1 September 1796, p.5.
2. Johnson, R. Brimley (1925), *The Letters of Mary Russell Mitford*. London: John Lane The Bodley Head, pp.65–6.
3. Alcohol mixed with aromatic plant extracts, usually wormwood.
4. *Letters* 9, 24 October 1798, pp.14–15.
5. *Ibid.*, 10, 27–8 October 1798, p.16.
6. Selwyn, David (ed.) (1996), *Collected Poems and Verse of The Austen Family. Dialogue between Death and Mrs A.* Manchester: Carcanet Press, p.30.
7. *Letters* 61, 20 November 1808, p.160.
8. Andrews, Cyril Bruyn (ed.) (1954), *op. cit.*, p.33.
9. *Traveller's Oracle*, Part 1, pp.30, 81–2.
10. *Ibid.*, p.95.
11. Raffald, Elizabeth (1799), *The Experienced English Housekeeper*, 12th edn. London: Printed For R. Baldwin, No. 47, In Pater-Noster Row, p.245.
12. *Ibid.*, pp.3–4.
13. *Letters* 19, 17 May 1799, p.41.
14. *Ibid.*, 35, 5–6 May 1801, p.85.
15. Everley on early-nineteenth-century maps.
16. Bradney-Smith, Adrienne (2010), 'Jane Austen and coaching inns', *The Jane Austen Society Report*. Chawton: Jane Austen Society, p.205.
17. *Letters* 35, 5–6 May 1801, p.86.
18. *Outlandish Cousin*, p.160.
19. *Letters* 29, 3–5 January 1801, p.71.
20. *Ibid.*, 30, 8–9 January 1801, p.74.
21. *Ibid.*, 29, 3–5 January 1801, p.71.
22. Cary, John (1819), *Cary's New Itinerary*, 8th edn. London: J. Cary, p.141.
23. Gilpin, William (1798), *Observations On The Western Parts of England*. London: T. Cadell Jun. and W. Davies, pp.130, 140, 148–150, 153.
24. Anonymous (1810), *A Guide to All The Watering and Sea-Bathing Places*. London: Richard Phillips, p.219.
25. *Letters* 104, 10–18 August 1814, p.279.
26. *FR*, p.137.
27. *P*, Vol. I, Ch. 11.
28. *P*, Vol. II, Ch. 8.
29. Austen-Leigh, R.A. (ed.) (1942), *Austen Papers 1704–1856*. London: Spottiswoode, Ballantyne and co., pp.235–6.

30. *Letters* 43, 8–11 April 1805, p.105.
31. *Ibid.*, 43, 8–11 April 1805, p.106.
32. *Ibid.*, 47, 30 August 1805, p.116.
33. Le Faye, Deirdre (2003), *Fanny Knight's Diaries*, second impression. Hampshire: Jane Austen Society, p.10.
34. *Letters* 55, 30 June–1 July 1808, p.144.
35. *NA*, Vol. II, Ch. 5.
36. *Ibid.*, Vol. II, Ch. 5.
37. Warner, Rev. Richard (1801), *Excursions From Bath*. Bath: Printed by Richard Cruttwell, pp.327, 332.
38. *FR*, p.155.
39. Huxley, Victoria (2013), *Jane Austen & Adlestrop*. Gloucestershire: Windrush, p.131.
40. Austen-Leigh, R.A. (ed.) (1942), *op. cit.*, p.245.
41. *Ibid.*, p.247.
42. http://www.stoneleighabbey.org/jane_austen.html.
43. *FR*, p.163.
44. *Letters* 52, 15–17 June 1808, pp.130, 131.
45. *Ibid.*, 52, p.131.
46. *Ibid.*, 52, p.131.
47. *Ibid.*, 52, p.133.
48. *Ibid.*, 53, 20–22 June 1808, p.134; *Ibid.* 54, 26 June 1808, p.138.
49. *Ibid.*, 54, 26 June 1808, pp.138, 139, 141.
50. *FR*, p.197.
51. *Letters* 84, 20 May 1813, pp.218–19.
52. Mogg, Edward (1826), *Paterson's Roads*, 18th edn. London: Longman, Rees, Orme, Brown, and Green, p.21.
53. *Letters* 84, 20 May 1813, p.219.
54. *FR*, p.206.
55. Chapman, R.W. (ed.), *Plan of a Novel & other Notes By Jane Austen*. Oxford: The Clarendon Press, 1926, p.17.
56. Gilpin, William (1798), *op. cit.*, pp.11–12.
57. Ibid., p.30.
58. *Letters* 159, 22 May 1817, p.356.
59. *Ibid.*, 160, 27 May 1817, p.358.
60. *Ibid.*, CEA/3, 29 July 1817, p.363.

Bibliography

Ackermann, Rudolf (1815), *The Repository of Arts, Literature, Commerce, Manufactures, Fashions and Politics*. London: R. Ackermann.

— (1816), 'Description of The Military Carriage Of Napoleon Bonaparte, Taken After The Battle Of Waterloo, And Now Exhibiting At The London Museum, Piccadilly', *Repository of Arts, Literature, Fashions &c*, new series. London: R. Ackermann.

A Lady of Distinction (1811), *The Mirror of Graces or The English Lady's Costume*. London: B. Crosby. (*Regency Etiquette: The Mirror of Graces*, facsimile edition (1997), Mendocino: R.L. Shep.)

Andrews, Cyril Bruyn (ed.) (1954), abridged by Fanny Andrews, *The Torrington Diaries*. London: Eyre & Spottiswoode.

— (ed.) (no date), *Clouds and Sunshine by An English Tourist of The Eighteenth Century Part I of the Tour of 1789 from the Torrington Diaries by The Hon. John Byng (1743–1813)*. Marlow: Roy Patrick Smith.

Andrews, Malcolm (1989), *The Search for the Picturesque*. California: Stanford University Press.

Anonymous (1810), *Guide to all the Seabathing Places*. London: Printed for Richard Phillips.

Anonymous (September 1789), 'Journal of a Tour from Oxford thro' the Peak of Derbyshire, etc.', *The Topographer*. London: Robson and Clarke.

Arnold, Hilary (1998), 'Mrs Margaret Graves and Her Letters From Bath, 1793–1807', *Bath History VII*. Bath: Millstream Books.

Austen, Caroline (1991), *My Aunt Jane Austen*. Chawton: The Jane Austen Society.

Austen-Leigh, R.A. (ed.) (1942), *Austen Papers 1704–1856*. London: Spottiswoode, Ballantyne & Co.

Bamford, Francis (ed.) (1936), *Dear Miss Heber*. London: Constable and Company.

Barchas, Janine (2012), *Matters of Fact in Jane Austen*. Baltimore: The Johns Hopkins University Press.

Beardsley, Martyn and Bennett, Nicholas (eds.) (2007), *Gratefull to Providence: The Diary and Accounts of Matthew Flinders, Surgeon, Apothecary and Man-Midwife 1775–1802*. Woodbridge: The Boydell Press.

Bennett, Francis (2007), *The Roads of Devon and Cornwall*. Exeter: The Short Run Press.

Beresford, John (ed.) (1968), *The Revd James Woodforde*. Oxford: Oxford University Press.

Birtwistle, Sue and Conklin, Susie (1995), *The Making of Pride and Prejudice*. London: Penguin.

Lord Brabourne, Edward (1884), *Letters of Jane Austen*. London: Richard Bentley & Son.

Bradney-Smith, Adrienne (2010), 'Jane Austen and coaching inns', *The Jane Austen Society Report*. Chawton: Jane Austen Society.

Bramston Archive, HRO 3A00W/A3/11.

Brander, Michael (1973), *The Georgian Gentleman*. London: Saxon House.

Brennan, Flora (trans.) (1987), *Puckler's Progress: The Adventures of Prince Puckler-Muskau in England, Wales and Ireland as Told in Letters to His Former Wife – 1826–9*. London: Collins.

Brook, Mrs (1795), *A Dialogue Between A Lady And Her Pupils, Describing A Journey through England and Wales; In Which Detail Of The Different Arts And Manufactures Of Each City And Town Is Accurately Given; Interspersed With Observations And Descriptions In Natural History. Designed for Young Ladies and Schools*. London: Printed for and sold by Thomas Clio Rickman.

Buchan, William MD (1798), *Domestic Medicine: or, A Treatise on the Prevention and Cure of Diseases by Regimen and Simple Medicines*, 16th edn. London: A. Strachan, T. Cadell Jun. and W. Davies.

Budworth, Joseph (1792), *A Fortnight's Ramble to the Lakes in Westmoreland, Lancashire, and Cumberland, By a Rambler*. 1st edn. London.

Colonel Byng, John (1996), *Rides Round Britain*. London: Folio Society.

Cary, John (1819), *Cary's Itinerary*, 8th edn. [first edn 1798] London: J. Cary.

— (1821), *Cary's New Itinerary* (8th edn). London: J. Cary.

Chapman, R.W. (ed.), *Plan of a Novel & other Notes By Jane Austen*. Oxford: The Clarendon Press, 1926.

Climenson, Emily J. (1899), *Passages From The Diaries Of Mrs. Philip Lybbe Powys*. London: Longmans, Green, and Co.

Cobbett, William (2010), *Rural Rides (1763–1835)*. London: Folio Society.

Combe, William and Rowlandson, Thomas (1815), *The Tour of Doctor Syntax In Search of the Picturesque*, 6th edn. London: R. Ackermann.

Darton, F.J. Harvey (ed.) (no date), *The Life and Times of Mrs Sherwood*. London: Wells Gardner, Darton & Co.

Day, Malcolm (2006), *Voices from the World of Jane Austen*. Newton Abbot: David & Charles.

Dolan, Brian (2002), *Ladies of the Grand Tour*. London: Flamingo.

Felton, William (Vol. 1: 1794, Vol. 2: 1796), *A Treatise On Carriages*. London: J. Debrett.

Fullerton, Susannah (2005), *Jane Austen & Crime*. Sydney: Jane Austen Society of Australia Inc.

Gatrell, Vic (2006), *City of Laughter Sex and Satire in Eighteenth-Century London*. London: Atlantic Books.

Gilpin, William (1792), *Observations Relative Chiefly to Picturesque Beauty. Made in the Year 1772, On several Parts of England; Particularly The Mountains and Lakes of Cumberland and Westmoreland*, 3rd edn. London: Printed for R. Blamire.

— (1798), *Observations On The Western Parts of England*. London: T. Cadell Jun. and W. Davies.

Gisborne, Thomas (1810), *An Enquiry Into The Duties Of The Female Sex*, 9th edn. London: T. Cadell and W. Davies.

Gregory, Dr John (1808), *A Father's Legacy to his Daughters*, new edn. London: T. Cadell and W. Davies.

Grey, J. David (ed.) (1986), *The Jane Austen Handbook*. London: The Athlone Press.

Hampshire Chronicle, 16 December 1805.

Harman, Claire (2009), *Jane's Fame*. London: Canongate.

Hewitt, Rachel (2010), *Map of a Nation*. London: Granta Books.

Hibbert, Christopher (ed.) (1991), *Captain Gronnow: His Reminiscences of Regency and Victorian Life, 1810–60*. London: Kyle Cathie.

Hill, Constance and Ellen G. (1902), *Jane Austen: Her Homes and Her Friends*. London and New York: John Lane.

Hill, George Birkbeck (ed.) (1934), *Boswell's Life of Johnson*, Oxford: The Clarendon Press.

Hurst, Jane (2008), *A History of Alton 1800–1850*. Alton: Jane Hurst.

Huxley, Victoria (2013), *Jane Austen & Adlestrop*. Gloucestershire: Windrush.

Ibbetson, Laporte, and Hassell, J., Mess. (1793), *A Picturesque Guide to Bath, Bristol Hot-Wells, the River Avon, and the Adjacent Country*. London: Hookham and Carpenter.

Irving, Washington (1820–21), *The Sketch Book of Geoffrey Crayon, Gent.* www.gutenberg.org.

Jenkins, Elizabeth (1959), '16th December. Sagittarius', *Jane Austen Society Collected Reports*. Chawton: Jane Austen Society.

Jennings, Paul (date unknown), extract from 'Jane in Vain', London: the *Observer*.

Johnson, R. Brimley (1925), *The Letters of Mary Russell Mitford*. London: John Lane The Bodley Head.

Kenyon Jones, Christine (2010), 'Portraying ambiguous cousinship: *Mansfield Park* and the family of the real Lord Mansfield', *Persuasions* Online. USA: JASNA.

Kitchiner, Dr William, MD (1827), *The Traveller's Oracle Or, Maxims For Locomotion*. London: Henry Colburn.

Lane, Maggie (1995), *Jane Austen's England*. London: Robert Hale.

— (1996), *A Charming Place: Bath in the Life and Novels of Jane Austen*. Bath: Millstream Books.

— (2003), *Jane Austen and Lyme Regis*. Hampshire: The Jane Austen Society.

Laver, James (1930), *Harriette Wilson's Memoirs*, 2nd edn. Plymouth: Peter Davies.

Le Faye, Deirdre (1986), *Reminiscences of Caroline Austen*. Chawton: The Jane Austen Society.

— (1999), 'Another book owned by Mr Austen', *The Jane Austen Society Report*. Chawton: Jane Austen Society.

— (2002), *Jane Austen: The World of Her Novels*. London: Frances Lincoln.

— (2002), *Jane Austen's 'Outlandish Cousin': The Life and Letters of Eliza de Feuillide*. London: The British Library.

— (2003), *Fanny Knight's Diaries*, second impression. Hampshire: Jane Austen Society.

— (2004), *Jane Austen: A Family Record*. Oxford: Oxford University Press.

— (2006), *A Chronology of Jane Austen*. Cambridge: Cambridge University Press..

— (ed.) (2011), *Jane Austen's Letters*. Oxford: Oxford University Press.

Lefroy, Helen and Turner, Gavin (eds.) (2007), *The Letters of Mrs Lefroy*. Chawton: The Jane Austen Society.

Lewis, W.S. (ed.) (1937), *Horace Walpole, Correspondence*, (42 vols). Oxford: Oxford University Press.

Lockhart, John Gibson (1837), *Memoirs of the Life of Sir Walter Scott*, (7 vols). Edinburgh: Robert Cadell.

Martin, Joanna (ed.) (1998), *A Governess in the Age of Jane Austen, The Journals and Letters of Agnes Porter*. London: The Hambledon Press.

Michaelis, Ruth and Merson, Jena and Willy (trans.) (1988), *A Lady Travels: The Diaries of Johanna Schopenhauer*. London: Routledge.

Mingay, Gordon (1981), *Mrs Hurst Dancing & Other Scenes From Regency Life 1812–1823*. London: Victor Gollancz.

Mitford, Mary Russell (1982), *Our Village*. Oxford: Oxford University Press.

Mogg, Edward (1826), *Paterson's Roads*, 18th edn. London: Longman, Rees, Orme, Brown, and Green.

Moir, Esther (1964), *The Discovery of Britain*. London: Routledge & Kegan Paul.

Morgan, Mrs Mary (1795), *A Tour To Milford Haven, In the Year 1791*. London: Printed for John Stockdale, in Piccadilly.

Murray, Venetia (1998), *High Society: A Social History of the Regency Period, 1788–1830*. London: Viking.

New Bath Guide (1790). Bath: Richard Cruttwell.

New Bath Guide (1800). Bath: Richard Cruttwell.

Ousby, Ian (ed.) (1992), *James Plumptre's Britain: The Journals of a Tourist in the 1790s*. London: Hutchinson.

Parry, Sarah (2008), 'The Pemberley Effect', *Persuasions*, No. 30. USA: JASNA.

Place Papers (unpublished), London: British Library.

Radcliffe, Ann (1795), *A Journey Made In The Summer of 1794, Through Holland and the Western Frontier of Germany, with a Return Down the Rhine: To Which Are Added, Observations During A Tour To The Lakes Of Lancashire, Westmoreland, and Cumberland*. Dublin: Printed by William Porter.

Raffael, Michael (2006), *Bath Curiosities*. Edinburgh: Birlinn.

Raffald, Elizabeth (1799), *The Experienced English Housekeeper*, 12th edn. London: Printed For R. Baldwin.

Reading Mercury, 19 August 1793.

Rochefoucauld, François de la and Scarfe, Norman (2011), *A Frenchman's Year in Suffolk, 1784*. London: The Boydell Press.

Rollins, Hyder Edward (ed.) (1958), *Letters of John Keats*. Cambridge, MA: Harvard University Press.

Sambrook, Pamela (2003), *A Country House At Work*. London: National Trust.

Selwyn, David (ed.) (1996), *Jane Austen: Collected Poems and Verse of the Austen Family*. Manchester: Carcanet Press.

Simond, Louis (1815), *Journal of a Tour and Residence in Great Britain During the Years 1810 and 1811 By A French Traveller*, Vol. I, Edinburgh: George Ramsay & Co.

— (1817), *Journal of a Tour and Residence in Great Britain During the Years 1810 and 1811 By A French Traveller*, Vol. II, Edinburgh: James Ballantyne & Company.

Simons, Paul (9 October 2002), 'Weather Eye', *The Times*.

Souden, David (ed.) (1991), *Byng's Tours: The Journals of the Hon. John Byng 1781–1792*. London: Century.

Southey, Robert (1807), *Letters From England By Don Manuel Alvarez Espriella*, 2nd American edn 1808. New York: David Longworth.

Spence, Elizabeth Isabella (1809), *Summer Excursions, Through Parts Of Oxfordshire, Gloucestershire, Warwickshire, Staffordshire, Herefordshire, Derbyshire, And South Wales.* London: Longman, Hurst, Rees, And Orme.

Sullivan, R.J. (1780), *Observations made during a Tour through parts of England, Scotland and Wales in a series of Letters.* London: T. Becket.

Sutherland, Kathryn (ed.) (2002), *A Memoir of Jane Austen: J.E. Austen-Leigh.* Oxford: Oxford University Press.

— (2005), *Jane Austen's Textual Lives.* Oxford: Oxford University Press.

Swift, Andrew and Elliott, Kirsten (2012), *Literary Walks in Bath.* Bath: Akeman Press.

Tennyson, Lord Hallam (1897), *Alfred Lord Tennyson: A Memoir by His Son.* London: Macmillan.

Tinniswood, Adrian (1998), *The Polite Tourist: A History of Country House Visiting.* London: National Trust.

Tomalin, Claire (1997), *Jane Austen: A Life.* London: Viking.

Tristram, W. Outram (1893), *Coaching Days and Coaching Ways.* London: Macmillan.

Trusler, John (1790), *The London Adviser and Guide: Containing every Instruction and Information useful and necessary to persons living in London and coming to reside there.* London: J. Trusler.

Vick, Robin (1996), 'Rural Crime', *The Jane Austen Society Report.* Chawton: Jane Austen Society.

— (1999), 'Mr Austen's Carriage', *The Jane Austen Society Report.* Chawton: Jane Austen Society.

Warner, the Rev Richard of Bath (1800), *A Walk Through Some of the Western Counties of England.* Bath: Richard Cruttwell.

— (1801), *Excursions From Bath.* Bath: Richard Cruttwell.

Watts, Susanna (1804), *A Walk Through Leicester.* London: Thomas Combe. (Facsimile edition, Leicester: Leicester University Press (1967).)

— (1805), *A Visit to London, Containing A Description of the Principal Curiosities In The British Metropolis.* London: Printed by J. Adlard, Duke-street, Smithfield, For Tabart and Co.

Works by Jane Austen

The Cambridge Edition of the Works of Jane Austen (Cambridge: Cambridge University Press):

Sense and Sensibility. Ed. Peter Copeland (2006).

Pride and Prejudice. Ed. Pat Rogers (2006).

Mansfield Park. Ed. John Wiltshire (2005).

Emma. Eds Richard Cronin and Dorothy McMillan (2005).

Northanger Abbey. Eds Barbara M. Benedict and Deirdre le Faye (2006).

Persuasion. Eds Janet Todd and Antje Blank (2006).

Juvenilia. Ed. Peter Sabor (2006).

Later Manuscripts. Eds Janet Todd and Linda Bree (2008).

The History of England. London: The British Library (1993).

Index

Onslow, Tommy, 79
ostlers, 72, 96, 103, 116, 121, 128, 134, 136
overnight travelling, 18, 49–52, 54, 88,
   108, 118, 125–6
Overton, 51–2, 69, 141
Oxford, 30, 39, 40, 49, 57, 71, 82, 102, 115,
   160, 161, 164–7, 220, 234
Oxfordshire, 39, 126, 221, 226

Palmer, John, 114–15, 117–18
Paterson, Daniel, *see* map makers
patriotism/patriotic travellers, 14, 15, 153,
   165, 215
pavements, 41–2, 100, 167, 185, 188
Peak District, 160, 161, 162–3, 172, 179
Pecchio, Count, 127
Persuasion, 13, 19, 26, 27, 29–30, 32, 34, 36–7,
   38, 41, 48, 60–61, 65, 67, 84, 85, 87, 88, 90,
   93, 107, 111, 114, 128, 129–31, 152, 159,
   183, 186–7, 193, 198–9, 201, 202–3, 205,
   211, 214, 215, 221, 227, 228, 230–31, 240
Petworth House, 205
picturesque, 19–21, 29, 141, 155, 161, 167–8,
   172, 184, 187, 206, 228–9, 239
Pitt, William, 99
Place, Francis, 101, 103
Plumptre, James, 12, 47, 153–4, 161, 172,
   176–7, 179–81
Plymouth, 38, 102
Porter, Agnes, 102–3, 206
Portsmouth, 18, 34, 42, 53, 102, 104, 107,
   115, 118, 134, 159, 195, 208, 221, 232, 237,
   239
post boys, *see* postilions
post masters, 75–6, 86, 110
Post Office, 45, 53, 116–17, 118–20, 196
postilions, 44, 53, 76, 79, 86, 87, 109, 110,
   111, 116, 118, 121, 133, 135, 222
Powlett, Charles, 54, 76
Pride and Prejudice, 18, 23, 31, 33, 56, 57–8,
   60, 63, 65, 80, 86, 89, 93, 97, 99, 100, 108,
   111, 119, 120, 123, 128–9, 139, 140, 147,
   148, 160–77, 190–93, 201, 202, 211–12, 214,
   215–16, 217, 221, 237
Prince Puckler-Muskau, 88
Prince of Wales (Prince Regent), 23, 64, 67,
   79, 102, 239
promenading, 185–7
Pynes House, 26
Pyrenees, 16, 24

de Quincey, Thomas, 40–41, 57

Radcliffe, Ann, 16, 156, 215
Raeburn, Henry, 59
Ramsgate, 24, 152, 185, 215
Reading, 39, 60, 71, 123

Repton, Humphry, 126–7, 230, 233
Rice, Henry, 84, 90
riding schools, 66–7
road books, 16–18, 23, 24–5, 45, 134, 141
road construction and maintenance,
   40–44, 46–9, 56–8
Rochefoucauld, François de la, 72, 73, 100,
   109
Rowlandson, Thomas, 8, 20, 64, 100, 217
Royal Naval Academy, 18

St John's College, Oxford, 164–5
Salisbury, 26, 42, 102, 115, 116, 134, 141
Sanditon, 26, 56, 60, 67, 84, 90, 112, 132–3
Sandling Park, 140, 231
Scarborough, 22
Schopenhauer, Johanna, 12, 40, 67, 76, 101,
   109, 112–13, 123, 128, 132, 135, 149, 154,
   157, 162, 163, 166, 169, 170, 171, 173–4,
   185, 188, 210, 214
Scotland, 14, 26, 56, 101, 155, 156, 179, 180
Scott, Sir Walter, 21, 156–7
sedan chair, 113–14, 135
Sense and Sensibility, 13, 18, 19, 20, 25, 26,
   30, 32–3, 38, 42, 46, 49, 57, 59, 60, 61–2, 64,
   68, 70, 74, 78, 85, 86, 91, 94–5, 96–8, 107,
   128, 131–2, 133, 139–40, 148–9, 159, 187,
   188, 189–90, 193, 195, 201, 206, 207, 217,
   221, 228, 229, 237
Sharp, Anne, 232, 240
Sherwood, Mrs Martha, 216
Shirreff, Miss, 108
side saddle, 62, 64
Sidmouth, 26, 27, 38, 128, 130, 227
signposts, 45–6, 64, 157, 161
Simond, Louis, 14, 146, 165, 169, 170, 172
Somerset, 18, 24, 25, 27, 38, 41, 124, 133,
   184, 208, 221
South Devon Militia, 26
Southampton, 17, 32, 51, 89, 102, 105, 107,
   108, 109, 115, 137, 140, 232, 234, 235, 236
Southey, Robert, 44, 106, 133
Spence, Elizabeth Isabella, 47, 154, 156,
   167, 170, 216
Sperling, Diana, 8, 43, 68
Spicer, Mr, 238
stable boys, 62, 72, 82
stables, 62, 67, 69, 73, 74, 101, 121, 125, 130,
   132, 134, 142, 238
Staffordshire, 49, 124, 160, 221, 232
Staines, 40, 222, 223
Steventon, 17, 24, 25, 32, 40, 47, 48, 51, 55,
   57, 65, 66, 69, 70, 71, 79, 86, 90, 104, 105,
   117, 124, 141, 157, 159, 160, 177, 178–9,
   188, 189, 217, 218, 221, 222, 226, 227, 232,
   234, 240
Stoke Canon, 27

271

Stonehenge, 141, 208
Stoneleigh Abbey, 26, 43, 45, 91, 140, 147, 167, 169, 232, 233, 234
Stourhead, 141, 145, 148
Stowe House, 8, 148, 149
Strawberry Hill, 147–8
street lighting, 50–51
Stuart, Mary (Queen of Scots), 21, 172–4
Stubbs, George, 7, 59, 64
Surrey, 17, 24, 25, 27, 30, 43, 53, 55, 58, 101, 107, 117, 124, 207, 221, 226, 239
Sussex, 25, 27, 32, 49, 159, 207, 221, 232, 237
Sweden, 15
Switzerland, 15, 16
Syntax, Dr, 20

Taunton, 38, 228
taxes, 44, 60, 62, 73, 80, 87, 99
Teignmouth, 27, 229
Telford, Thomas, 56
Tennyson, Alfred Lord, 159
Tetbury, 45, 73, 227, 233
Three Sisters, The, 61, 97
toll house and tolls, 44–5, 46
Topographer, The, 160, 175
travel literature, 14, 15–16, 17–18, 20, 22–3, 155, 161, 206–11, 214–15, 228, 237
travel sickness, 222–6, 240
travelling clothes, 7, 81, 82, 85, 103, 211–12, 214
Trusler, John, 132
Tunbridge Wells, 51, 185, 205
turnpike roads, 13, 14, 17, 24, 38–9, 42–3, 44–9, 56, 107, 164, 167, 203, 227, 232
turnpike trusts, 38, 42–3, 44–9, 56
Twickenham, 147

Usk, 24, 47

Vanbrugh, Sir John, 143, 165
Venice, 15

Wales, 7, 24, 47, 101, 116, 143, 154, 161, 179–80, 181, 206, 209, 213
walking, 12, 19, 20, 38, 47, 50, 53, 61, 65, 77, 81, 93, 98, 100, 159, 161, 166, 178–200, 225, 230, 238
  clothes, 7, 161, 180–81, 185–6, 211–12
Walpole, Horace, 100, 147–8, 149
Walter, Philadelphia, 51, 104
Warner, Revd Richard, 38–9, 143, 182–3, 233
Warwick, 160, 161, 167
Warwick Castle, 140, 147, 167
Warwickshire, 154, 221, 232
watches, 52, 54, 99, 116, 127
Watsons, The, 43, 48, 61, 64, 74, 81, 86, 107, 136, 186
weather, 21, 38–42, 50, 53–4, 56, 60, 61, 65, 67, 69, 76, 81, 90, 94, 112, 137, 151, 179, 185, 189–90, 191, 213–14, 222, 223, 225, 227, 235, 237–8
Wedgwood, Josiah, 49
Weymouth, 15, 92, 102
Whip Club, 79
Williams
  Charles, 64
  Jane (*née* Cooper), 90
Wilton House, 141, 145, 148, 149
Wiltshire, 26, 27, 42, 105, 124, 159, 208, 221
Winchester, 40, 70, 72, 76, 86, 107, 114, 126, 140, 157, 158, 188, 200, 208, 235, 236, 240
Woburn Abbey, 148, 205
Wollstonecraft, Mary, 214, 215
Woodforde, James, 41, 50
Wordsworth, William, 21, 155
Worthing, 26, 185, 231–2
Wyards, 77, 189, 199

Yalden, Mr, 103, 106–7
Yorkshire, 42, 73, 173, 179
Young, Arthur, 42, 43